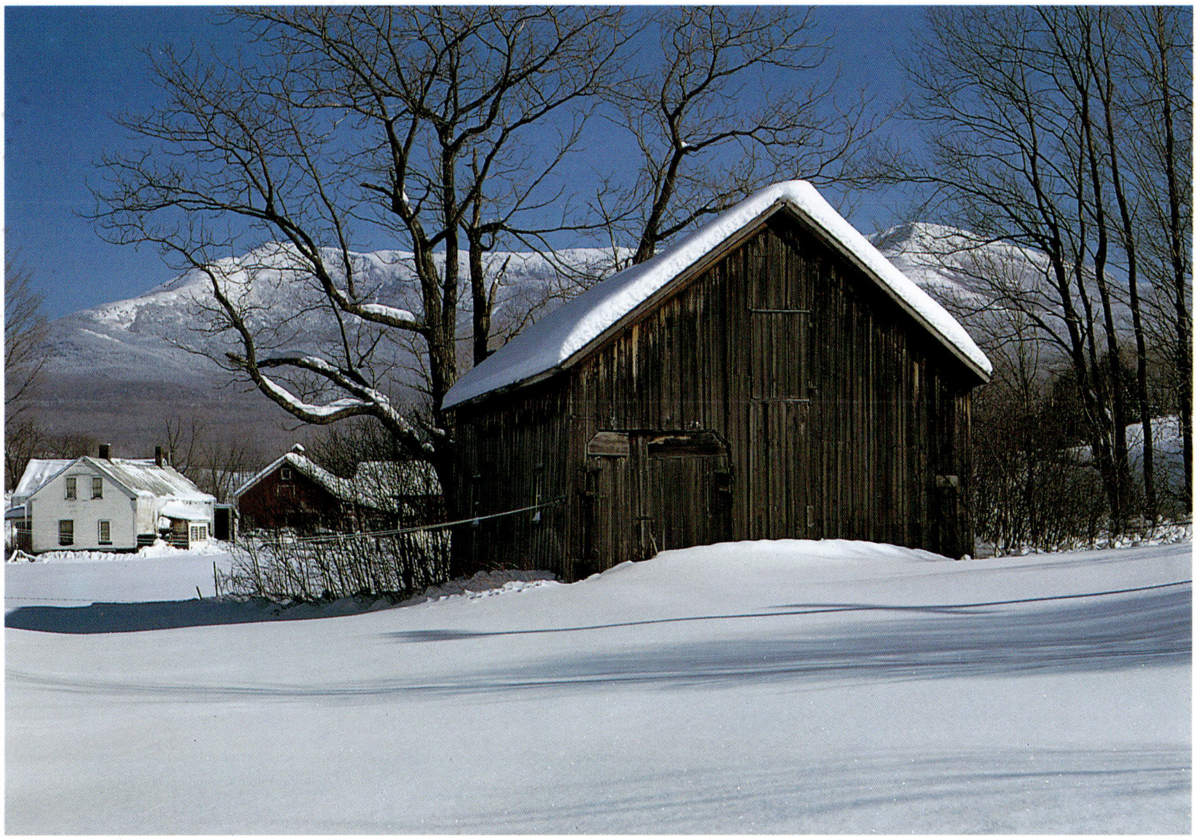

Underhill Center

Overleaf: Connecticut River and Barnet

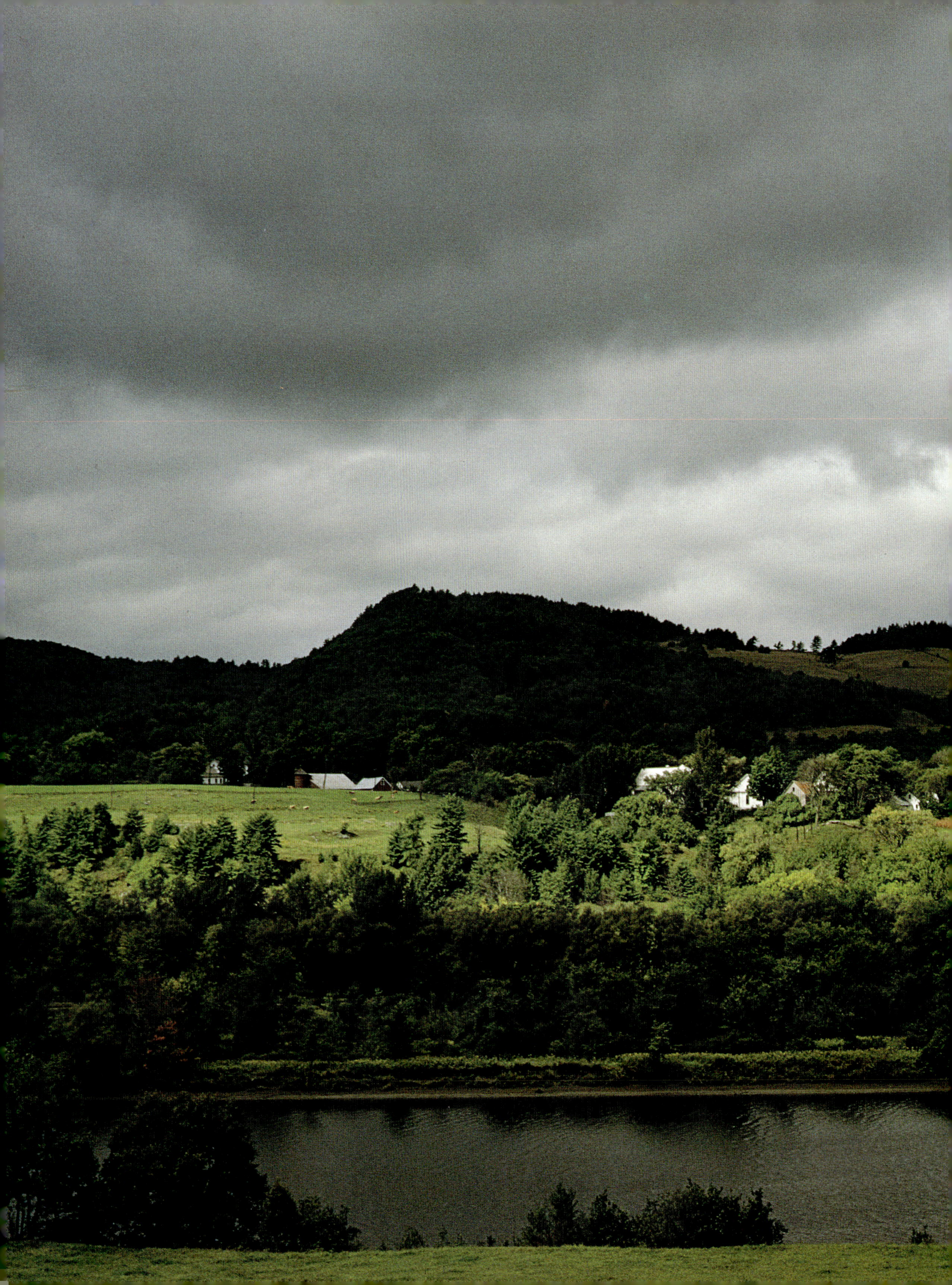

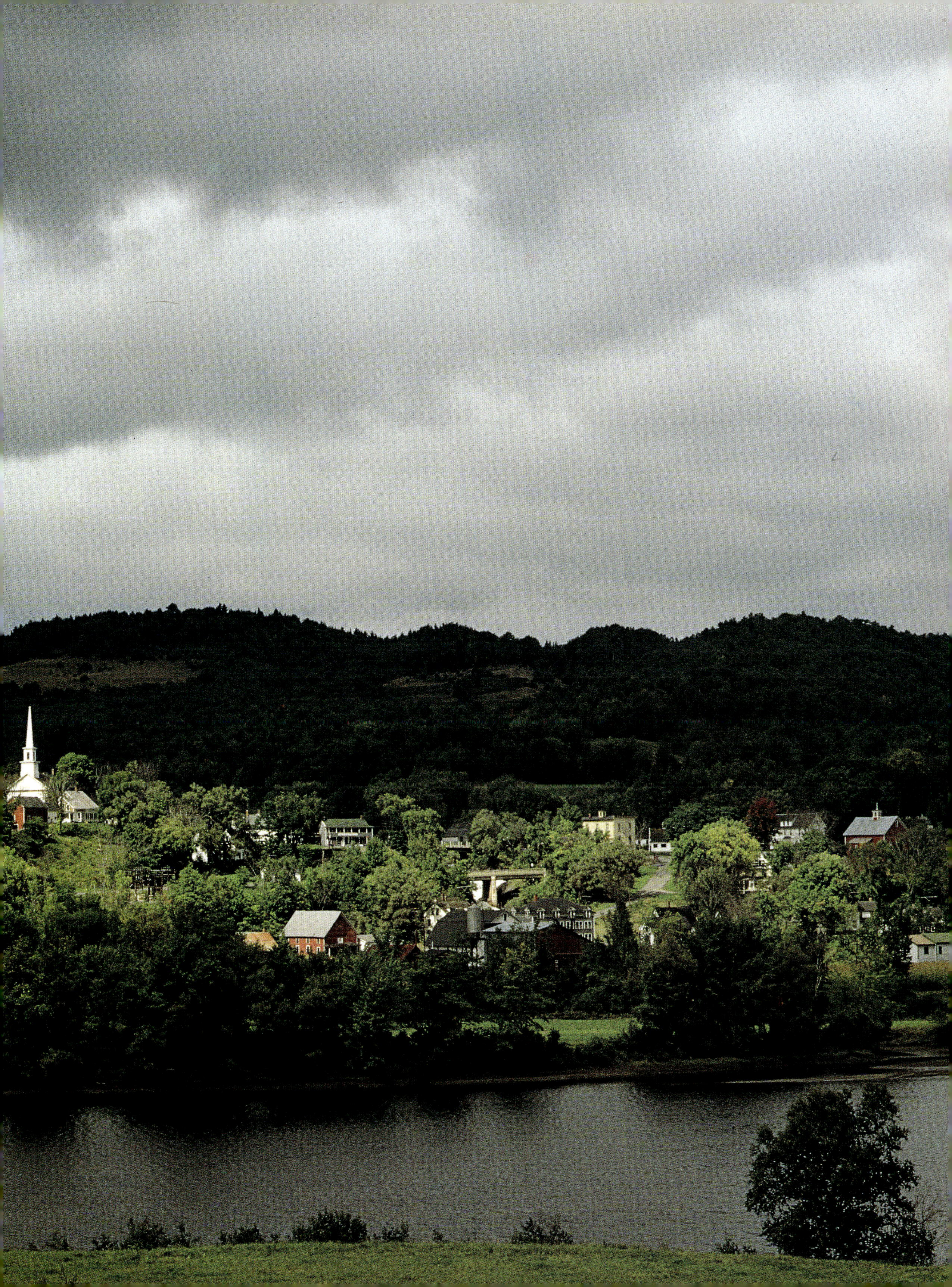

Dedication

If I were asked to describe VERMONT in a single word, I'd call it magical! There are, for example, few natural spectacles on earth that can match Vermont's dazzling seasonal transitions. When its sugar maples slowly dissolve from summer greens to speckles of yellow and finally brilliant red, Vermont's countryside becomes a bewitching paint-pot spectacular! And, you don't have to be a great photographer with lots of fancy equipment to capture it on film either. Simply be there. Any camera will do; but since I'm often asked, I use Nikon cameras and lenses. The film is Kodachrome 64.

Vermont is where I launched my career in photography over twenty years ago. How could I miss with so many calendar views around every corner! Vermont is also where I raised three daughters. We explored the state's Green Mountains together, camping, hiking and canoeing many of its white-water rivers. In summer we bicycled back country roads and in winter we zoomed down nearly every ski area in the state. Five bucks got you an all day lift ticket in those days!

Vermont's eternal magic is etched into my very soul. I'm especially delighted to share a bit of its everlasting charm through the pages of this book. And, I would like to dedicate this work to my daughters – Sally, Robin and Tracey, who lived in and loved this special world we call Vermont.

Clyde H. Smith

Edited by James B. Patrick

Designed by Donald G. Paulhus

Printed in Japan

ISBN 0-89909-128-8

Published by Foremost Publishers, Inc.
An affiliate of Yankee Publishing Inc.
Dublin, NH 03444

VERMONT

A Scenic Discovery

Photography by Clyde H. Smith
Introduction by Brian Vachon

Published by Foremost Publishers, Inc.
An affiliate of Yankee Publishing Inc.

Overleaf: Mt. Mansfield from Pleasant Valley

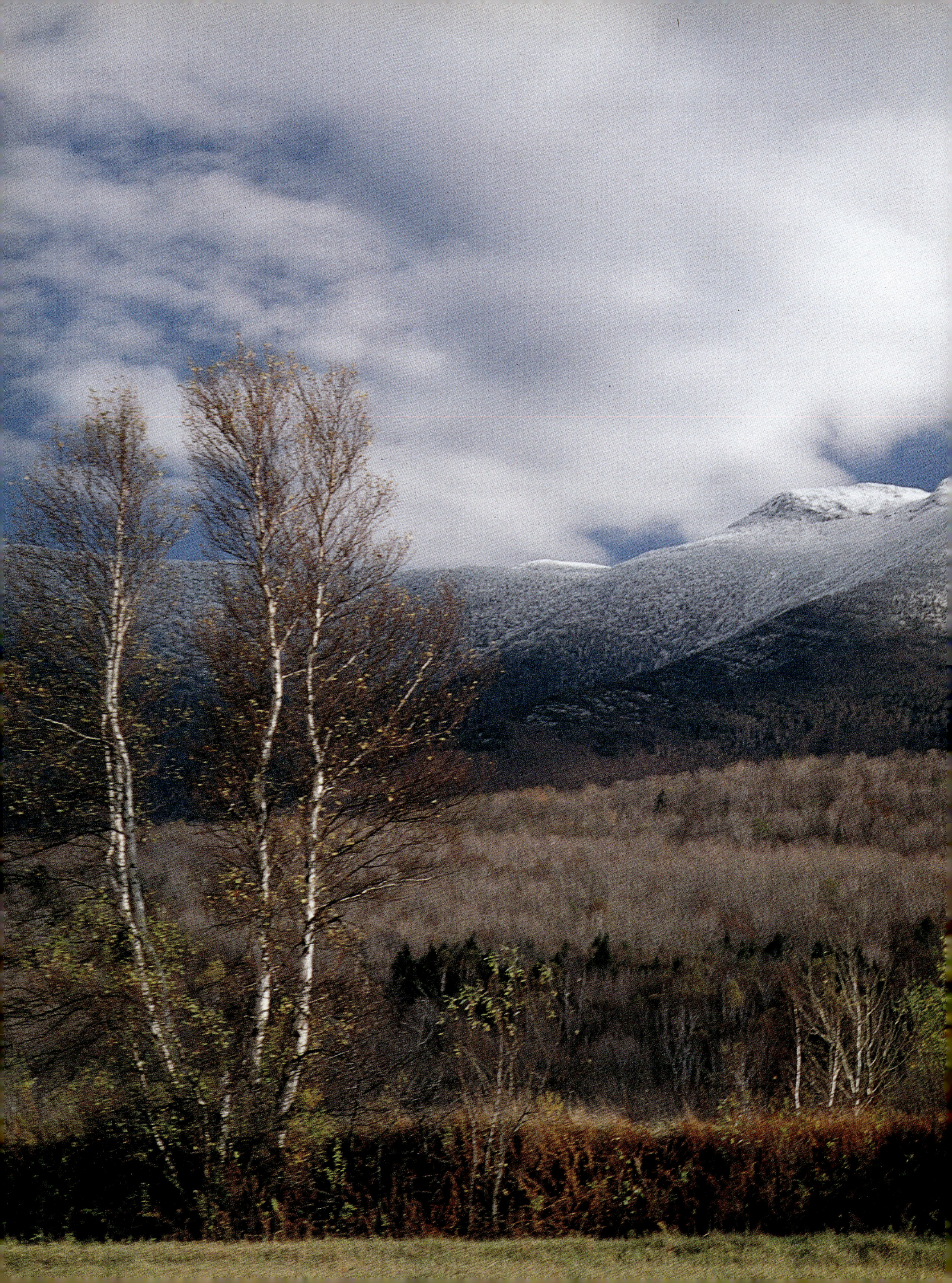

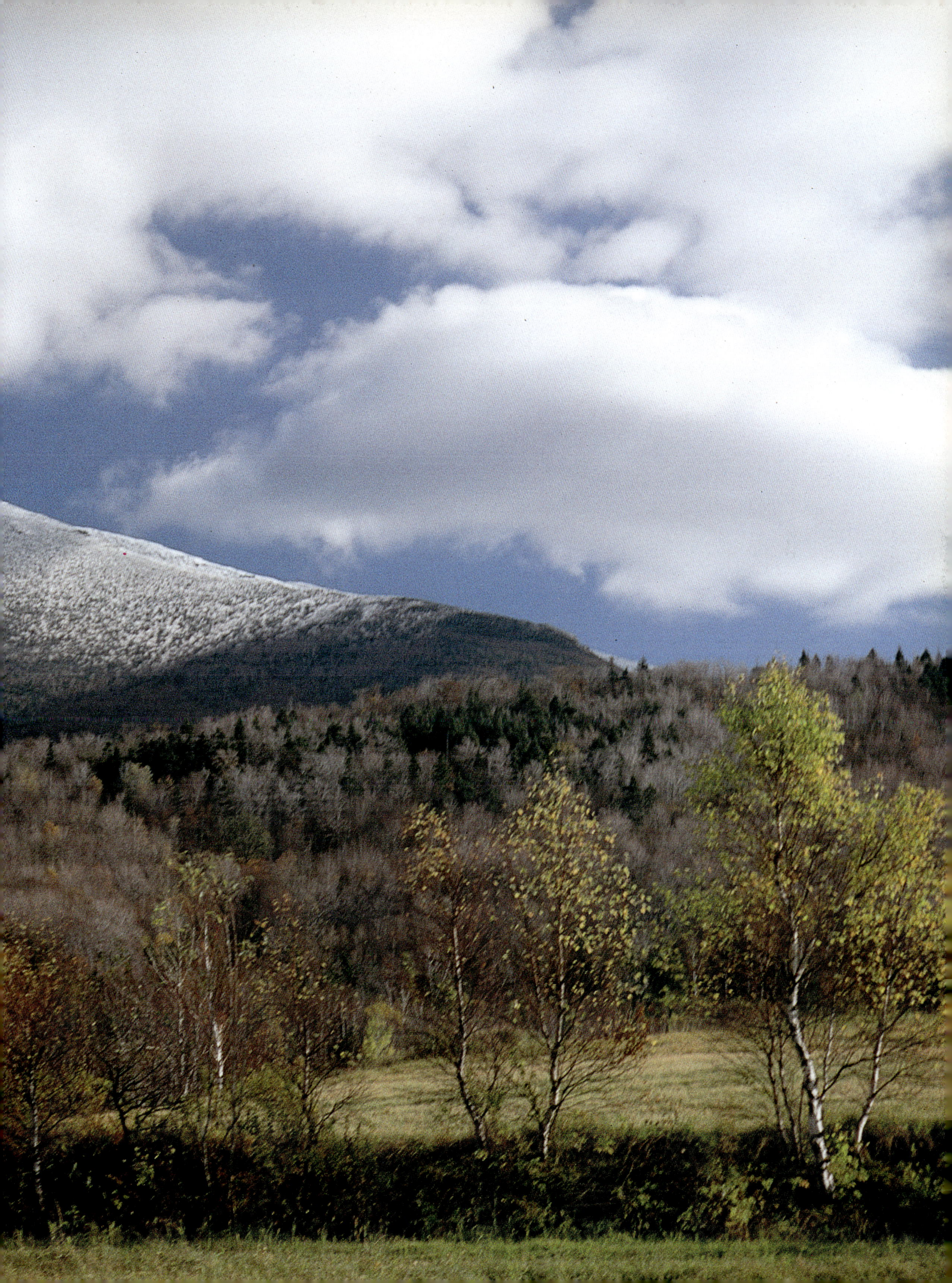

There's this thing about Vermont.

Well, that may be a bit of an over-simplification. Actually, there are lots of things about Vermont – cultural, historical, architectural, anthropological, physical and even (perhaps essentially) spiritual – that separate this particular place from any other on earth.

But it's this *thing* about Vermont – this singular and rather pertinacious essence – that is worthy of note. Not, it should be quickly pointed out, because it hasn't been noted before. It gets noted all the time. Books and songs and stories and magazine articles and poems and simple slogans frequently pay homage to this central and vital element of Vermont. And they do this with, depending on one's point of view and measure of affection, varying degrees of accuracy. But this thing does get noted, and noticed.

Slogans do it most succinctly. Vermont, a special world. Vermont, the beloved state. Vermont, the way America used to be. Vermont, every American's second home. And on and on. Extravagant catch-phrases attempt to define the qualities of this rocky, hilly, under-populated, over-forested slice of New England and translate the sum total into something tangible. They succeed, those slogans, only in proportion to the degree those who hear them and use them have already somehow experienced the place. Calling Vermont "special" doesn't mean anything to anyone who hasn't. Calling Vermont "beloved," on the other hand, is – to most anyone who has lived in, visited or thought seriously about the Green Mountain State – an acknowledgement of the obvious.

We're talking here about a quality most illusive. But because its very illusiveness has been captured to a very significant degree by the photographic artistry of Clyde Smith, whose portraits of Vermont adorn this book, we're talking also about a quality that can be sensed and recognized. And most particularly, seen.

One thing about Vermont is that while it is small (less than ten thousand square miles) and mostly unpretentious, it is also dramatically visual. One can *look* at Vermont and get a pungent sense of what the mystique is all about. The state photographs about as well as any, and when the photographs are as telling as those that fill these pages, the slogans and the poetry and the praises of Vermont become enhanced with some real substance. The words lose their notional inference and begin to *mean* something. Viewers of Vermont almost immediately get the idea.

It's mainly a very positive idea. People all over the globe who have any feelings at all for Vermont have predominantly affirmative feelings. Those folks on the outside generally think of the state as being rural, quaint, unspoiled and uncrowded. Those inside occasionally think of Vermont as being precariously balanced, sometimes self-conscious and potentially vulnerable to all those people outside who love it so much. But that's the way it has been for a very long time, and both views – the one looking in and the one looking out – aren't really likely to change any time soon.

Nor should they. Vermont isn't likely to. This is a state that is looking at national trends from a singularly contrary perspective.

As the entire country shifts and groans under the weight of population growth and premeditated development, Vermont slips rather decidedly in the opposite direction. Already vying for the title, it will officially be the least populous state – by Census Bureau reckoning – in the year 2,000. There are less than one half million folks who call Vermont home today and while that number isn't likely to drop, it is hardly surging. The positive side of that statistic is stability. Vermont's sons and daughters, who at one time celebrated adulthood by moving out of (and often far from) the Green Mountains, are now generally staying put. A certain *lure* may still be out there, but increasingly the opportunities for employment are close by.

Vermont *is* developing. And because there are vocal groups who claim, with about equal vigor, that the development is either happening too fast or not fast enough, it is probably safe to say that the state's economic base is being enriched at a pace that is mostly reasonable. The existing environmental laws (again, lamented because of their restrictiveness or discredited for their frailty) allow expansion to happen about the way one would expect it to happen in a state where, until only recently, there were more cows than people. It occurs very deliberately.

Now that cow thing used to be a sticking point. There was a time when a lot of Vermonters didn't particularly care to admit that the bovine population exceeded the human one. There was an insinuation in that condition that seemed, somehow, unseemly. But now that the trend has been reversed (it happened in the early sixties) and its implications soothed, there is a growing internal acceptance of the fact that Vermont's status as America's most rural state is a valuable one. Or at least not one that should undergo random tampering. Growth, at whatever rate deemed acceptable by whatever group, is seen to be linked – at least in the foreseeable future – to tourism. And tourism in Vermont is linked to agriculture. That's what gives the place its topographical distinction, its horizontal nuances. It's the gentle backdrop of what people come to see.

And people really *do* have to drop in now and then. They might be invited to do a little skiing or a little historic sighting or just share in the annual autumn spectacular, but they *are* vital to the scheme of things. Tourism is an industry in Vermont – the second largest – and it would very quickly be a lot less if the state's essential farming character disappeared.

And so farms and farmers are accorded a fairly universal degree of respect within Vermont's borders. Their products – those provided by the Holsteins, Jerseys and Brown Swiss as well as the products that spring up from the soil – are important exports. And agriculture's impressions and influence on the landscape are an integral part of that image the state projects and protects. Vermonters may be willing, even eager, to make *subtle* transformations in the essential character of their state. Rendering it inert and left hopelessly behind is only an agreeable notion to the very new or the very rich. But non-trivial changes – the kind that would happen if family farms began to disappear or factories began to sprout like fiddlehead ferns – have no champions whatsoever. People know a very good thing when they live it. And Vermonters live in a place where suggestions for major modifications get viewed with considerable suspicion. This special place doesn't stay special by accident.

Nor did it begin that way. Unless one can call the inexorable creep of a continental glacier an accident. Because that is how Vermont got started. The ice masses that invaded the northern parts of this hemisphere left permanent marks on what they covered and what they left behind, trimming peaks and carving valleys, leaving countless tons of rubble as well as cradles for ponds and lakes. The earliest visitors who wandered in to survey the aftermath of that geological event were mostly not inclined to stay. It was not a particularly inviting place and so they made their permanent settlements elsewhere – in the Saint Lawrence Valley to the north and the Connecticut Valley to the east.

But it was a fine place for hunting and fishing, and both the great eastern nations of Indians – the Algonquins (particularly the Abnaki tribe) and the Iroquois – visited frequently. They were not, however, on particularly good terms with one another. When the first known European explorers appeared near the vastly wooded, often impermeable scene, they did what most European explorers did in those days of geopolitical disquietude. They brought their grievances with them and took sides.

In 1609, Samuel de Champlain, the French explorer, sailed down a lake he named after himself. He is generally credited as being the first white man to take a look at what is now Vermont, but he evidently didn't take a particularly good look. What he saw on the eastern shores of the lake was a dense wilderness that he was apparently content to leave uninspected. He did, however, make an alliance with the Algonquins whom he encountered in his journeys. Together, they engaged in a temporarily successful battle with the Iroquois – a relatively small battle that was to have major and lasting repercussions in the ultimate settlement of that part of the world. Ultimately, the French and their Indian allies would lose control of the region to the English and *their* Indian allies in a grisly counterpart to the enduring political wars of Europe.

Throughout the seventeenth and well into the eighteenth century, Vermont served largely as a forested corridor through which the French and their confederates moved back and forth in order to harass the English settlements to the south and east. It was not until 1763 that the French relinquished all claims to the region to the English, despite the fact that England had already claimed most of the territory as its own. What was claimed by the emissaries of George the 3rd, however, and what was conceded by the newest settlers of the area were matters of vastly differing perspectives. Most of those differences got settled, if not amiably at least finally, by the American Revolution. But not in Vermont. The newest Vermonters proved to be contrarians of the first order.

The passage of time has both glamorized and obscured the motives of those early Vermonters, who were led, most notably, by Ethan Allen and his famed Green Mountain Boys. It is known that when the first thirteen colonies declared their independence, Vermont wasn't among them. It was declaring its *own* independence in what must surely be recognized as an early manifestation of what today has become recognized as an indigenous mindset.

For fourteen years, right in the middle of the newest republic on earth, sat Vermont, which for that brief period of history was the second newest republic on earth. Ultimately, however, Vermont ratified and adopted the Constitution of the United States and joined the team. As a member, it prospered significantly. It transformed itself from the game-filled wilderness that the Indians had enjoyed and Champlain had largely ignored to a state with a rapidly growing population, a high degree of self-sufficiency and a dedication to agriculture and small industry that literally changed the face of the countryside.

By 1840, there were not more cows than people in Vermont, but sheep – six times as many. And as sheep raising grew more popular, the land was stripped to accommodate their grazing needs. The virgin forests in which game had once been so plentiful were hacked down and in their place, thousands of homesteads and tens of thousands of acres of cultivated fields, divided by stone walls, were established. The new pioneers established centers of population on the banks of rivers and there, small villages – seemingly designed by like-minded architects – sprang up supporting lumber and woolen mills, with town halls and steepled churches in their centers and clapboard residences ringing their imprecise borders.

But the economics of the times would eventually affect both the wood and wool crops and leave its own permanent marks on the emerging state – marks which are clearly visible today. Dairy herds supplanted sheep as the primary activity of Vermont farmers. And throughout the state, where pastures had once been the predominant feature on the hillsides, forests began to grow back. Modern methods of production and distribution proved the undoing of countless small factories, mills, forges and distilleries. The state's self-sufficiency proved to be only temporary and Vermont eventually began to build its economy and reputation on a skilled and dedicated labor force and on products it could shape, manufacture and export.

The first urban areas grew in the state – in Burlington where wood products were made and shipped throughout the world; in Barre where the cash crop became granite; in Springfield which became an international center of the machine tool industry; in St. Johnsbury with the manufacture of the world's finest precision scales, and in Rutland which prospered as a railroading and manufacturing center.

When the Civil War came, Vermont reacted swiftly and paid a bitter price as its male residents enlisted in the Union forces in record numbers. War memorials in virtually each of the state's 251 towns give testimony to the fact that many of them never came home from that conflict. And when the war was over, Vermont settled into a period of slow recovery and even slower growth.

But the growth that did happen largely came from overseas. Italians from the quarry towns of northern Italy, as well as Scots, Irish and Spaniards, brought their skills to the granite centers in Barre and Proctor. The slate quarries near Poultney were manned by an influx of Welch immigrants. Central Europeans came to fill the populations of the small manufacturing towns of Springfield and Windsor. The French came to work in the textile mills and Scandinavians migrated to Vermont for work in the lumber industry. The Irish helped build the state's hundreds of miles of railroads.

These new residents brought their own traditions and helped shape new ones. Vermont, which had led the nation in banning slavery, was the first state in New England to allow women to vote in school district elections. It also was among the first states to pass temperance laws. It entered the Second World War officially even before the U.S. Congress made its declaration and during the Vietnam conflict, one of Vermont's most famous sons – the late Sen. George Aiken – suggested (with a wisdom that was only later acknowledged) that America should simply declare victory and leave.

But the tradition in Vermont which took hold in the previous century and which plays such an important part in the fabric of the state today is the one that welcomes visitors. That is a tradition which may have been caused as much by the state's location – it lies relatively close to the eastern seaboard cities and Montreal – as by its natural endowments and its mostly undisturbed landscape. But it is not a tradition that is taken lightly.

Vermont established the first publicity service of any state in the nation in 1891, but for years before that, railroad trains brought scores of visitors from throughout the east to favored spas and resorts in and around the state. The automobile only made Vermont more accessible to vacationers and a highway program was vigorously promoted.

The ski industry helped bring people into Vermont as much as any enterprise and it brought them at a time when the state clearly needed a little company. The first rope tow in the United States, powered by a Model T engine, was put into place in Woodstock in 1935. Today, over 40 ski resorts have cut trails on the hills and mountains and dozens of other cross-country skiing centers take advantage of what is clearly Vermont's most abundant winter commodity – snow.

In Vermont, the snow lingers. The state can have as many as 250 inches fall in that period loosely defined as winter (which, in fact, is a six-month, extended season that causes autumn to cancel early and helps itself to more of spring than almost anyone is willing to accept). The ski people are generally delighted with this climatic protraction and most Vermonters, who are generally *not* ski people, have learned long ago to live with it. But it makes for difficult driving, and the temperatures hover persistently around the uncomfortable.

When winter finally leaves, and it does so reluctantly, the season that descends upon the state is the least inviting to everyone encountering it. Spring, according to a Vermont maxim that gets proven accurate more often than not, is much less than a short season. Sometimes it's a short week. Mud season, which precedes spring with mucky regularity, attacks the state's thousands of miles of dirt roads with almost diabolic determination. Driving on them becomes even trickier than excursions through the ice and snow.

But finally summer comes – warm and rich and as full as anyone could imagine – and visitors arrive to enjoy the leisure activities with which Vermont so clearly and thoroughly abounds. Shorefront property on all but the most secluded ponds are dotted with cottages and camps and the entire state seems to become dedicated to offering pleasure and recreation to its own citizens and to those who have come to call.

And then there is autumn. Every year, as dependable as a calendar, the season performs its ultimate magic act and the land is splashed with magnificent waves of color in infinite shades and variety. Strictly speaking, of course, the distinctions are caused primarily by a slowdown in the photosynthesis process and subsequent breakdown of elements in reaction to the chemical and climatic conditions. But who can speak strictly of autumn in Vermont? It is a time of peculiar warmth that can be smelled and seen. It is a time of harvest and flamboyance and a time when – more than any other – visitors come to see and feel this *thing* about Vermont.

It is perhaps least illusive in the fall. The valley towns, white and serene and preparing for the season to come, seem to exude the sense of permanence that Vermont has come to symbolize. America the way it used to be? Perhaps not precisely. But the state does seem to emanate those characteristics which most of us somehow think America used to have. There is a tranquility that transcends the myth and lends credibility to the mystique. Vermont is somehow comforting and reassuring. We're glad it's there. We take pleasure in knowing that a place like this still exists.

Vermont historian Ralph Nading Hill writes that "perhaps the people of a rootless age find something admirable about a slice of hillcountry that has resisted being made over into the latest fashionable image." And perhaps that is it, as succinctly as it possibly can be said. This thing about Vermont is not so much what it is as what it represents. The illusive quality is linked somehow to the whims and ideals and fantasies in ourselves. And Vermont somehow brings them to the surface and lets them play. We often see, in this abundantly generous place, what we have always been promised. Graciously, delicately, sharply, sweetly, those promises are kept.

And that's the thing about Vermont.

Brian Vachon

Overleaf: Pleasant Valley

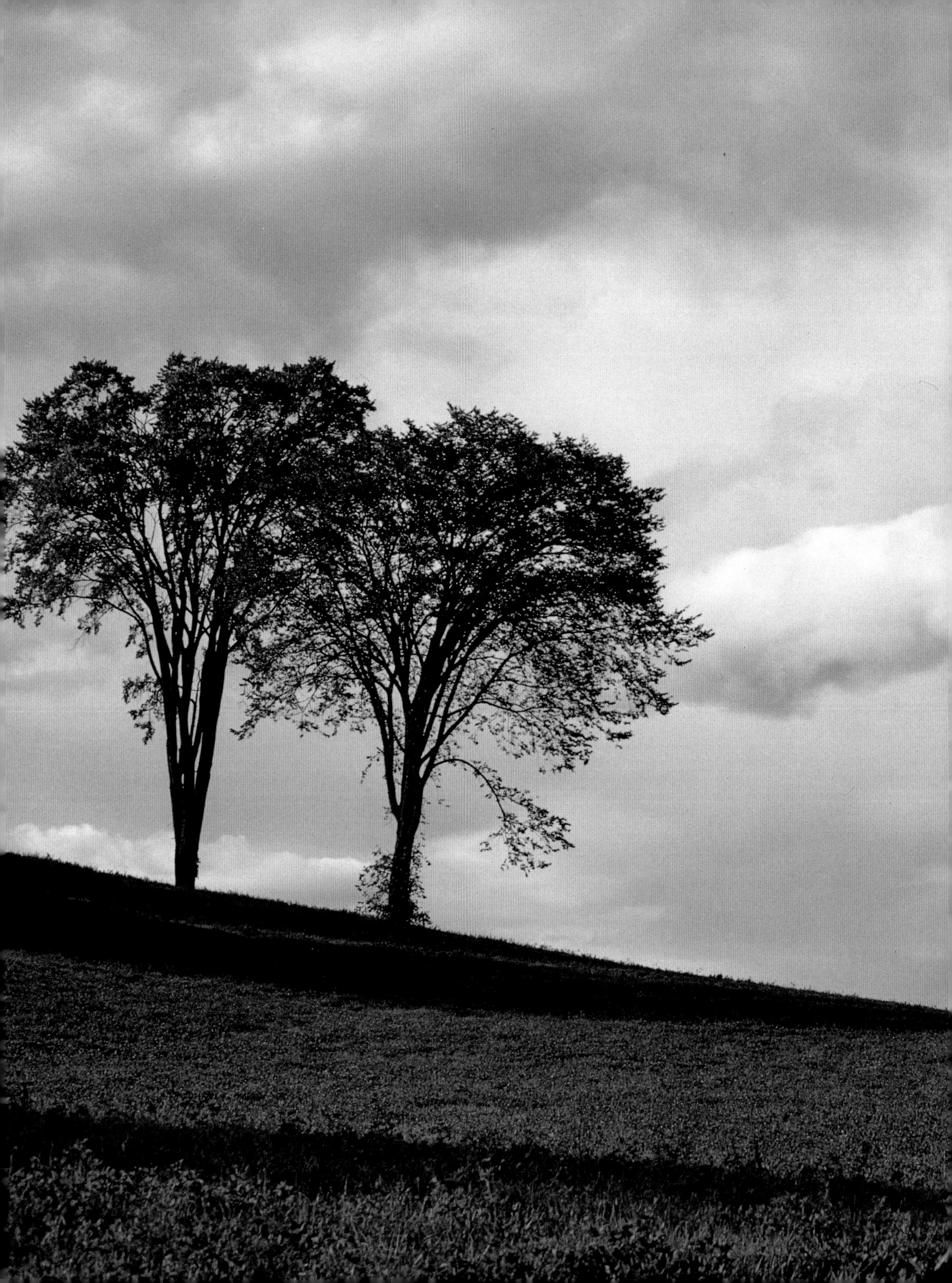

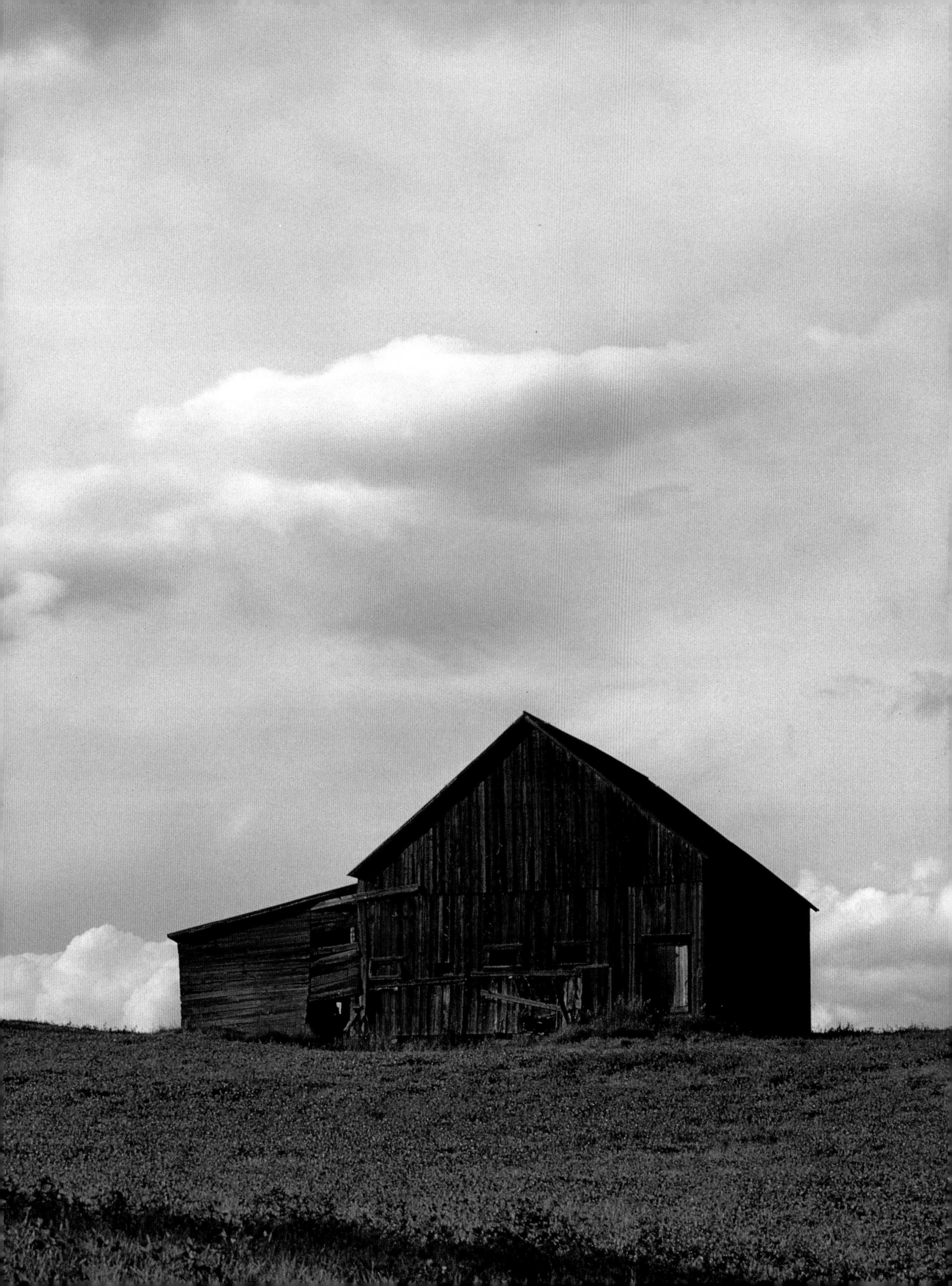

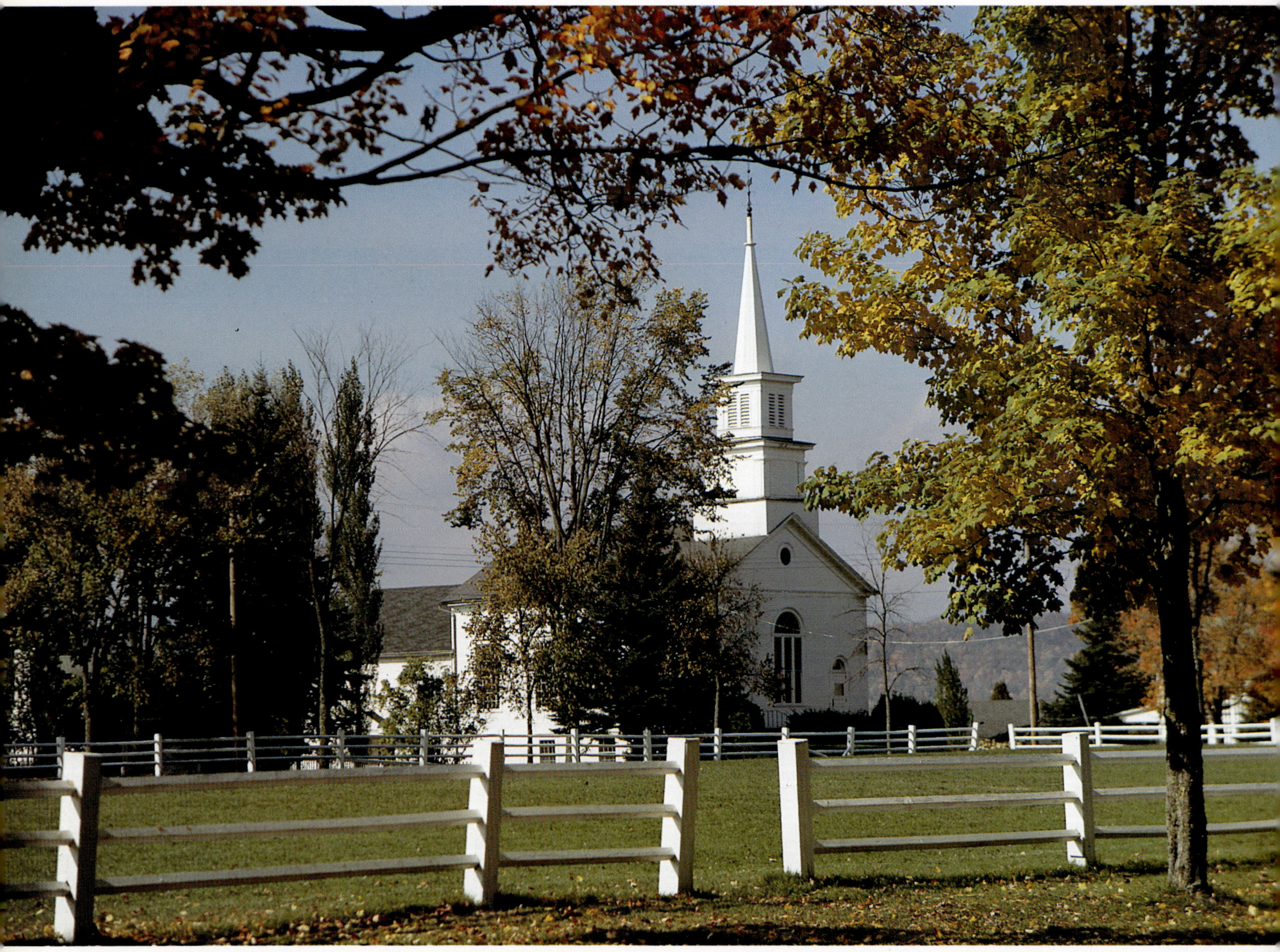

Craftsbury Common

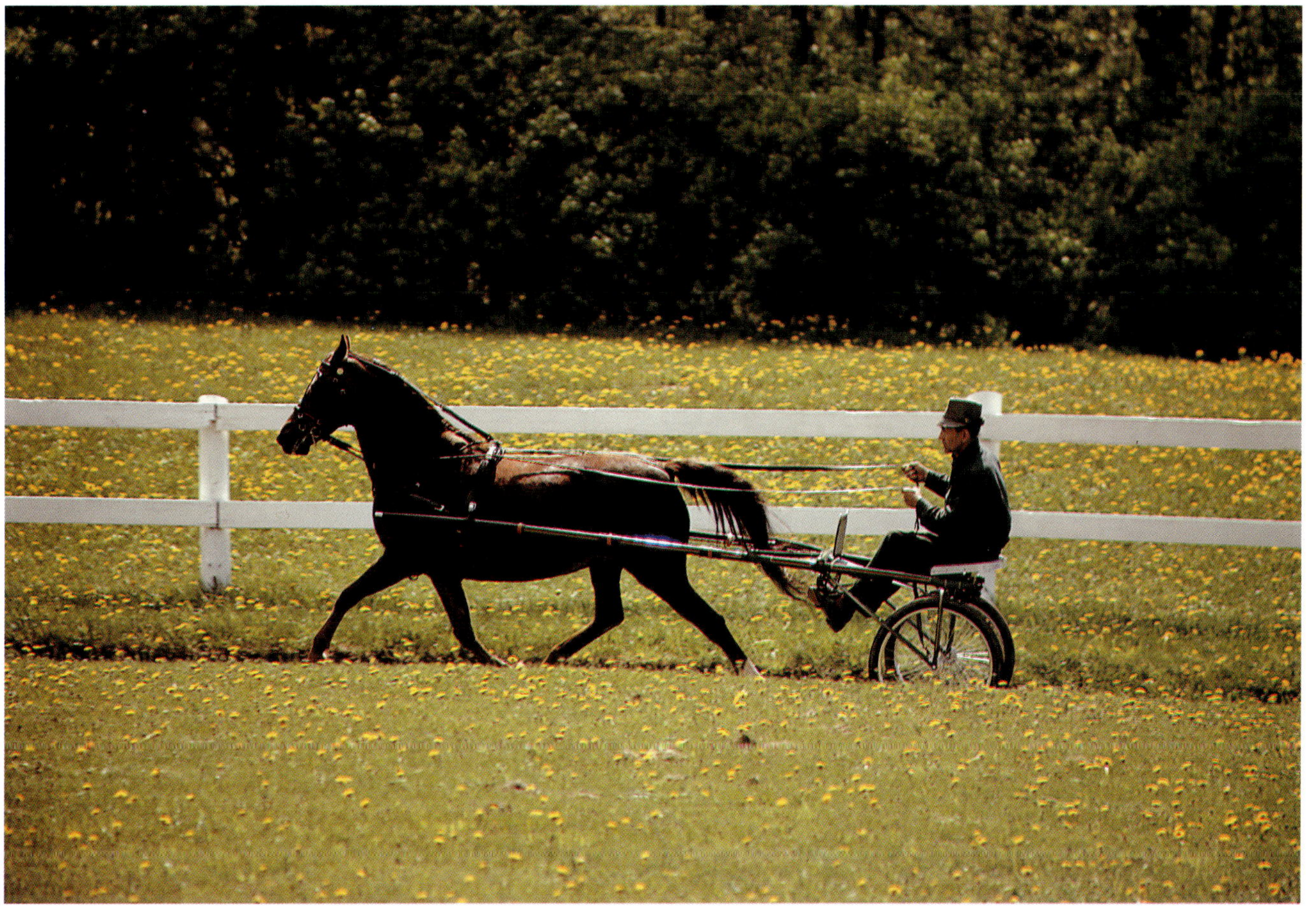

Morgan Horse Farm, Middlebury

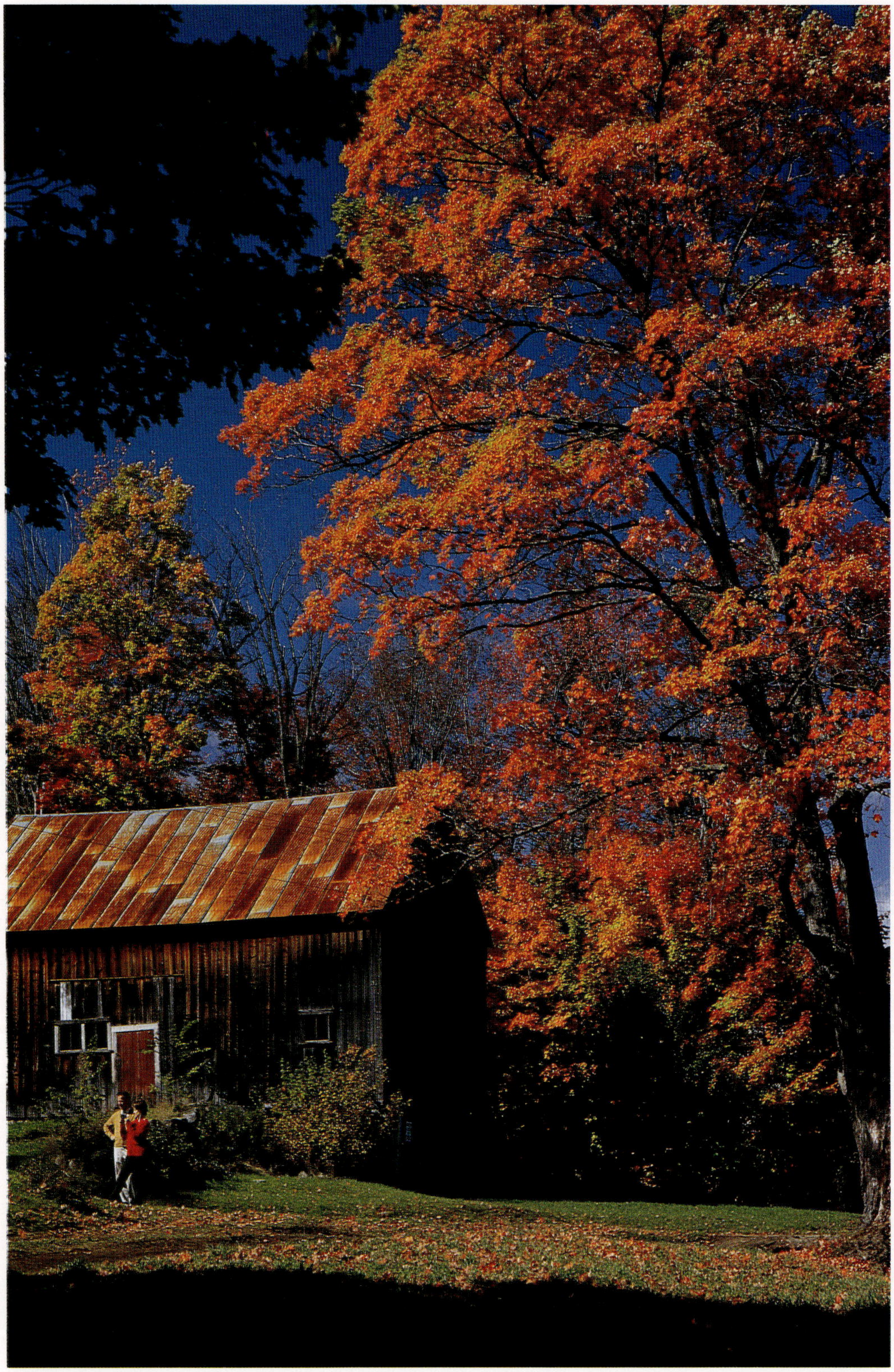

Waits River

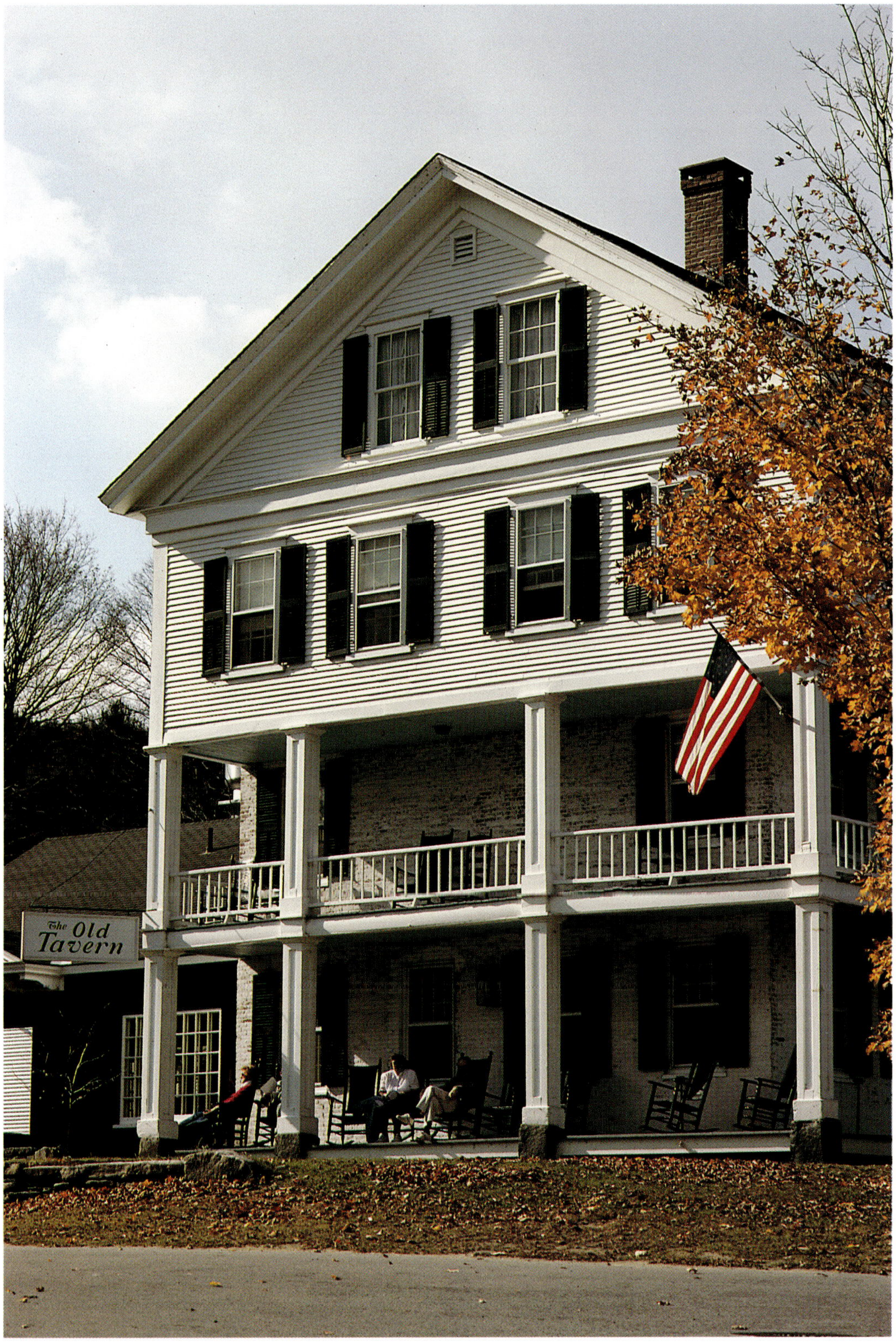

Grafton

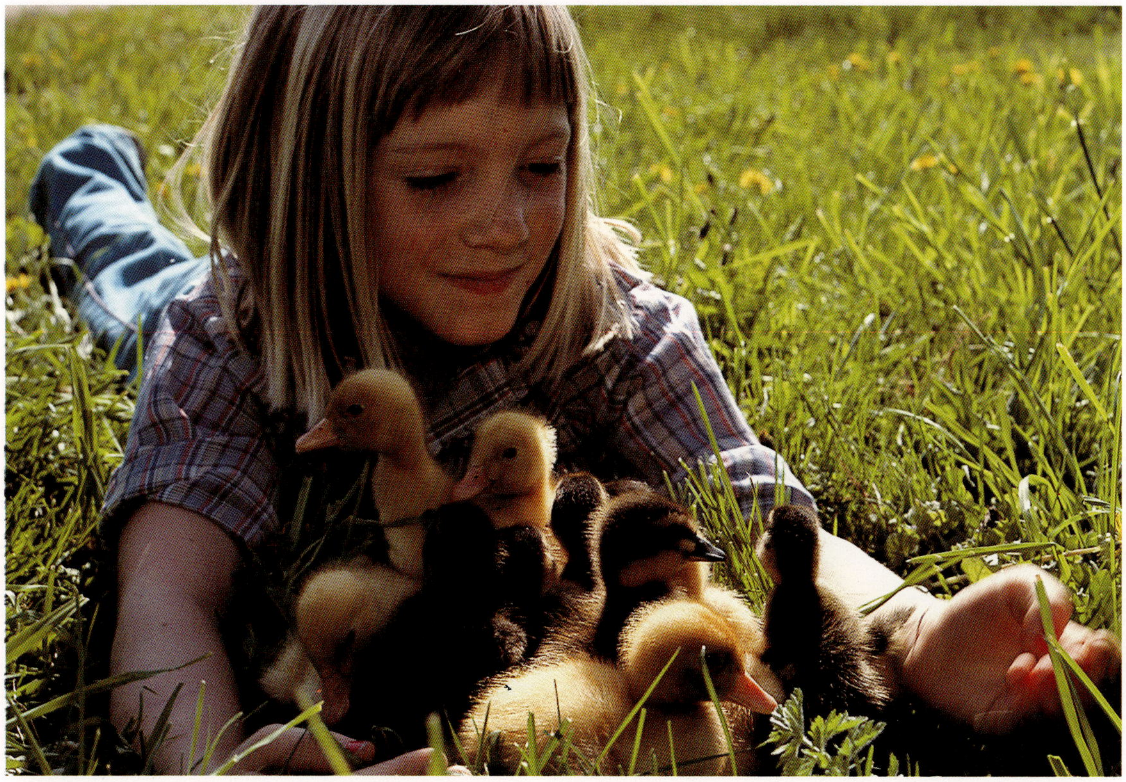

Heather with baby ducks

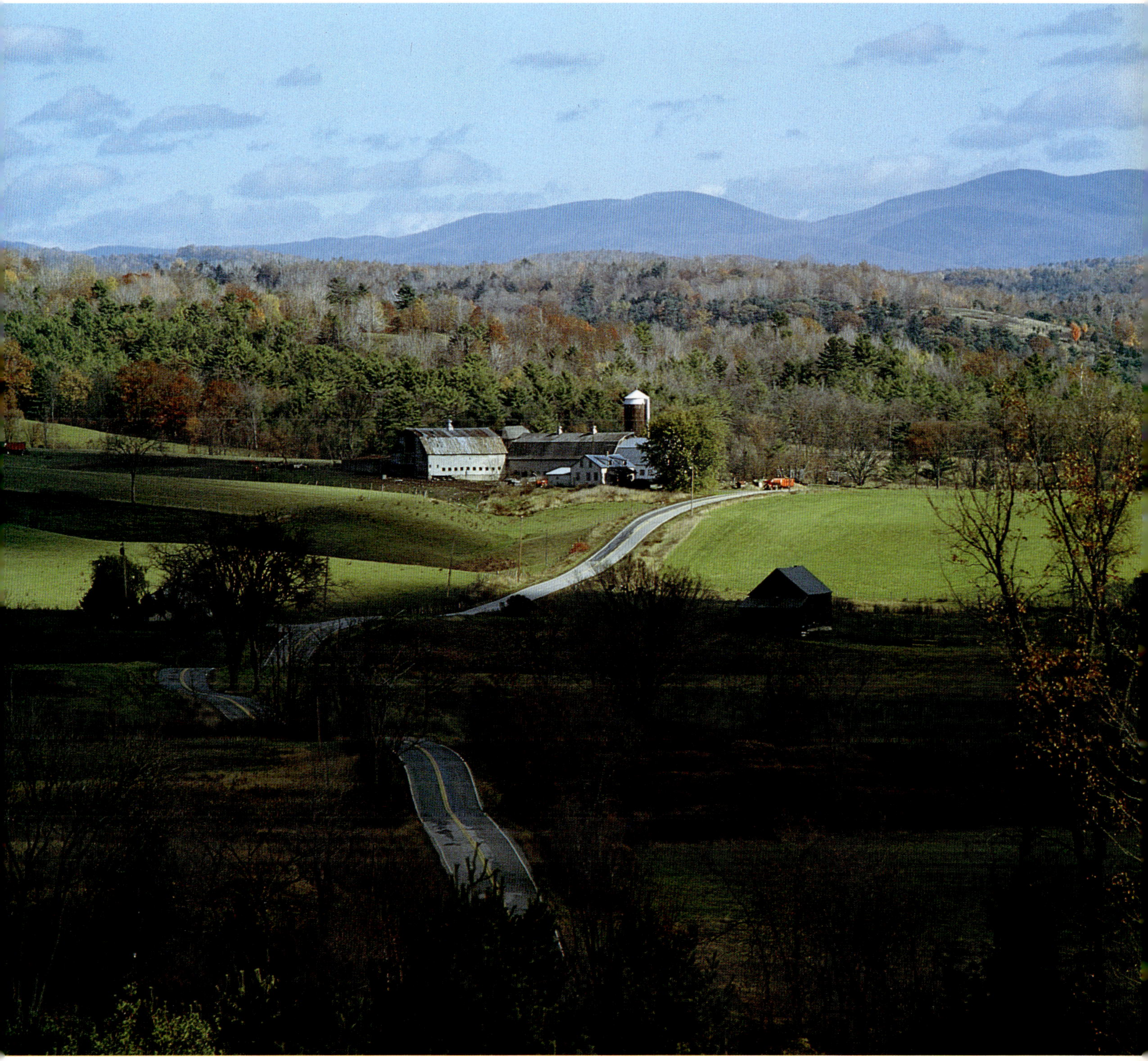

West Haven

Overleaf: Winooski River Valley

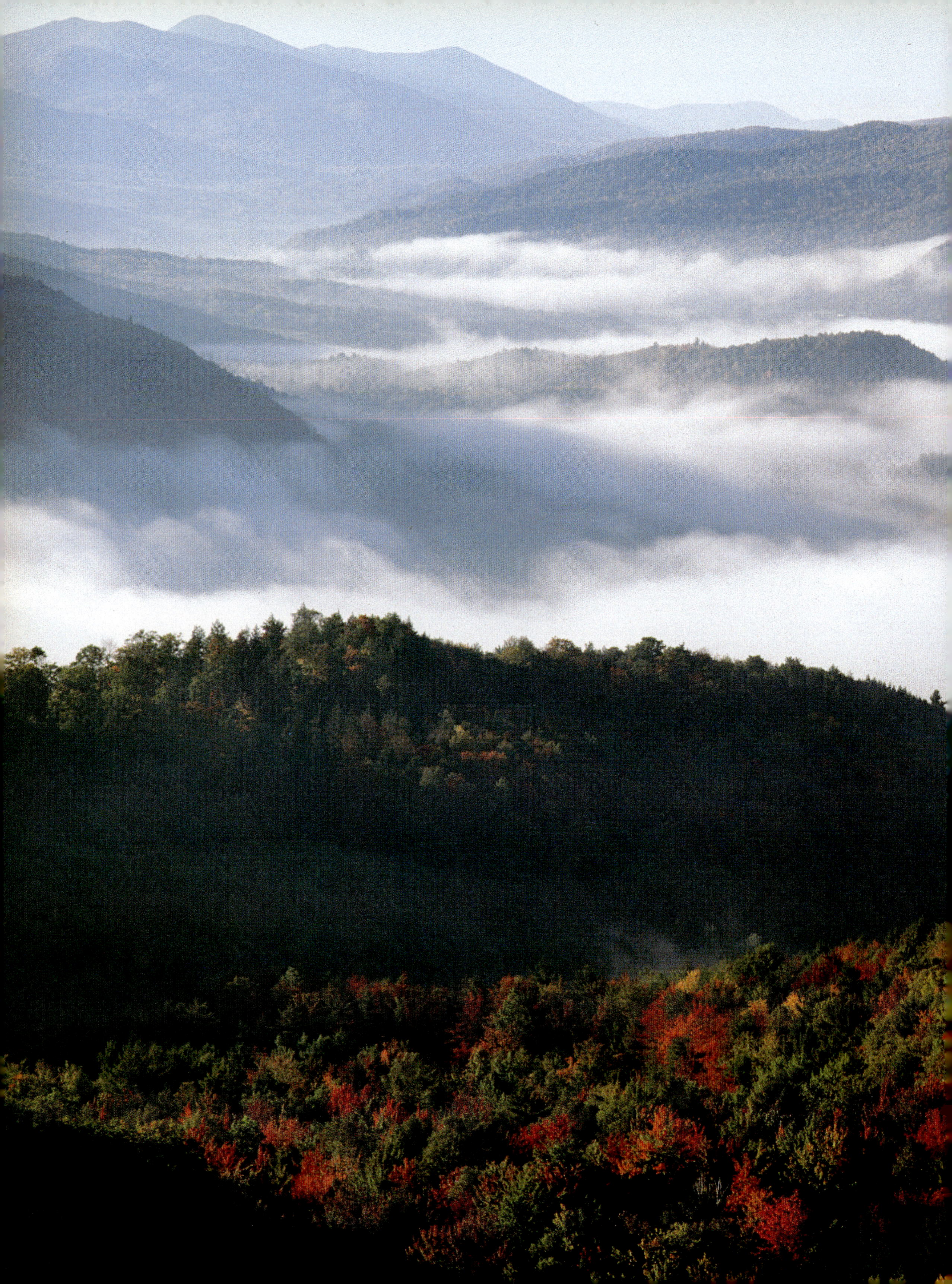

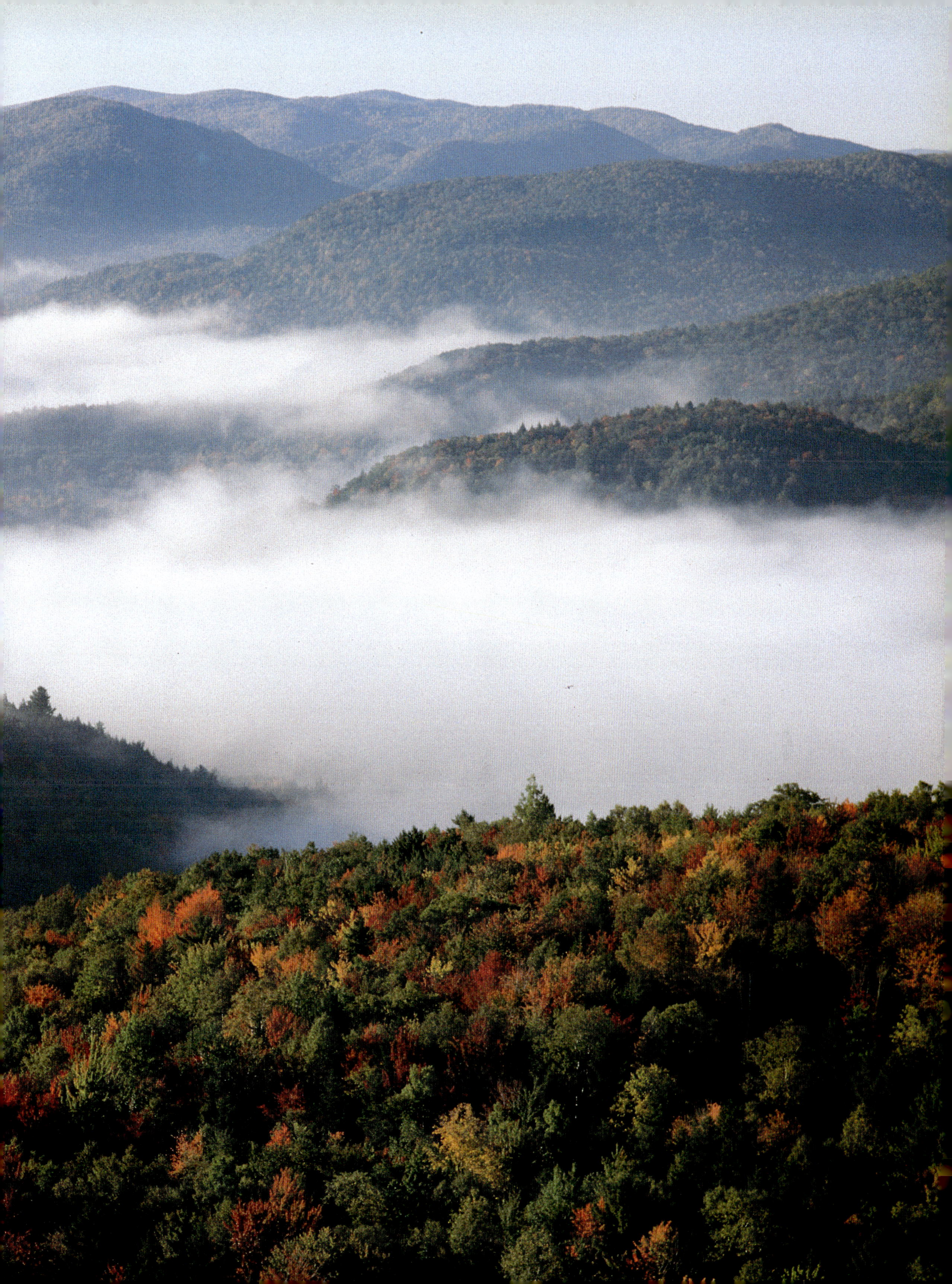

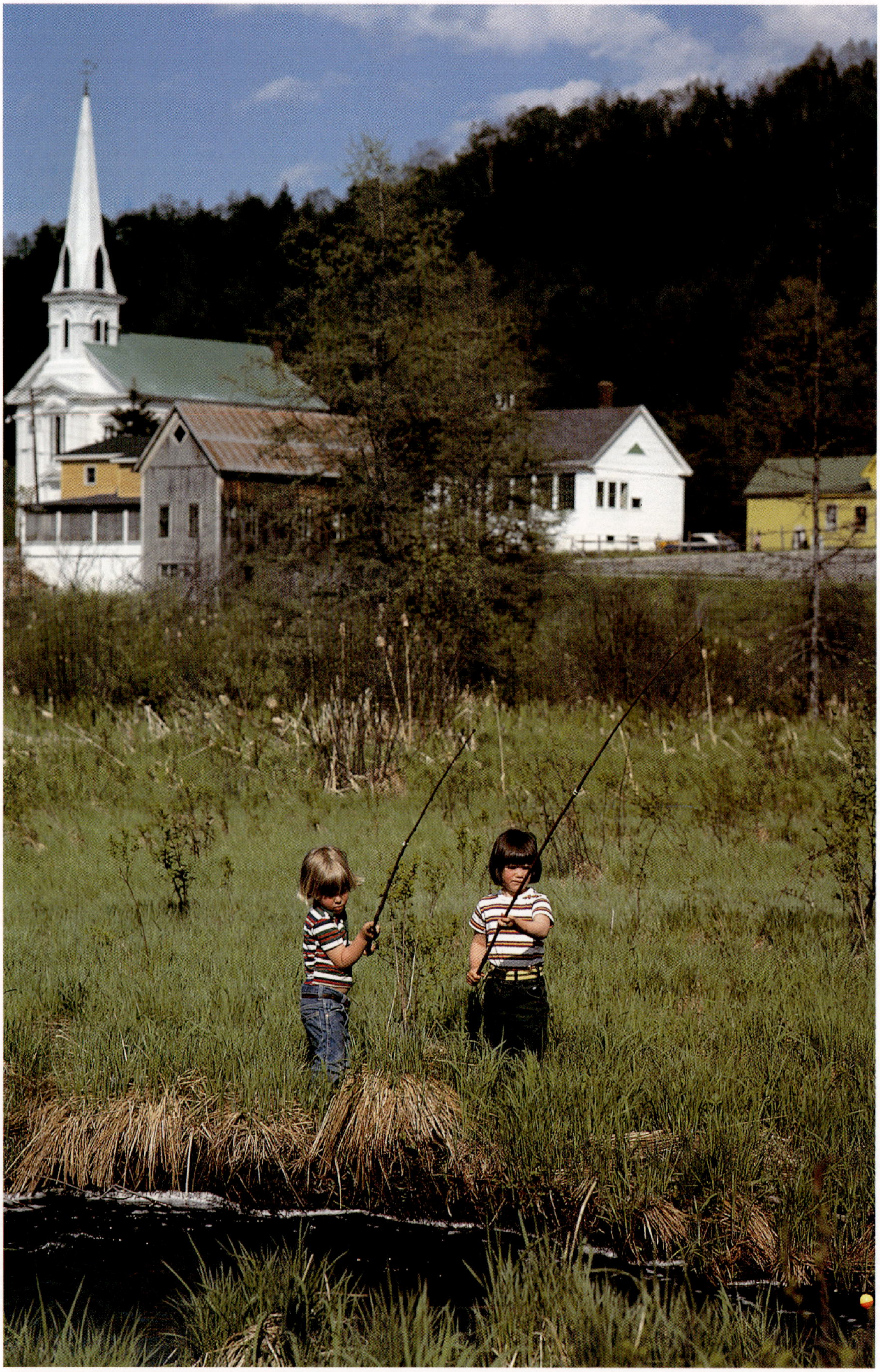

South Woodbury

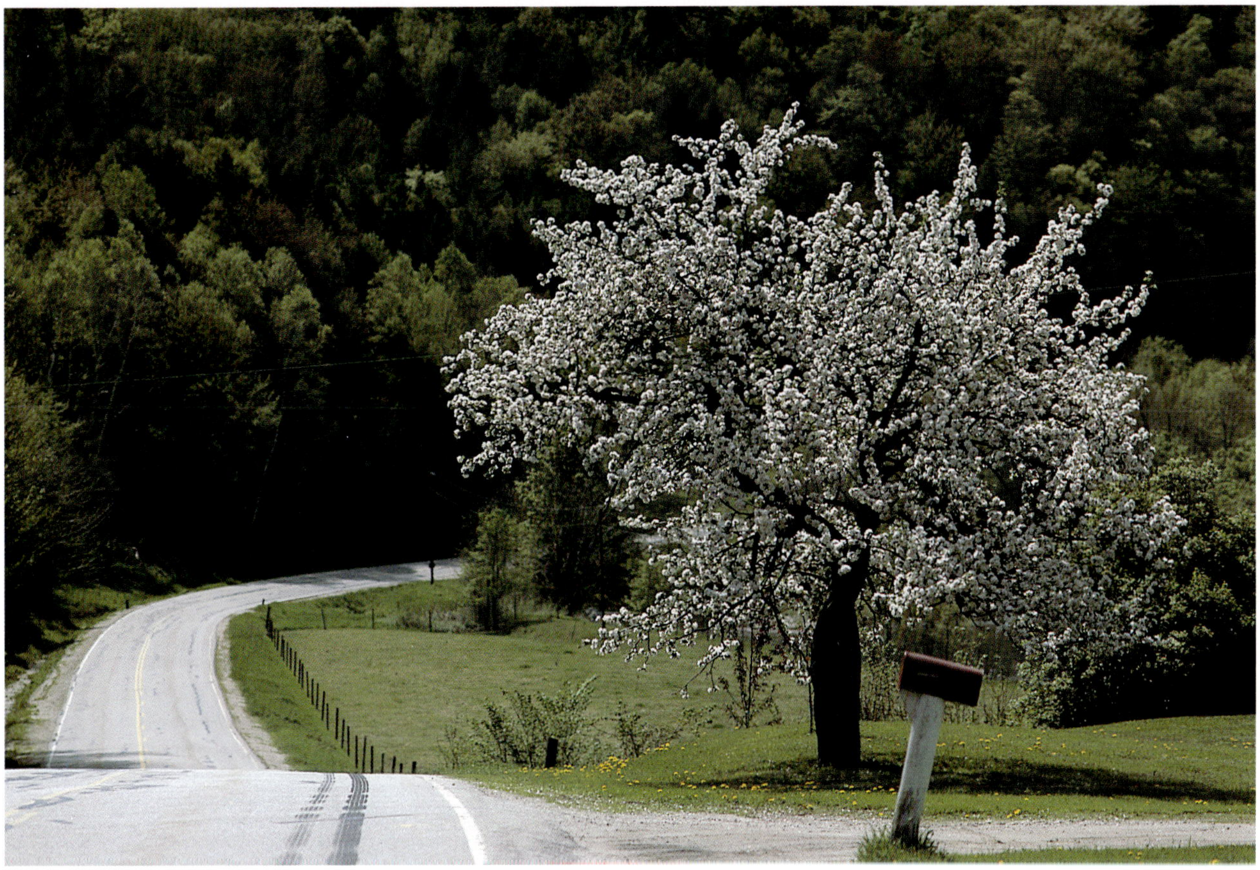

Rochester

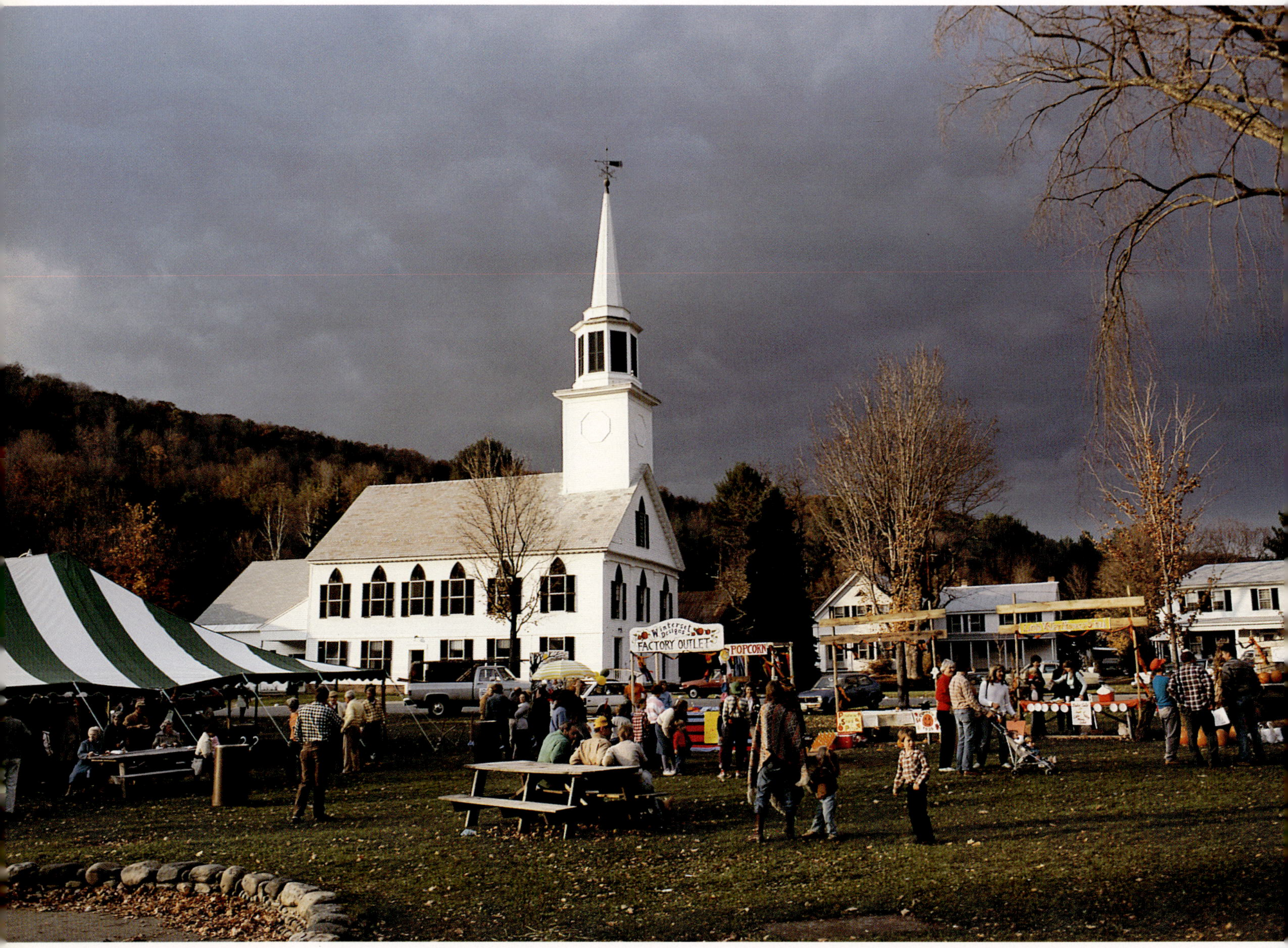
FACTORY OUTLET
POPCORN

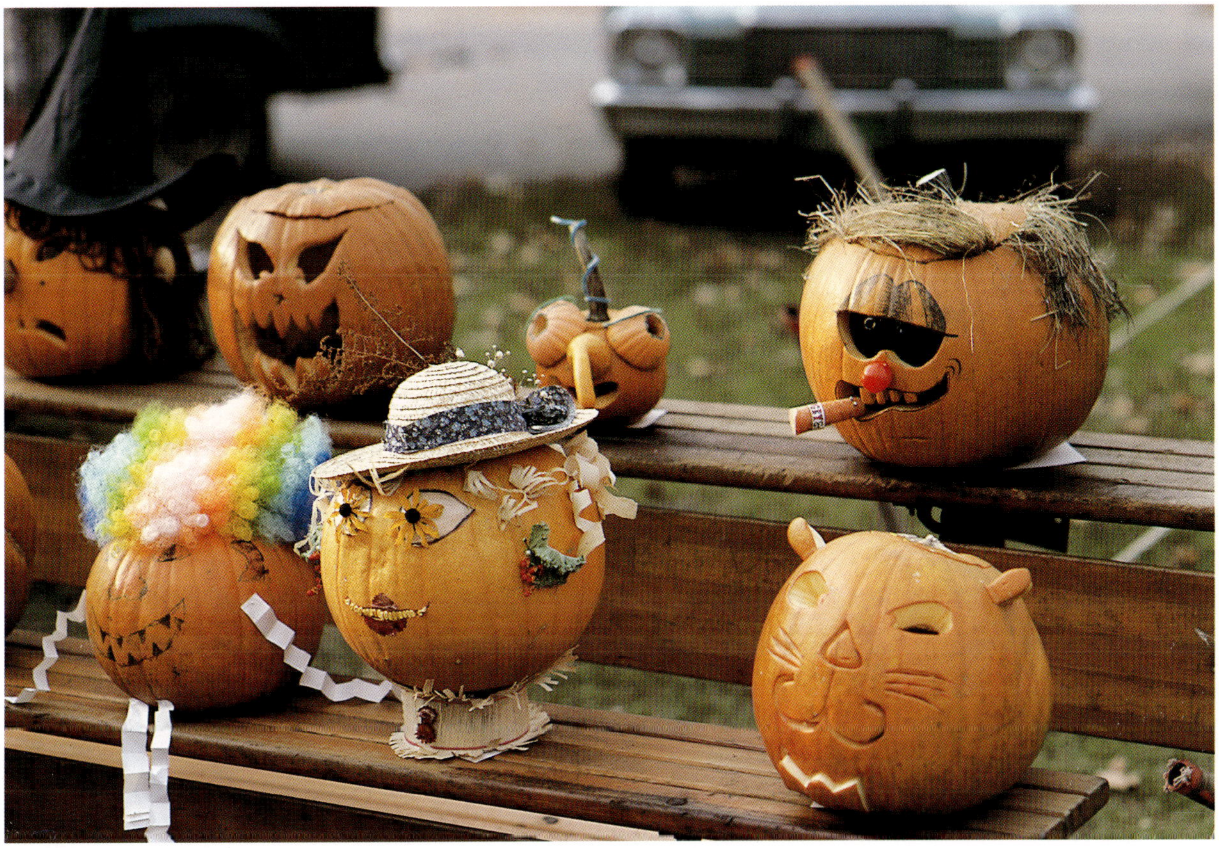

Townshend

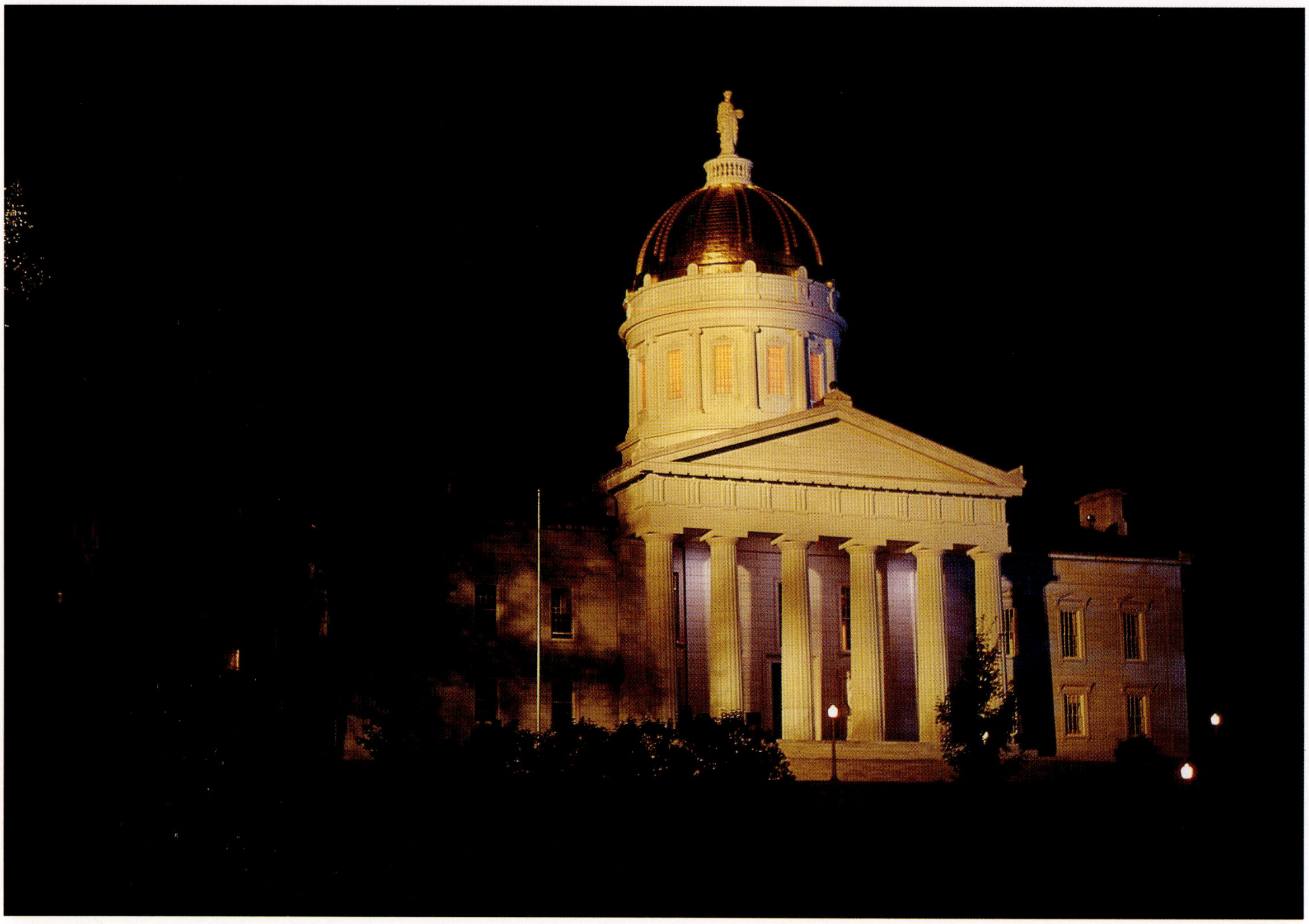

Montpelier

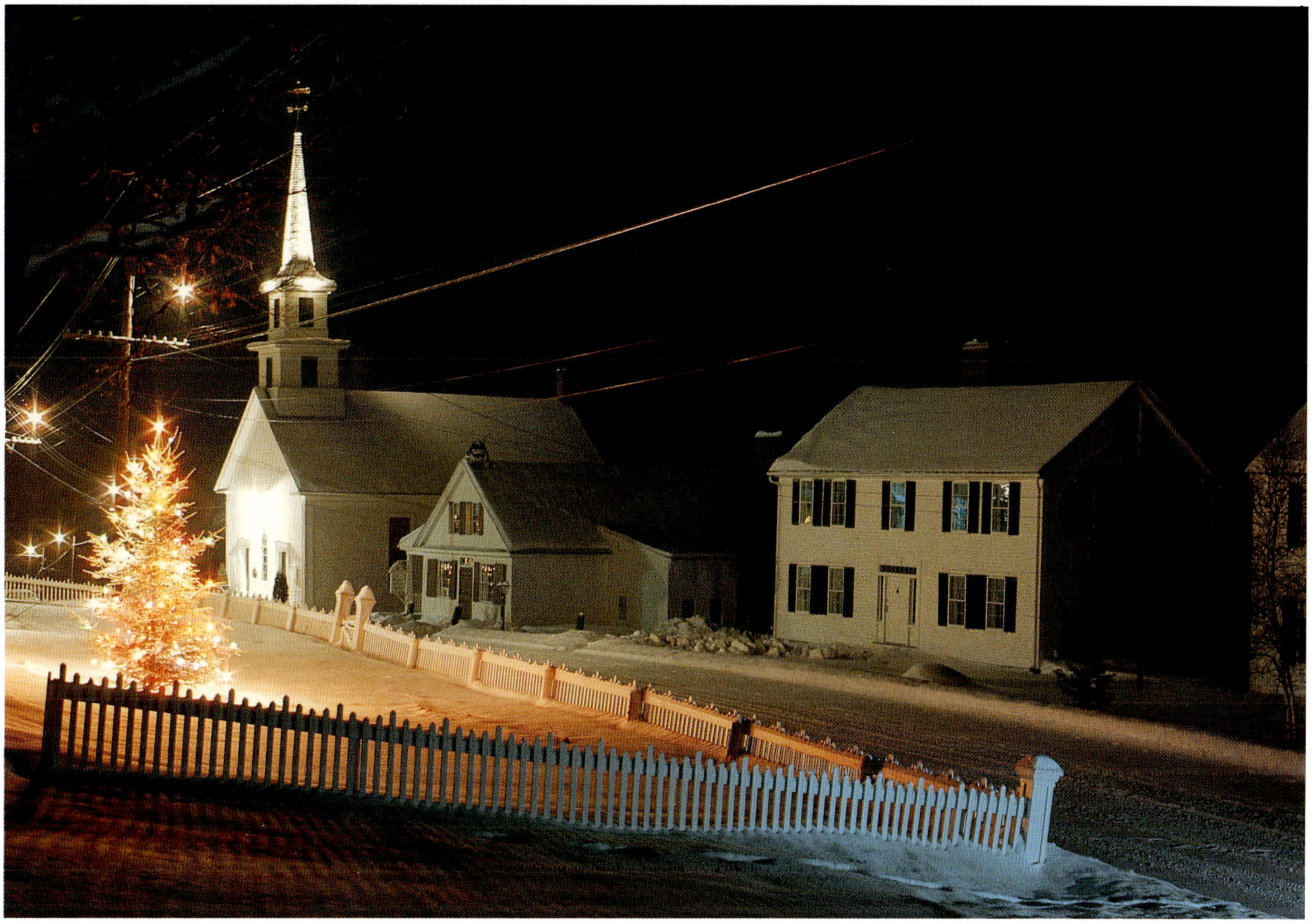

Lower Waterford

Overleaf: Summit of Camels Hump

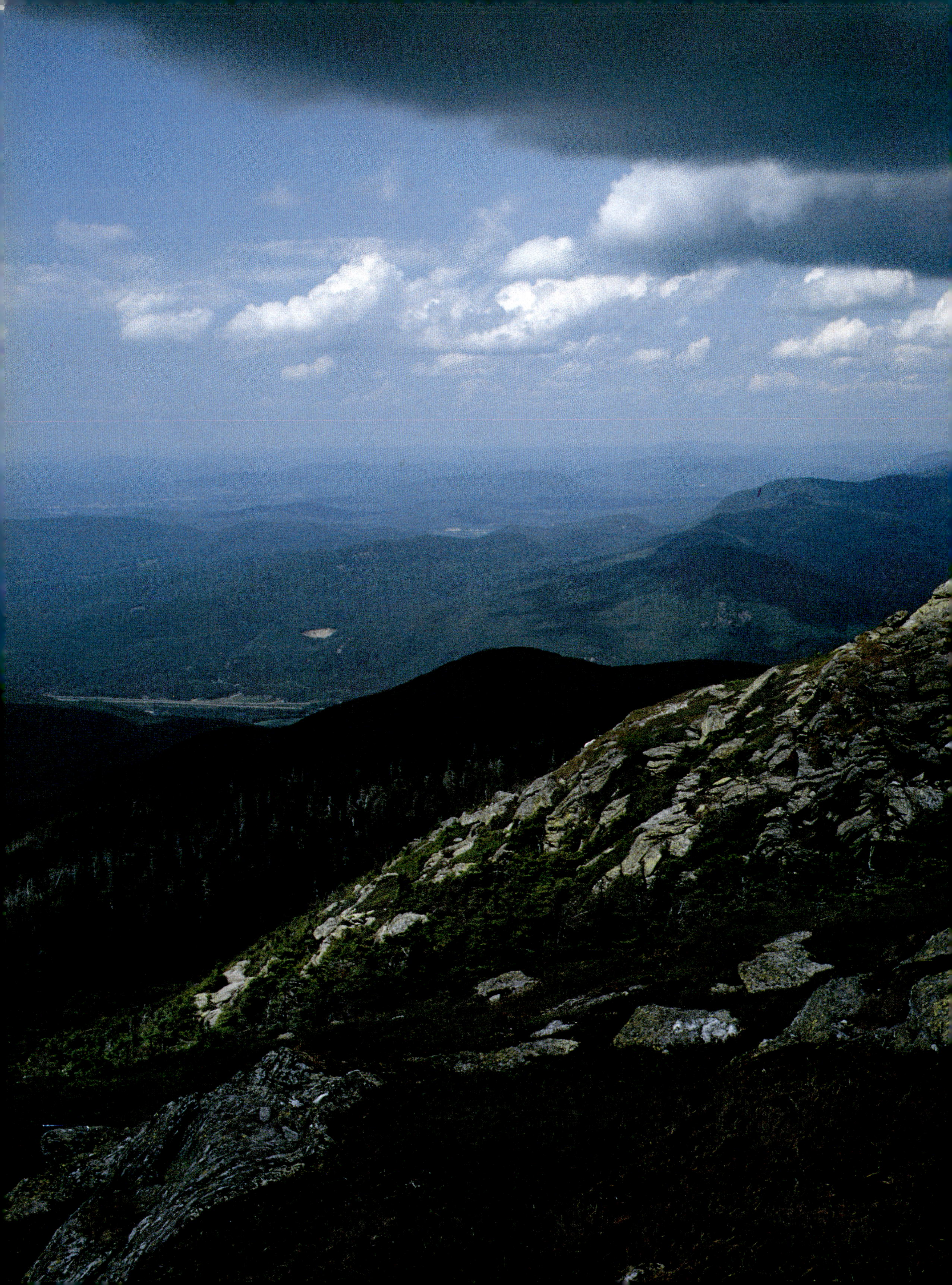

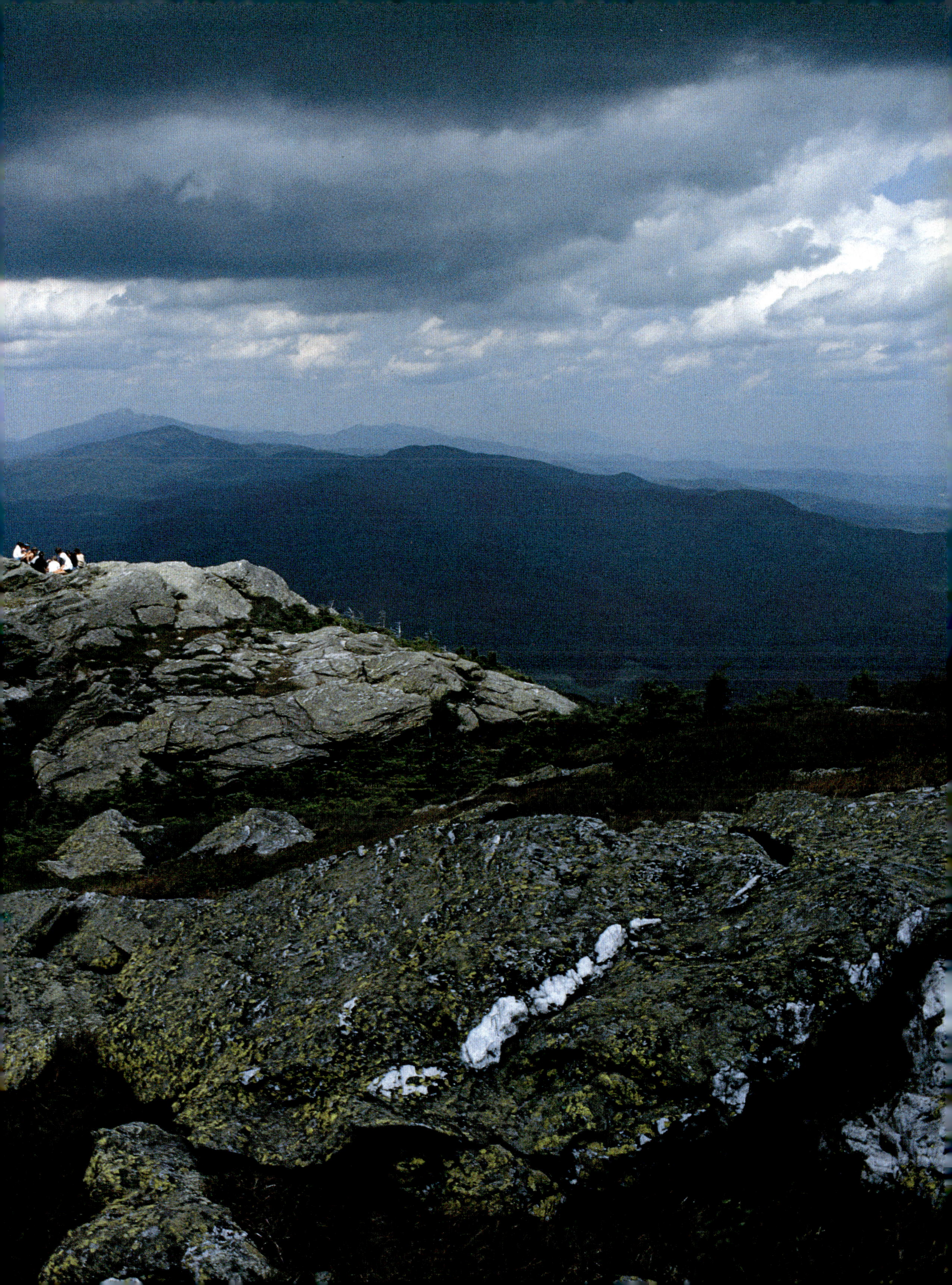

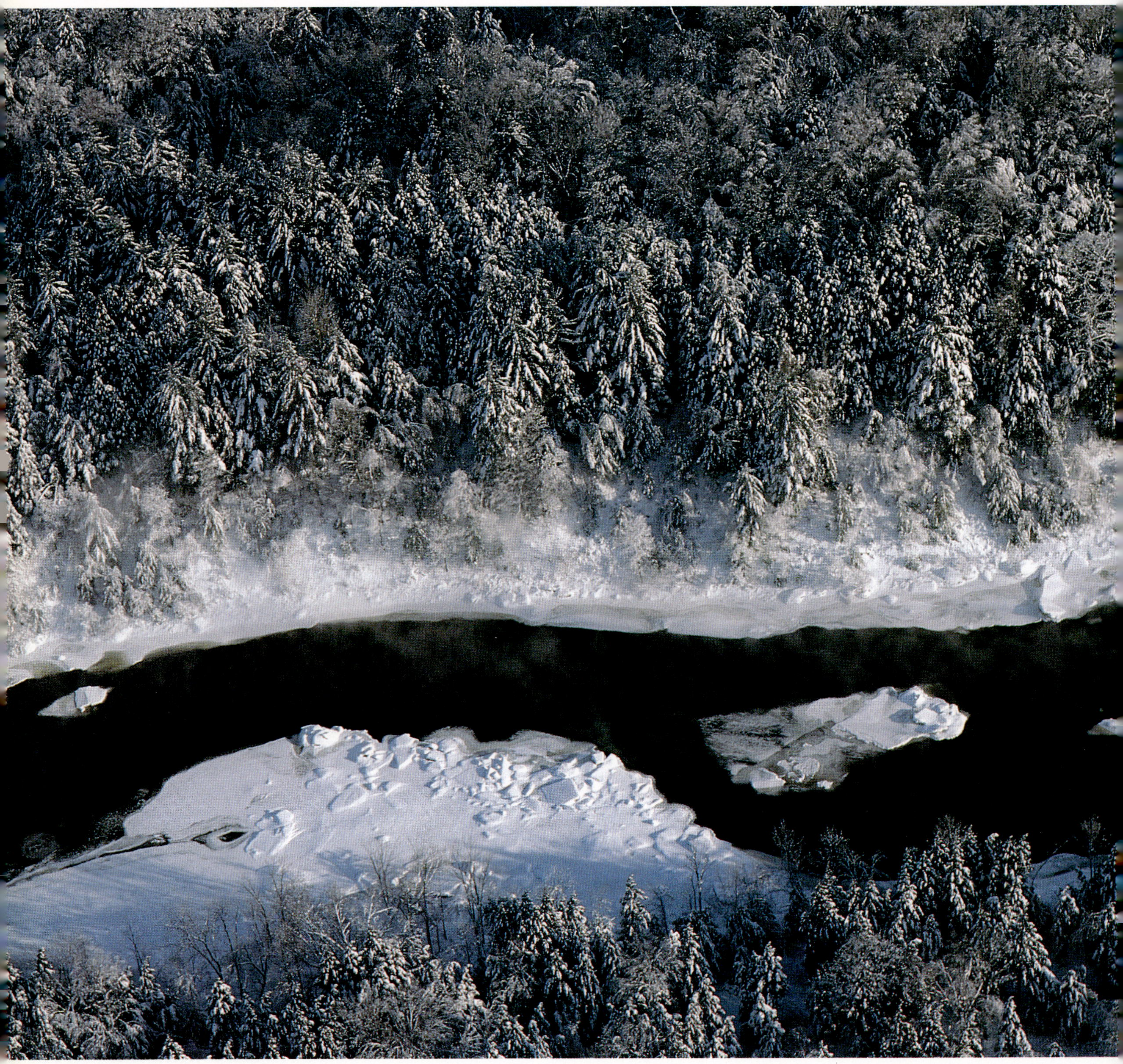

Lamoille River, Johnson

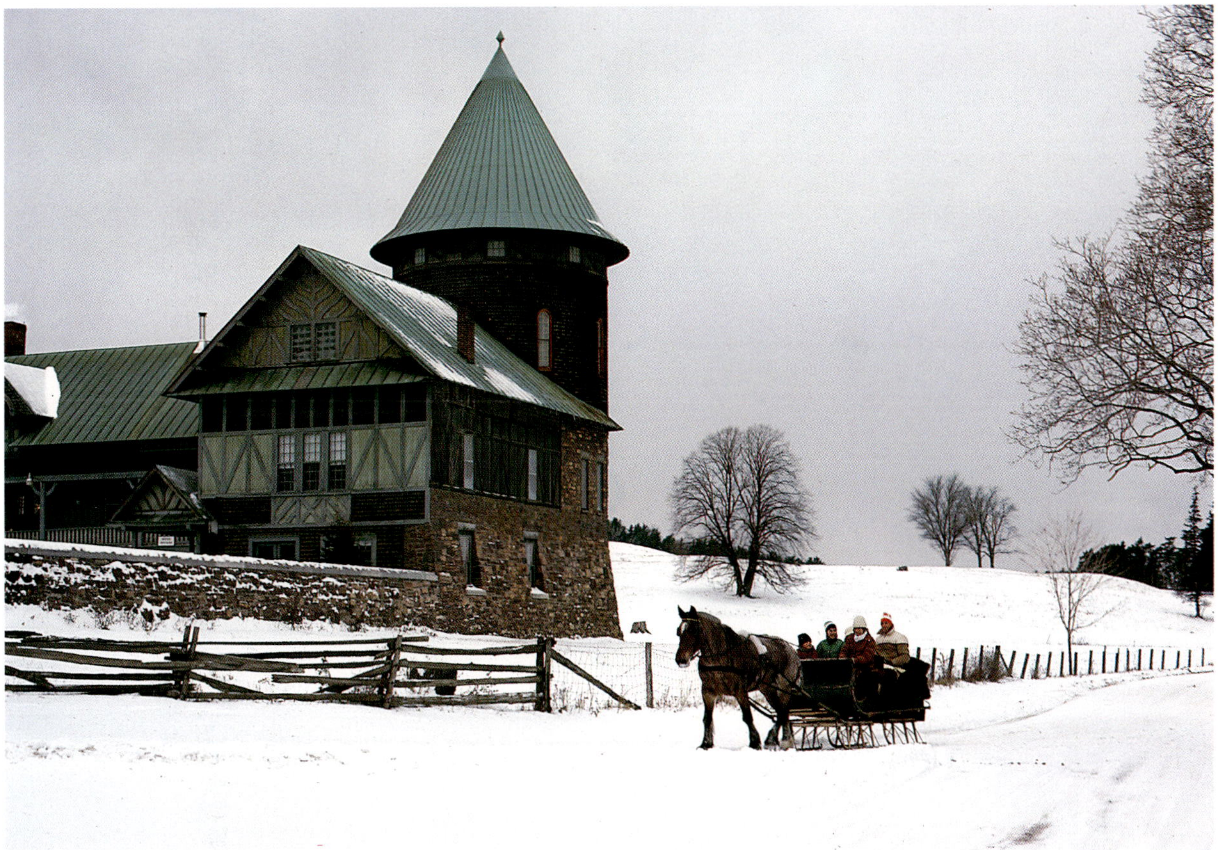

Shelburne Farms, Shelburne

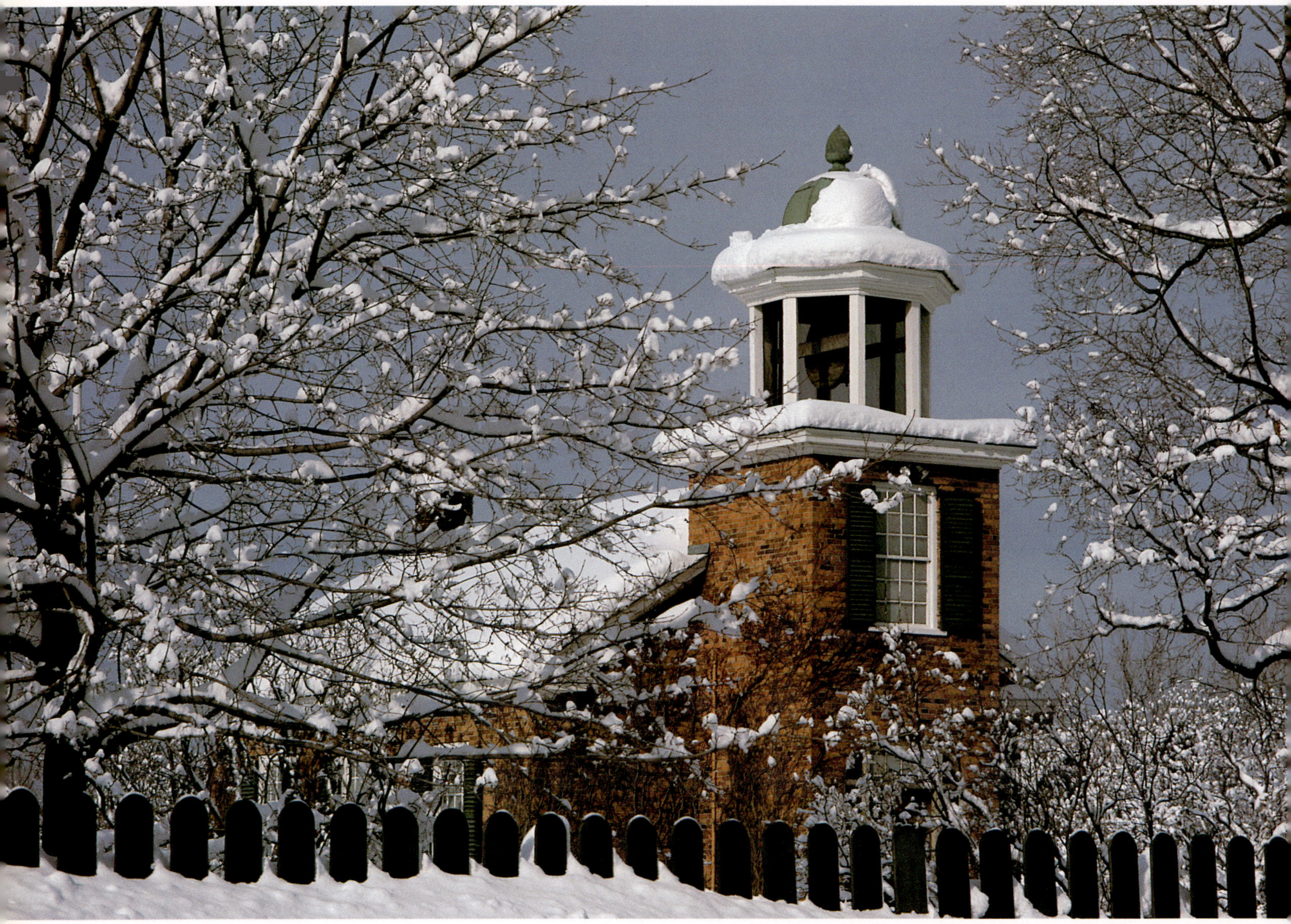

Vergennes School House

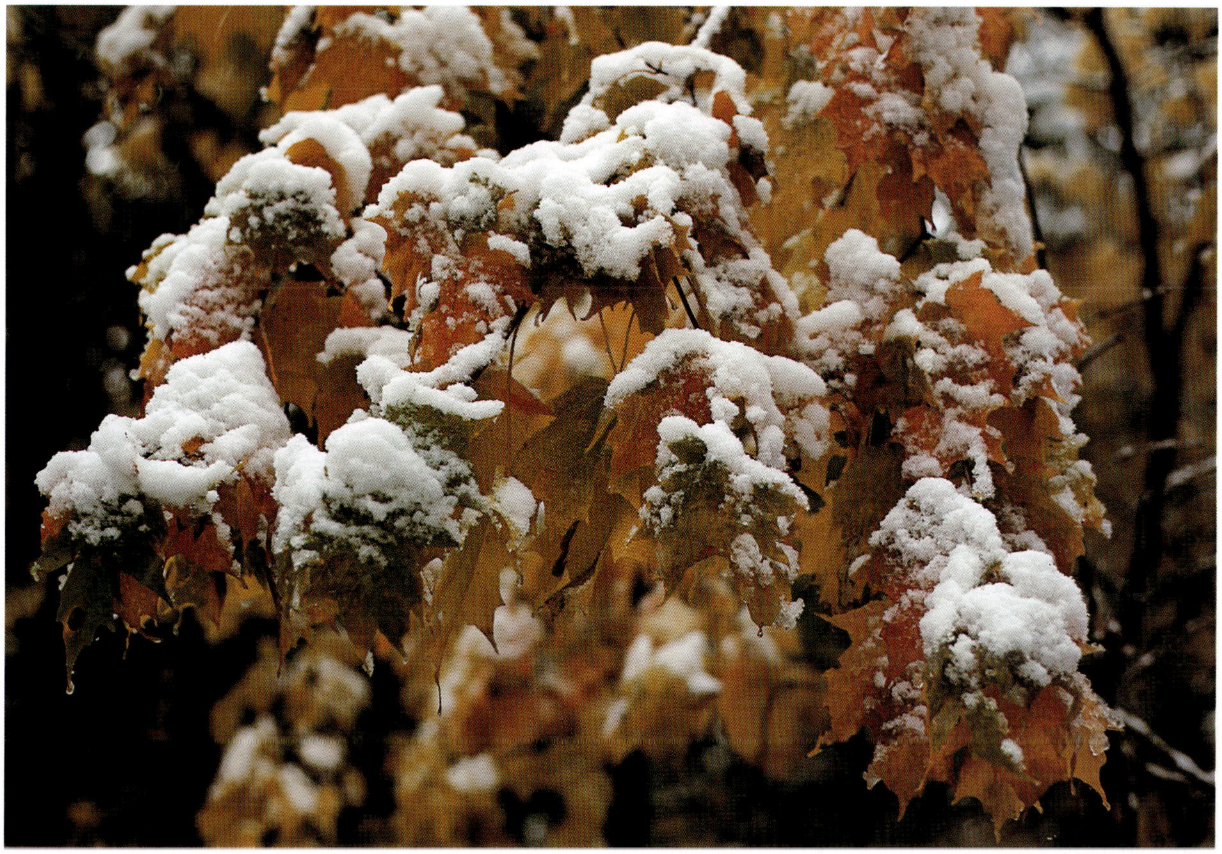

Sugar Maple

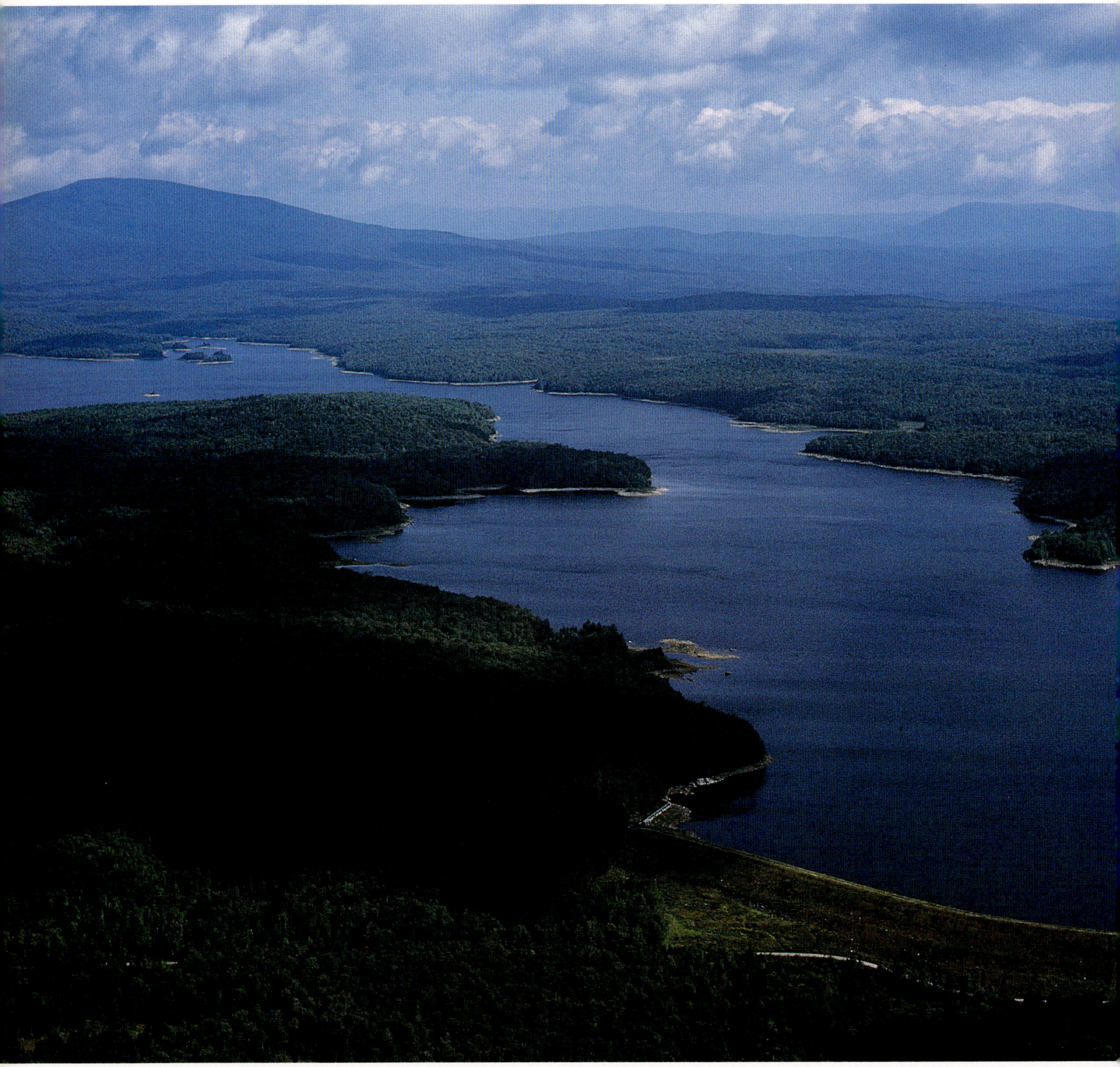

Somerset Reservoir and Mt. Stratton

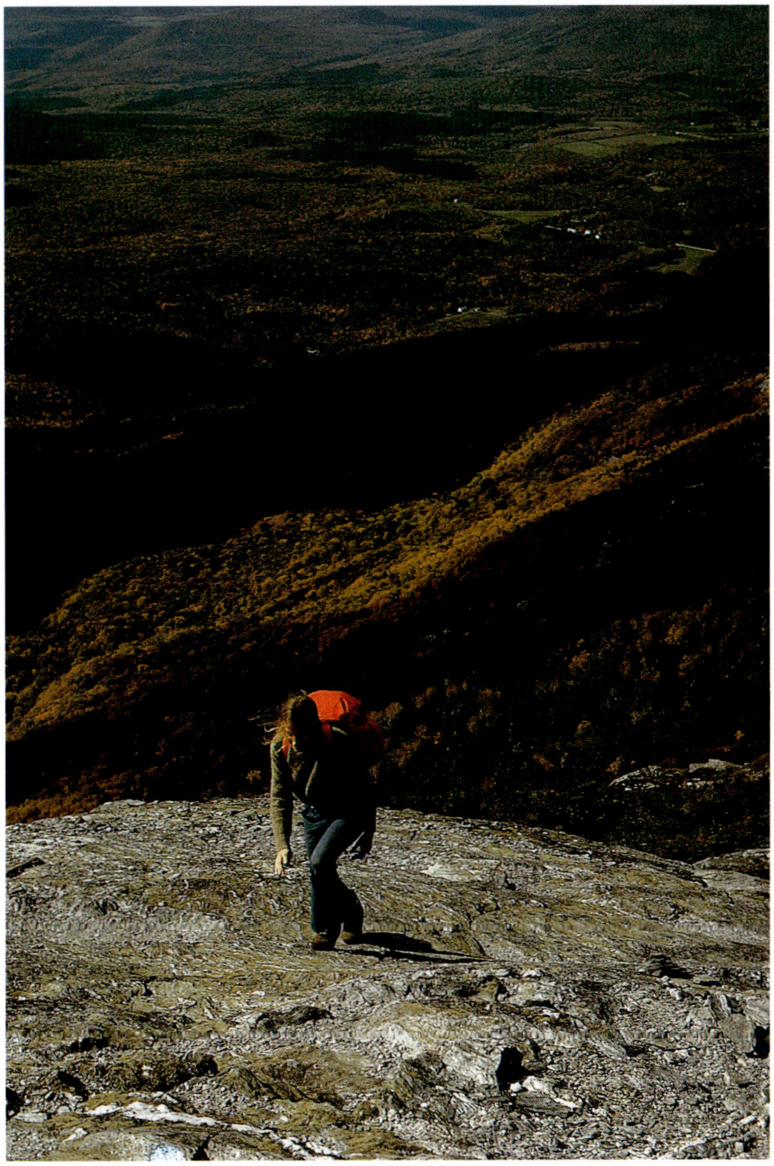

Long Trail, Mt. Mansfield

Overleaf: Worcester

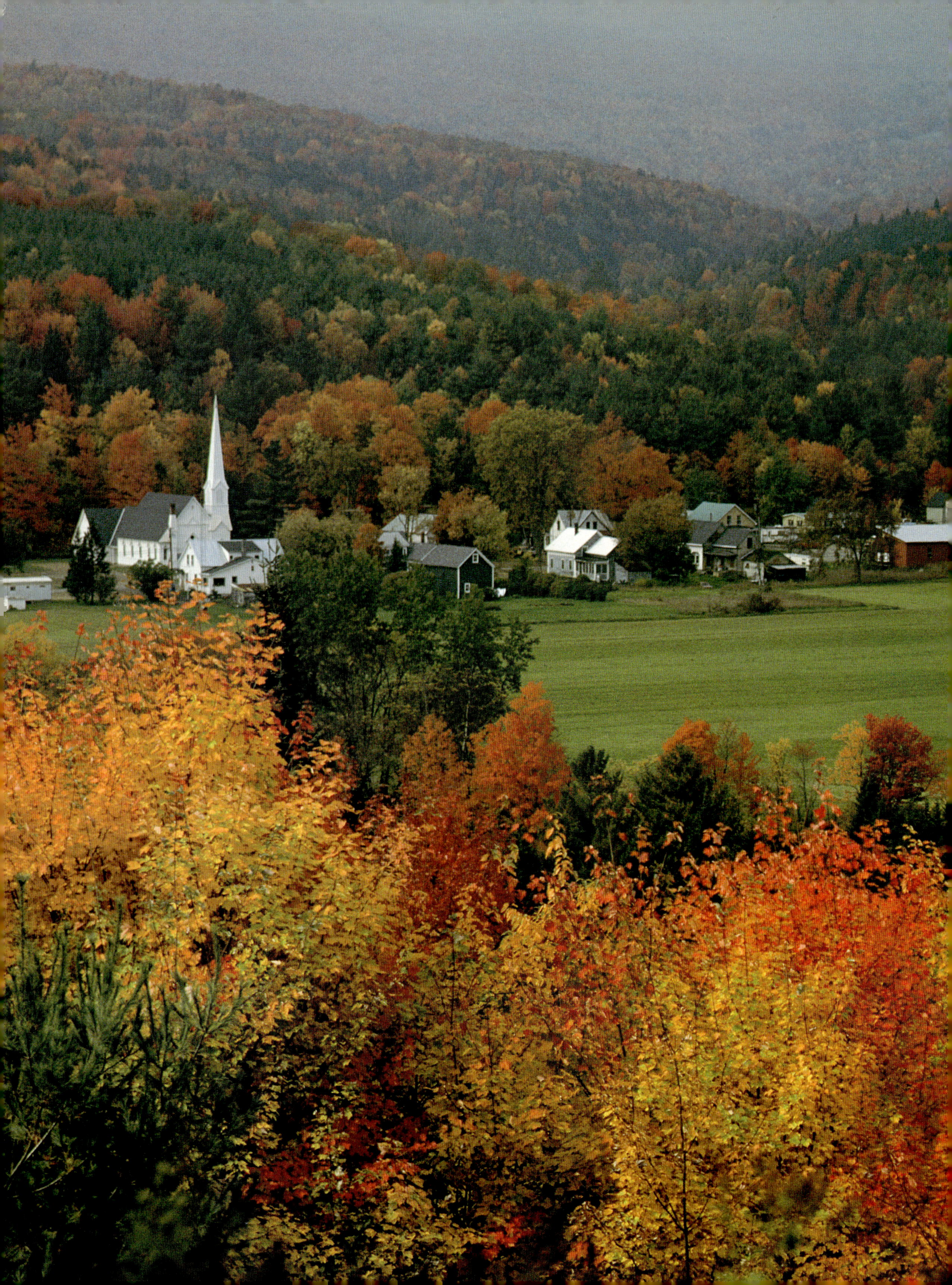

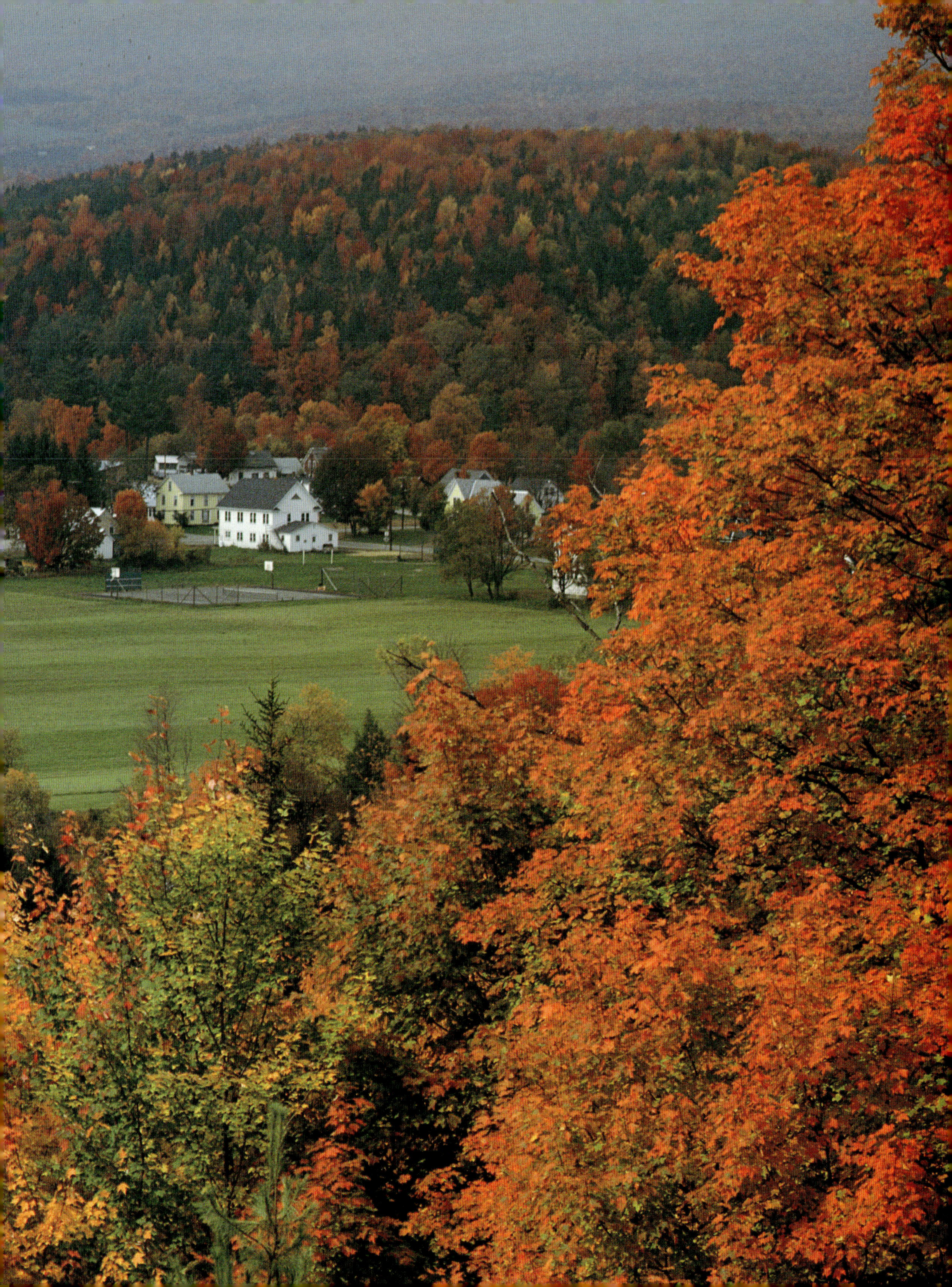

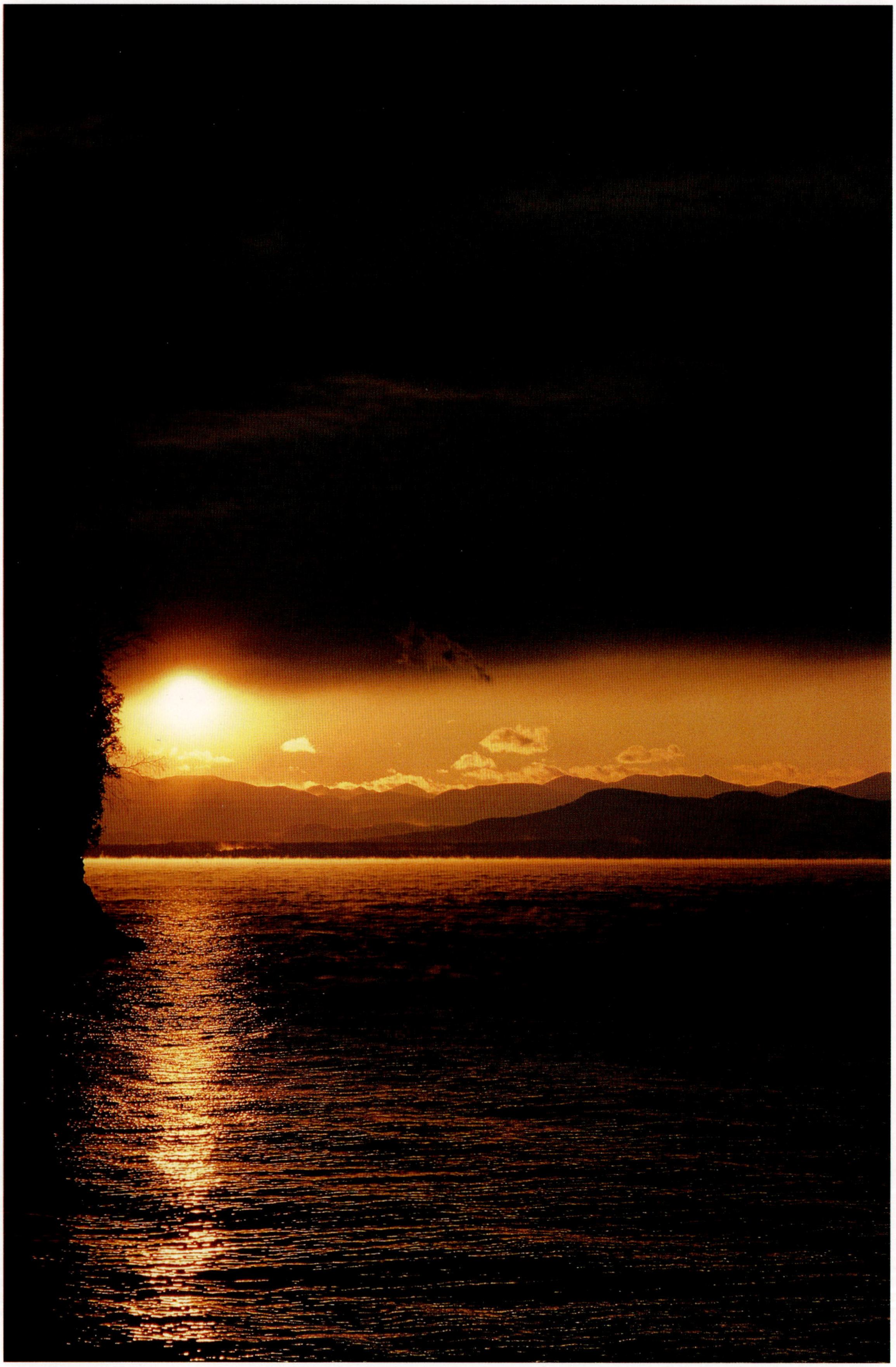

Lake Champlain

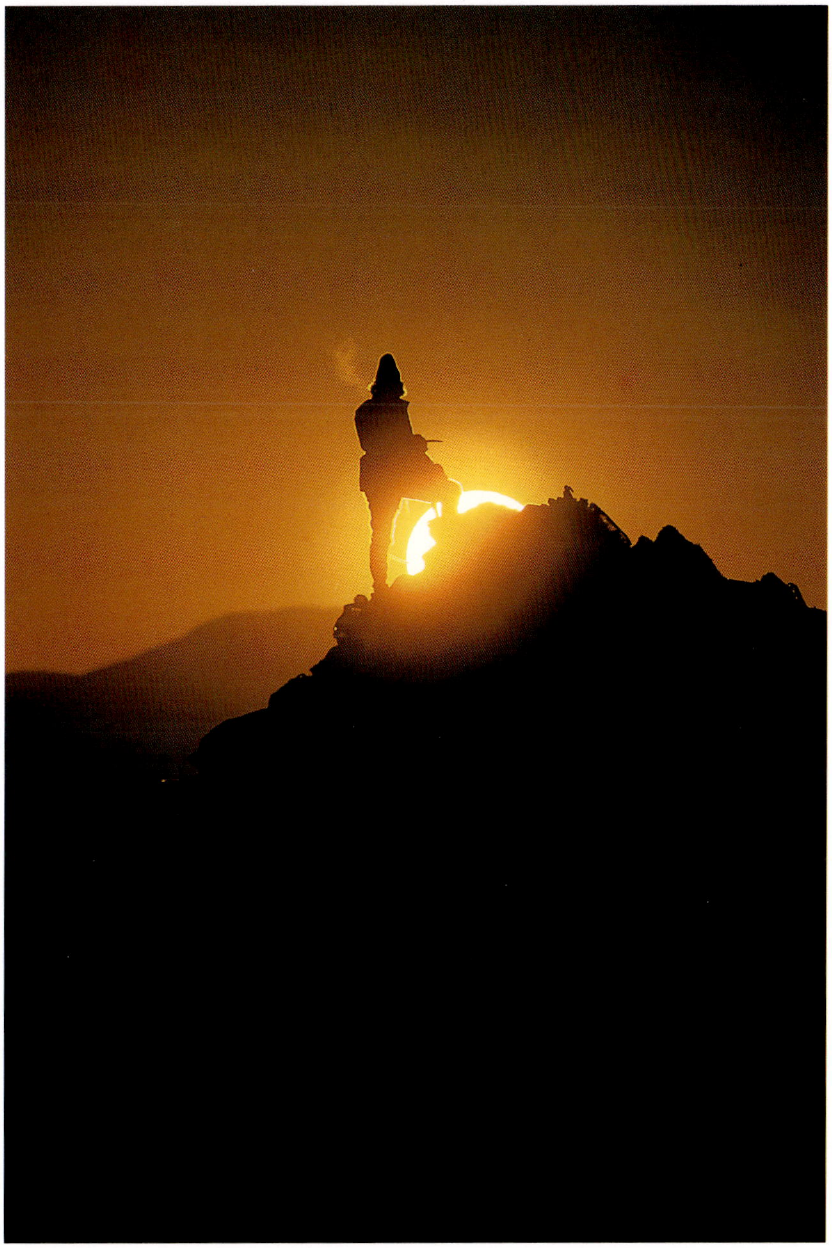

Snow drift, Lake Champlain

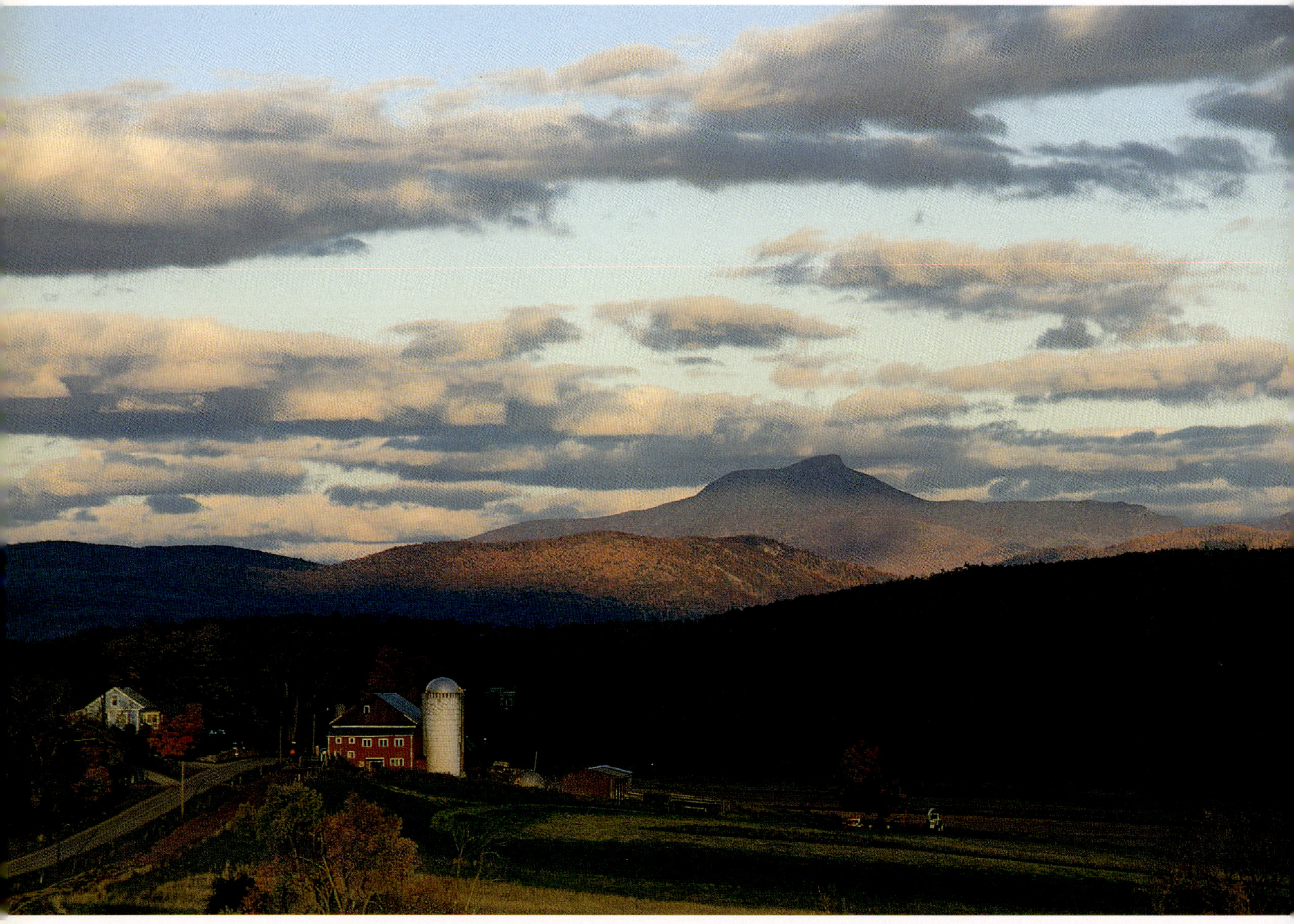

North Ferrisburg

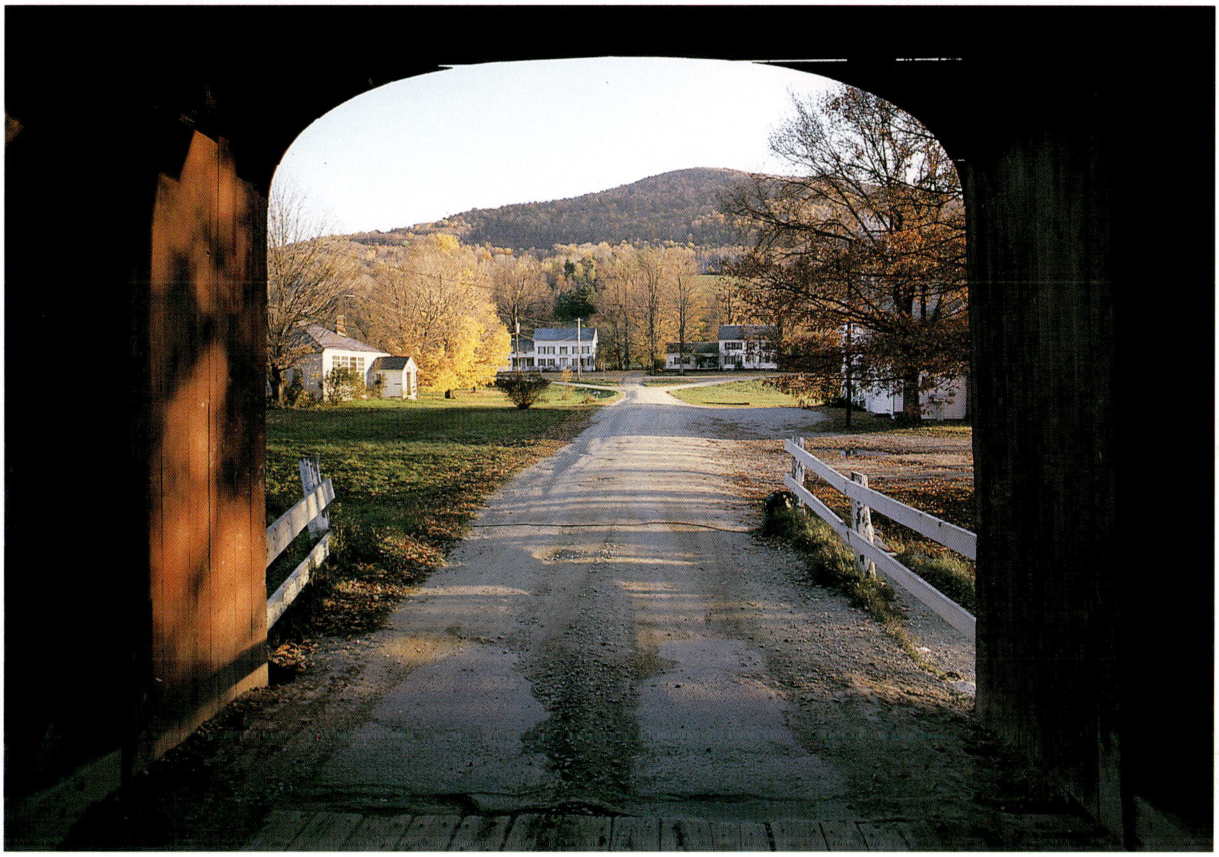

West Arlington

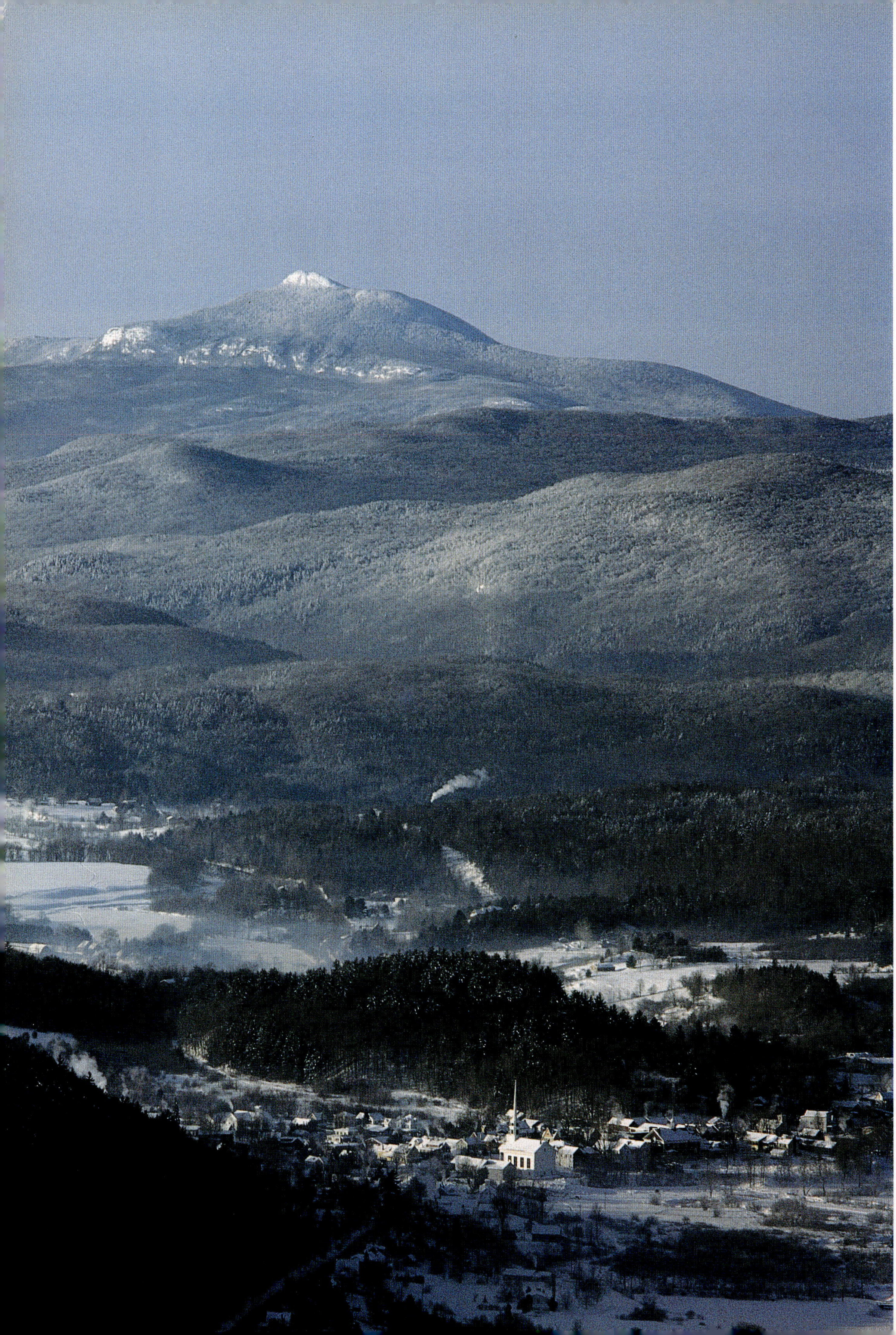

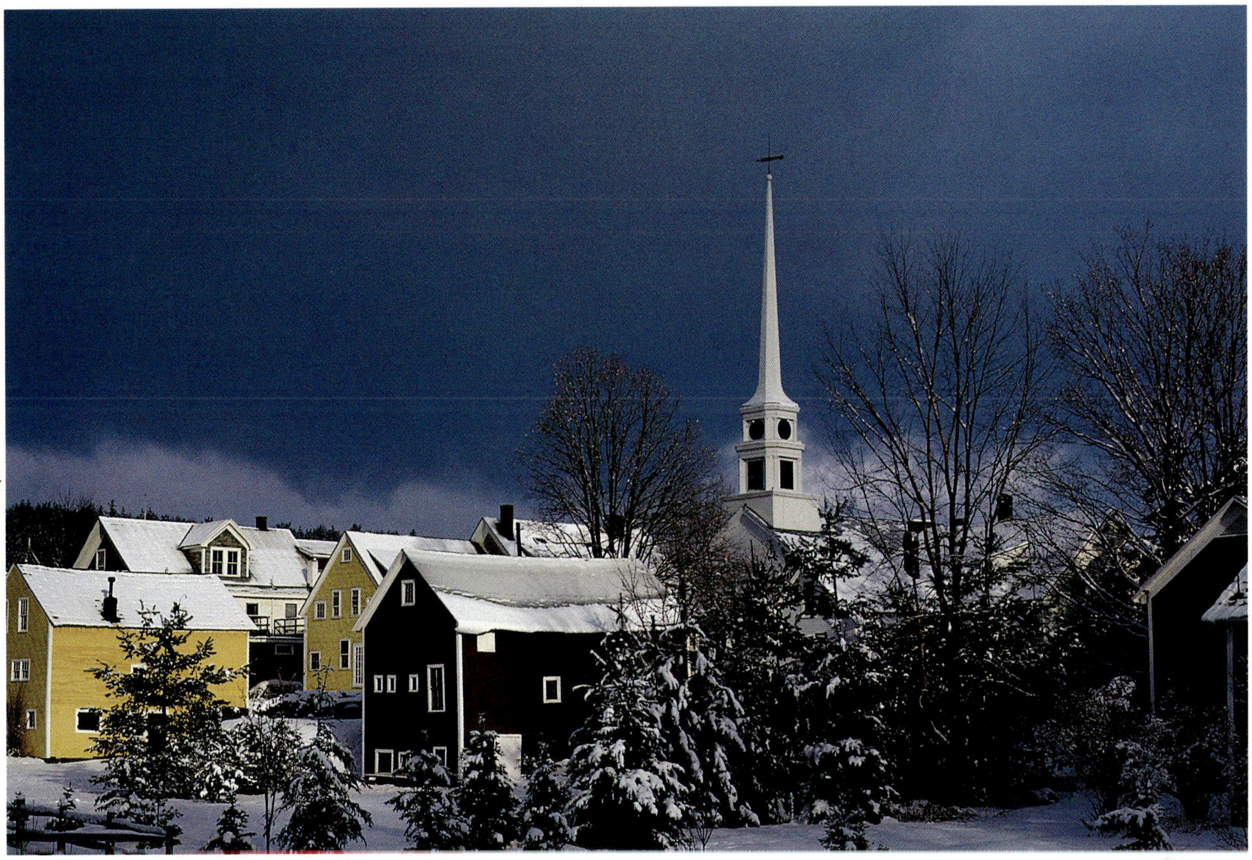

Stowe and Camels Hump

Stowe

Overleaf: Mt. Mansfield

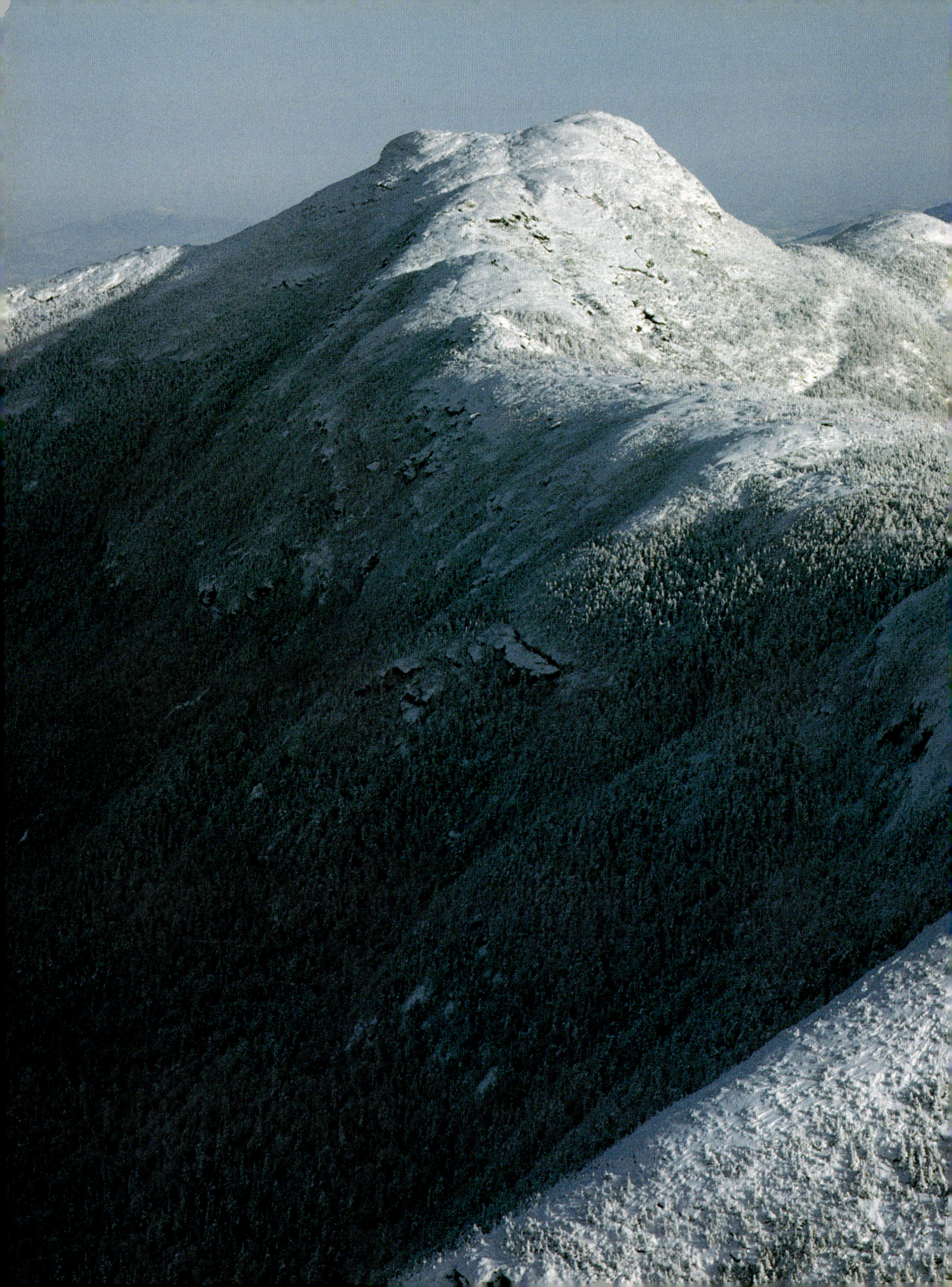

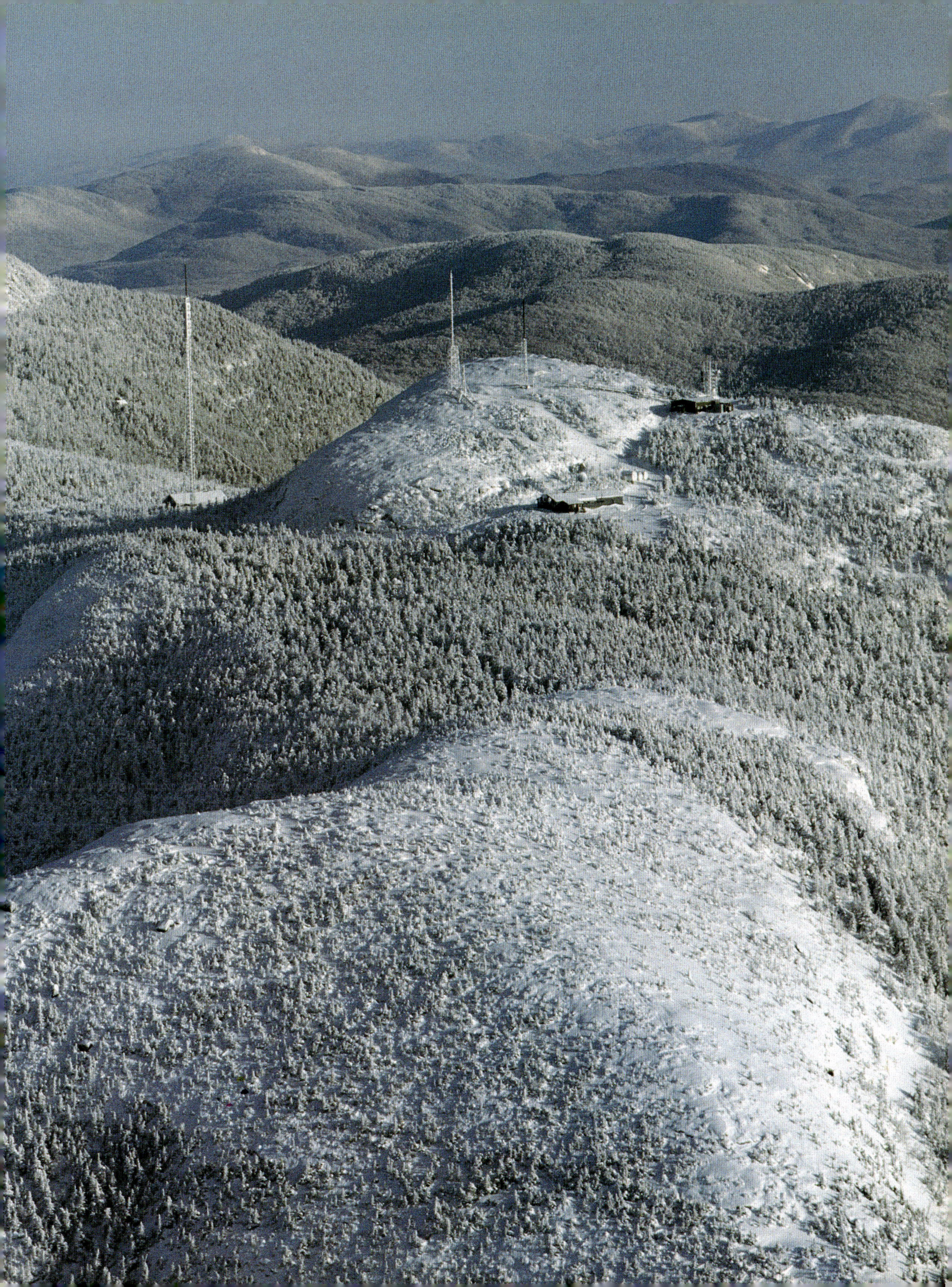

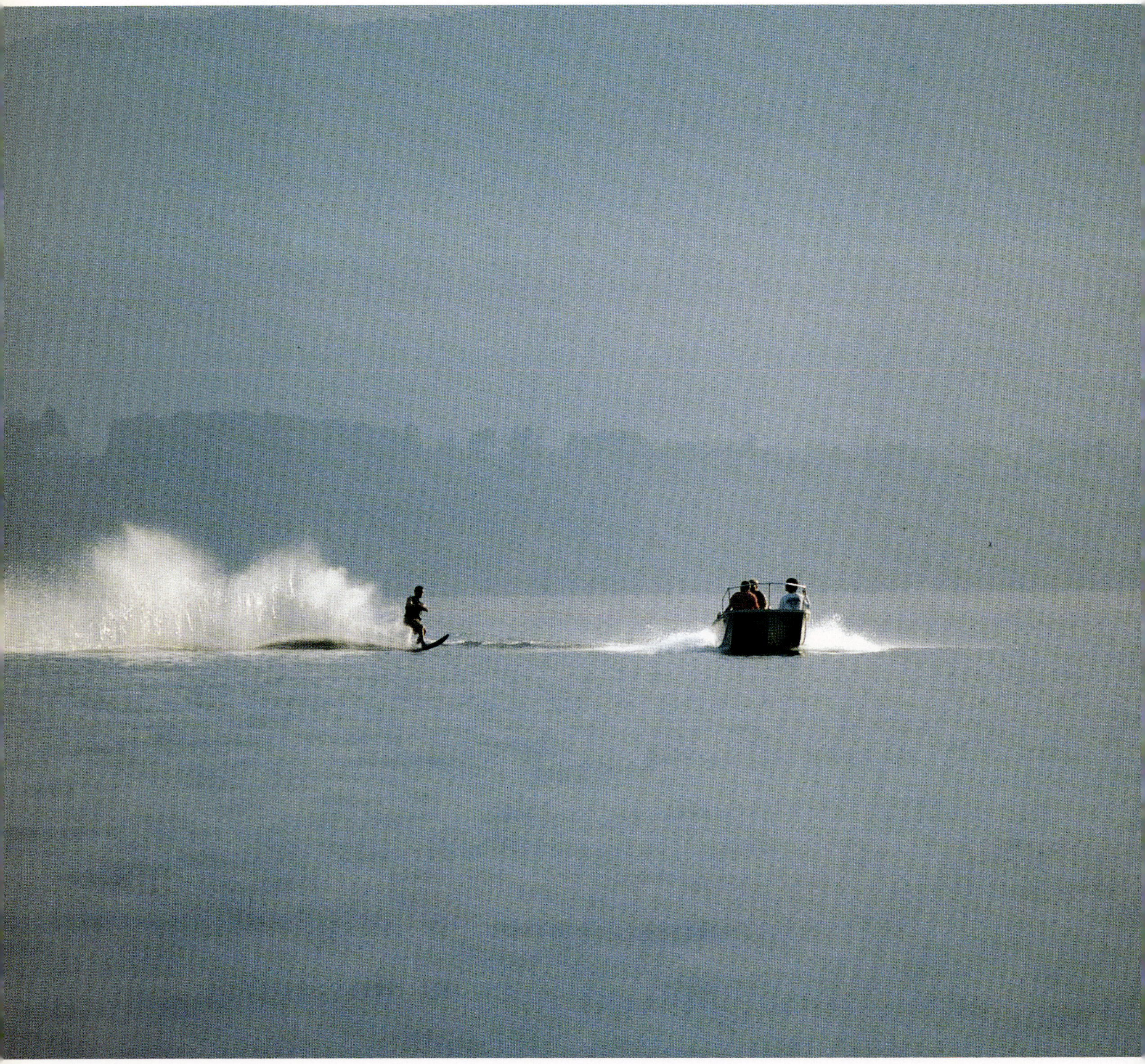

Basin Harbor, Vergennes

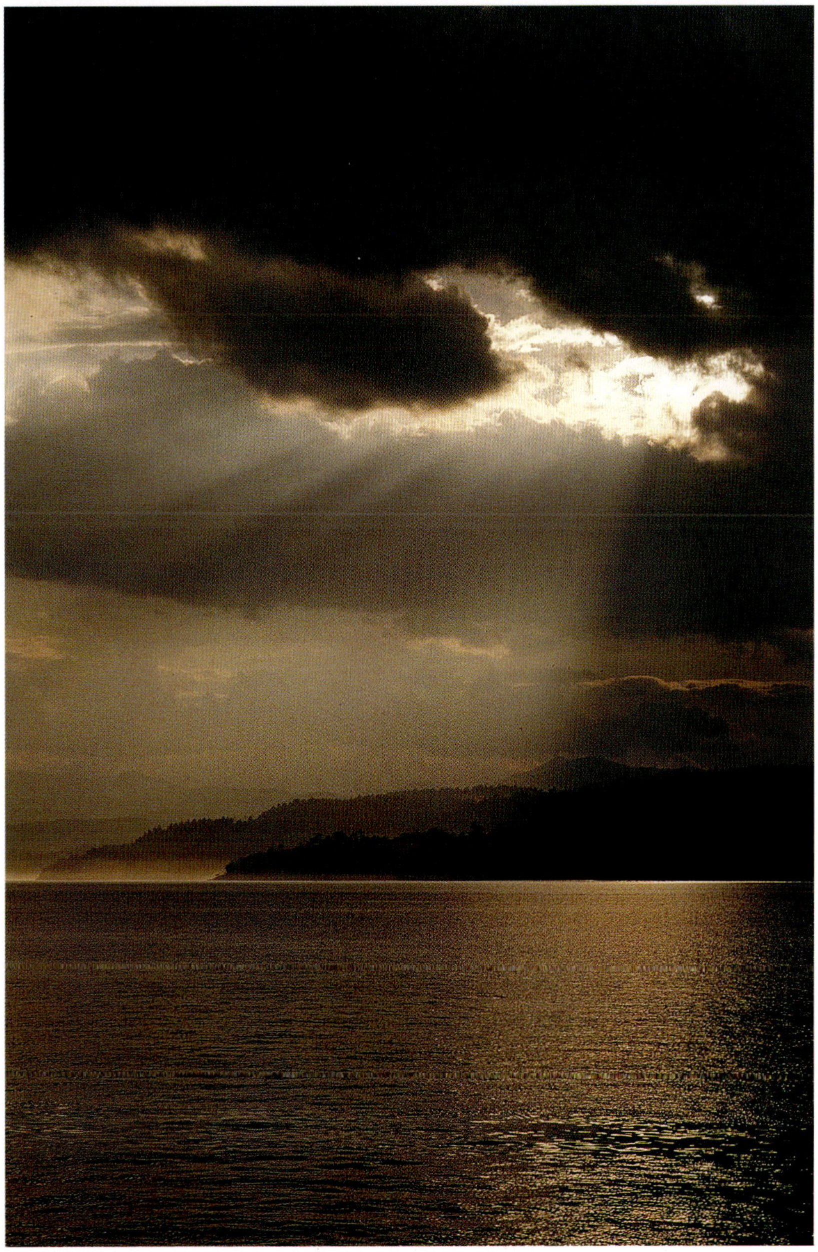

Basin Harbor

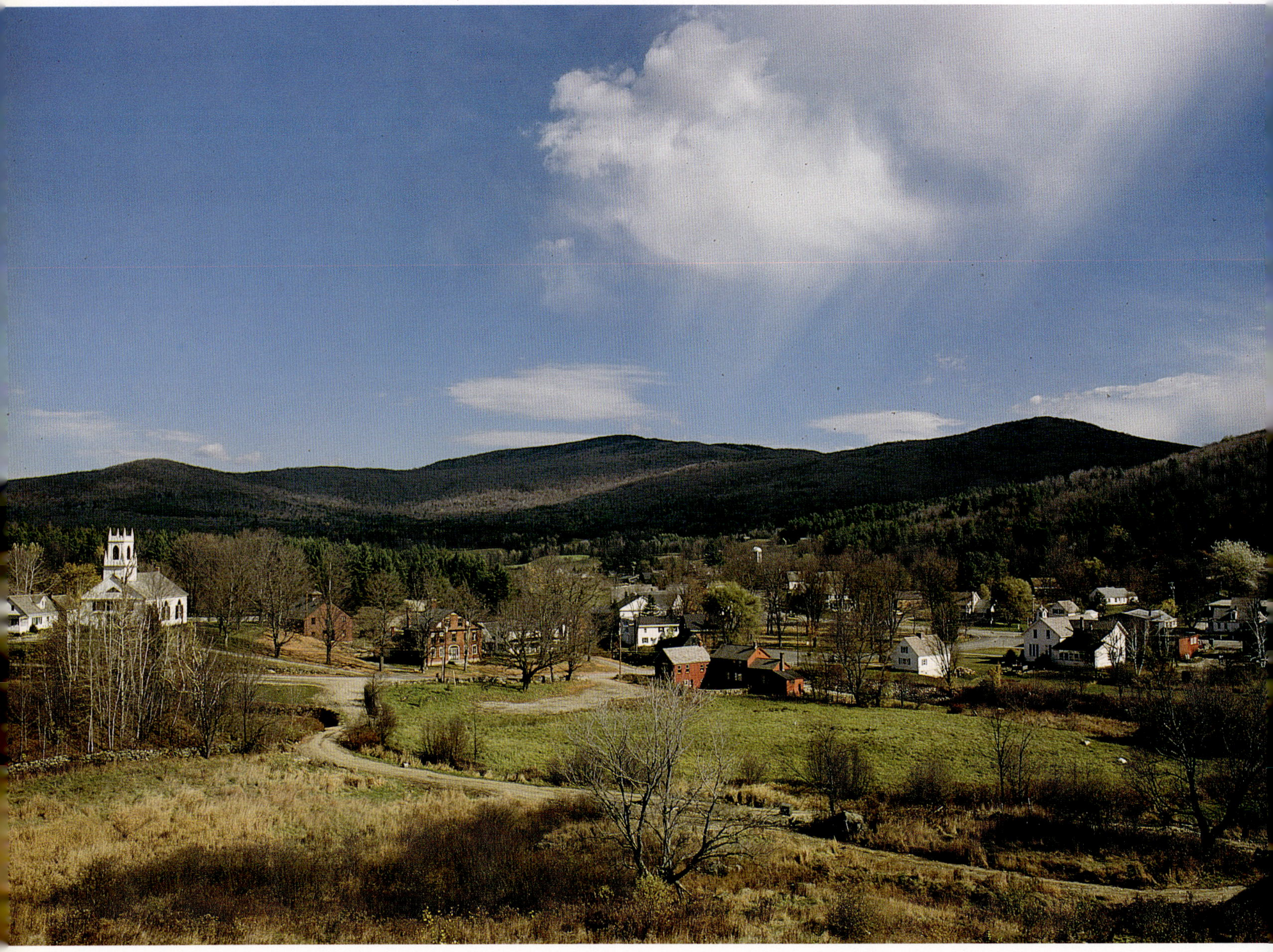

Weston

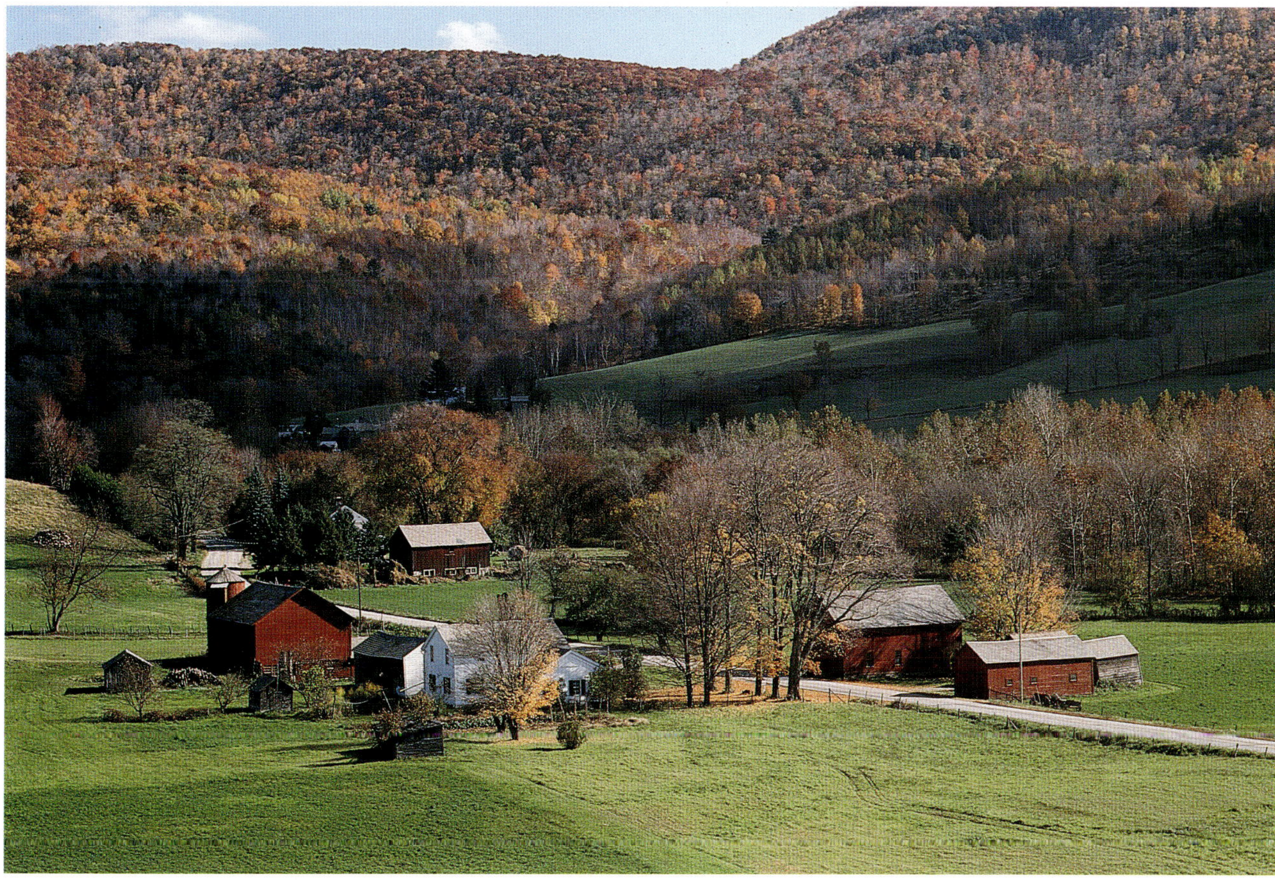

West Pawlet

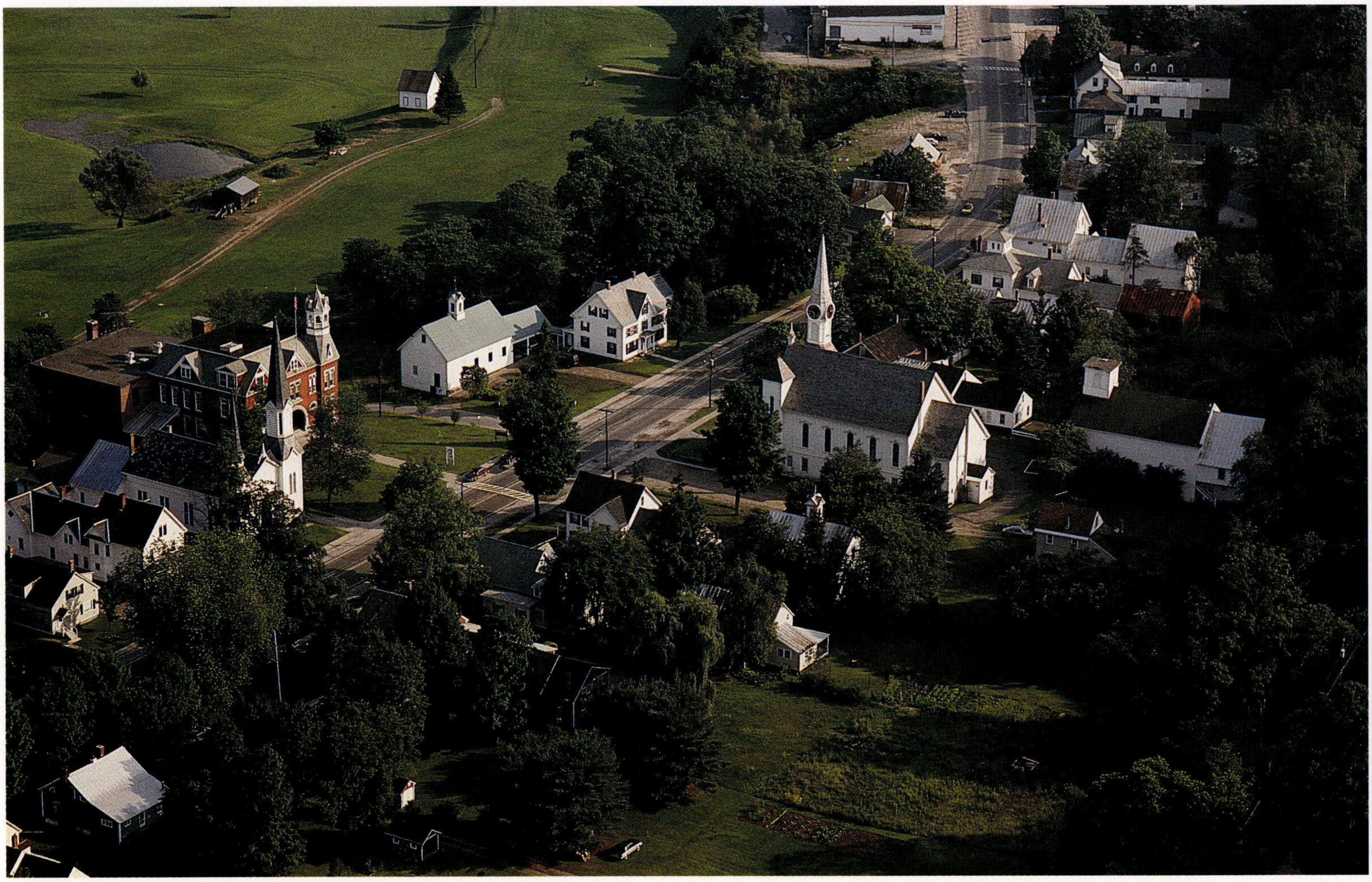

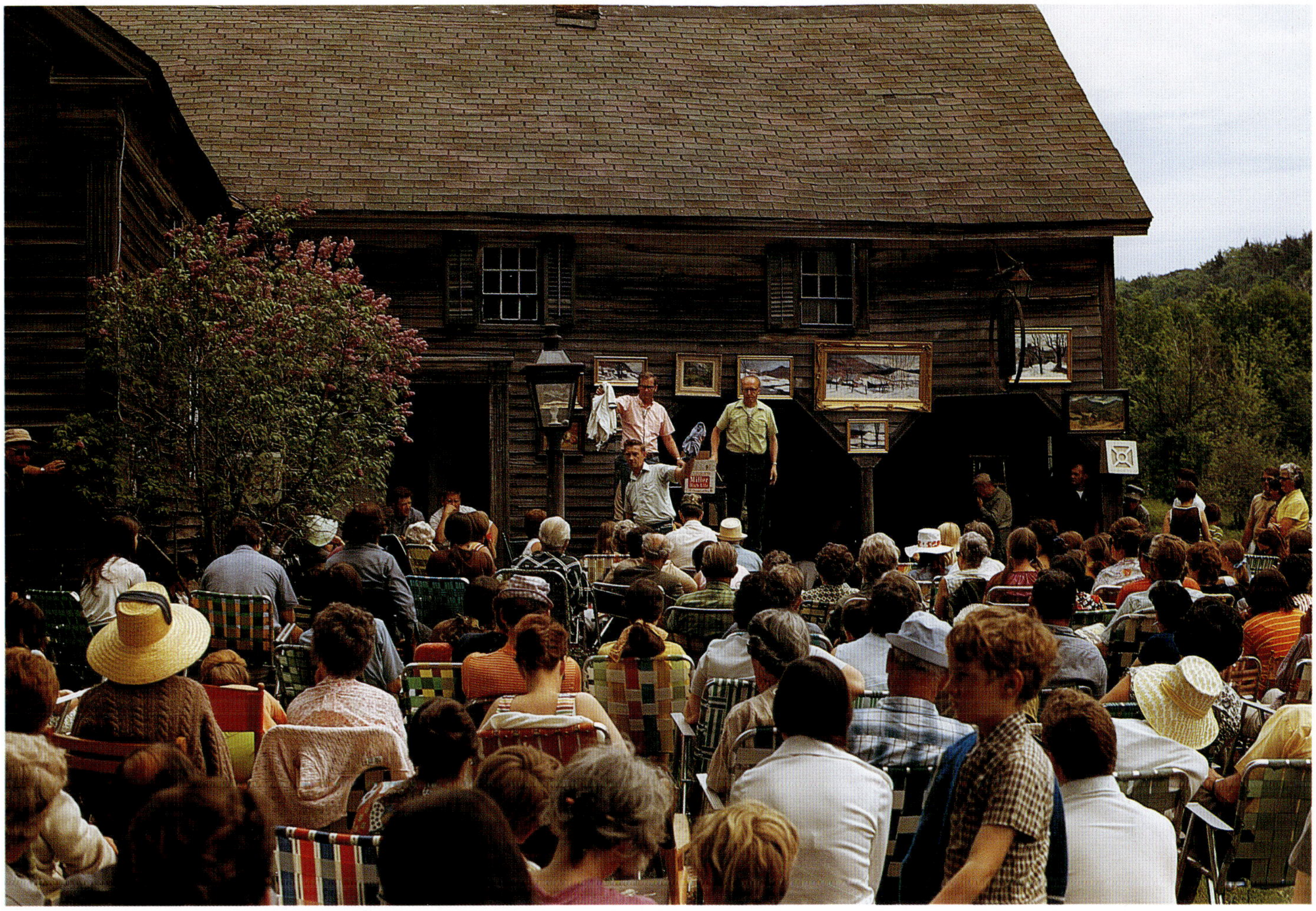

Starksboro

Overleaf: Camels Hump

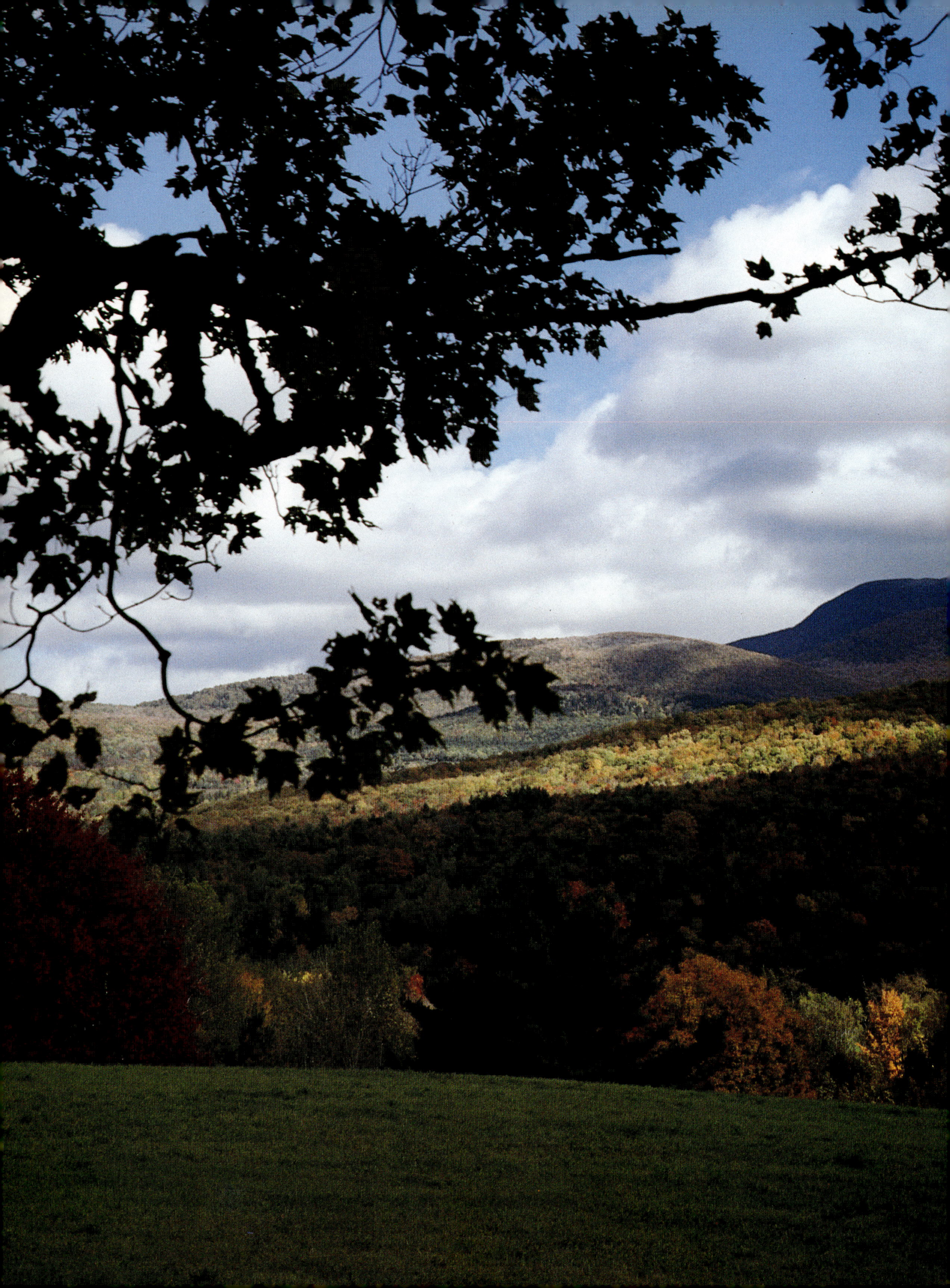

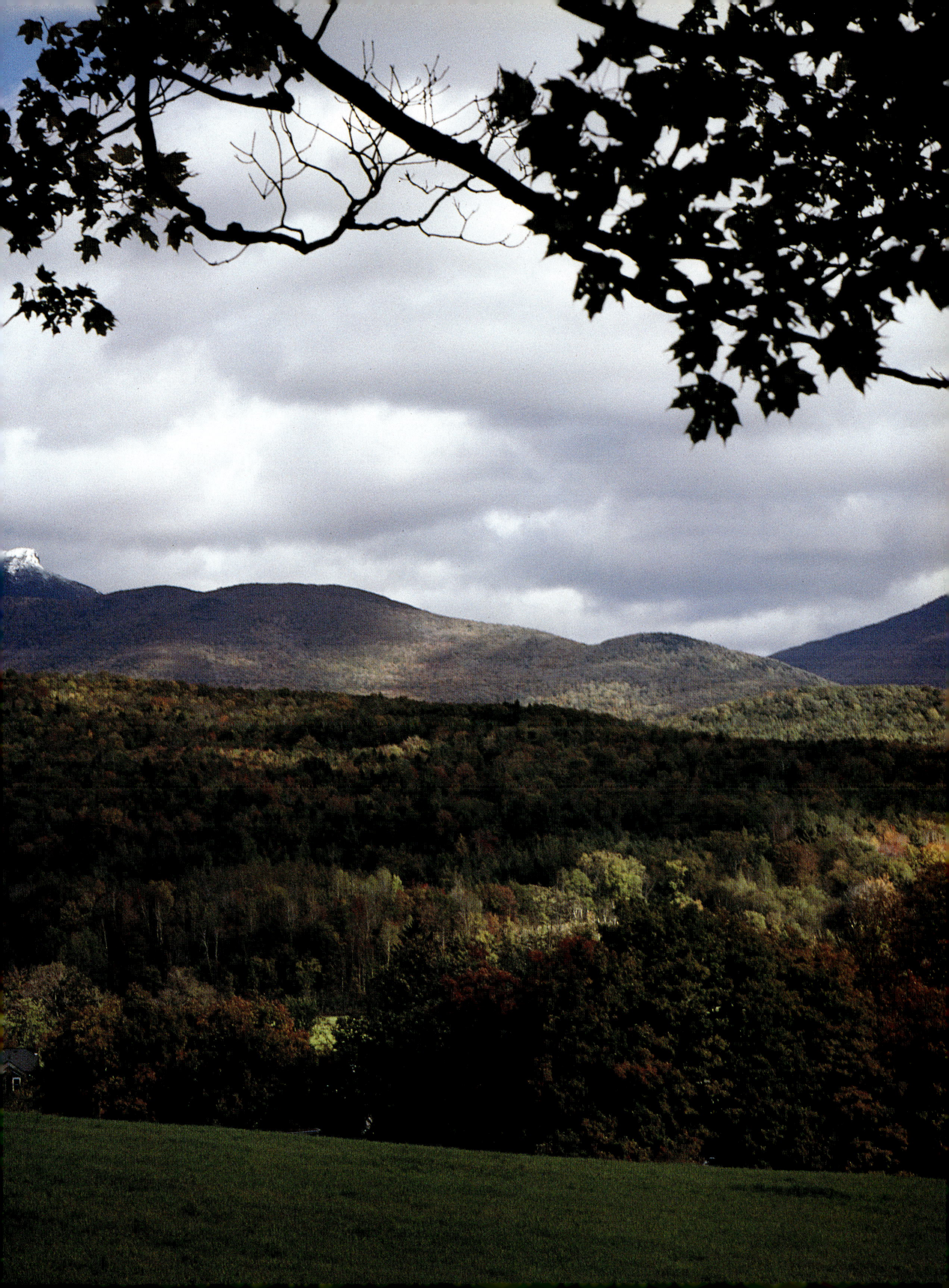

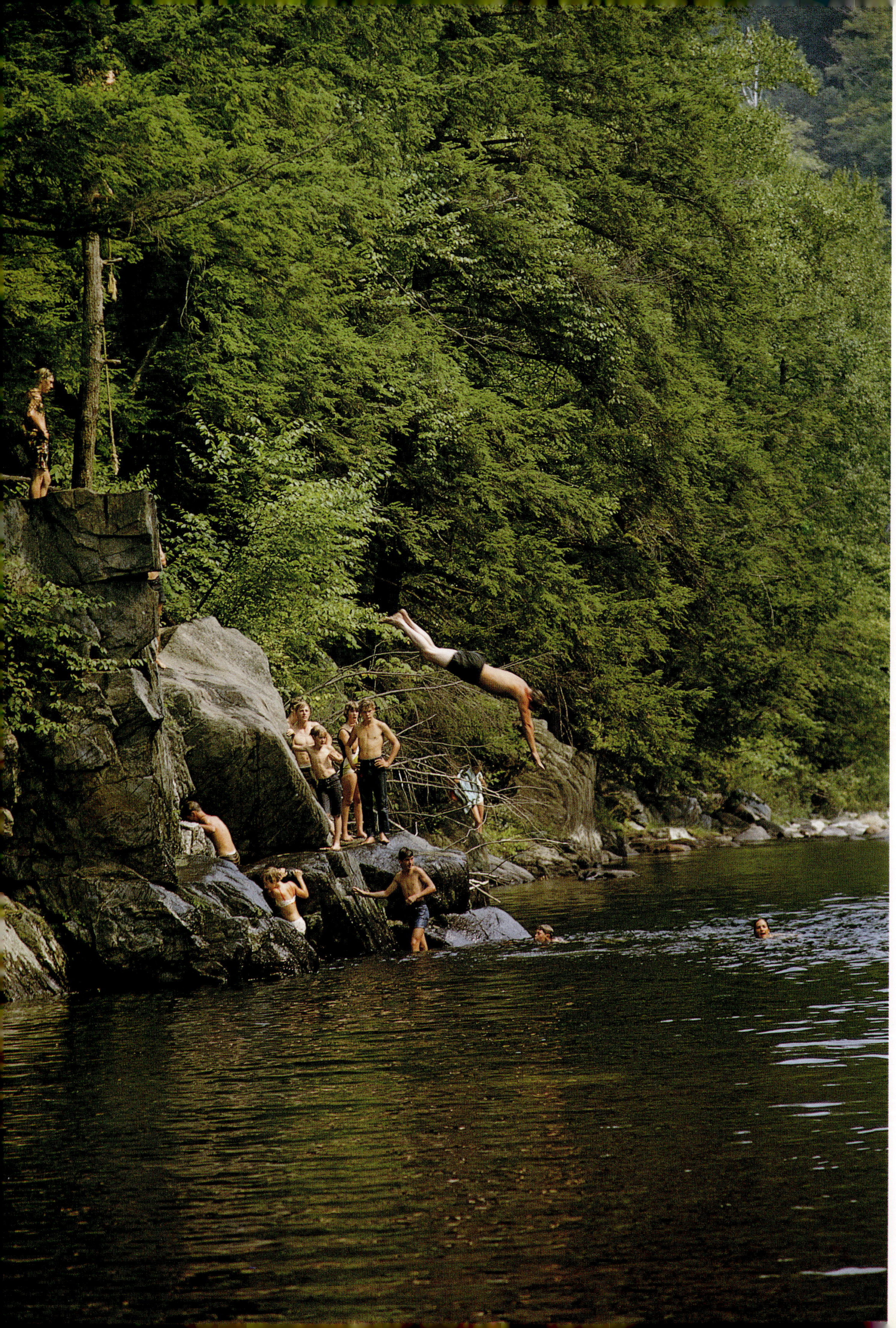

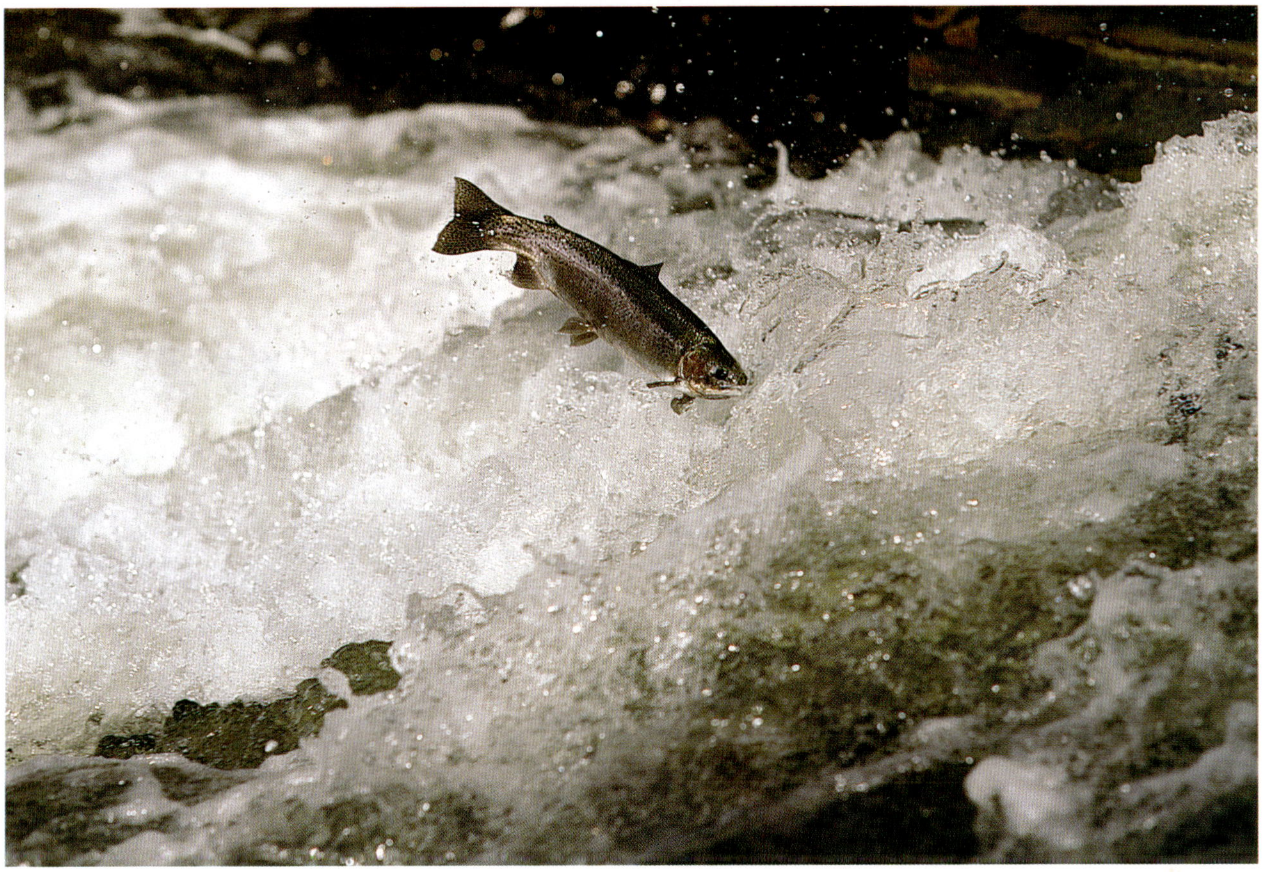

Willoughby River

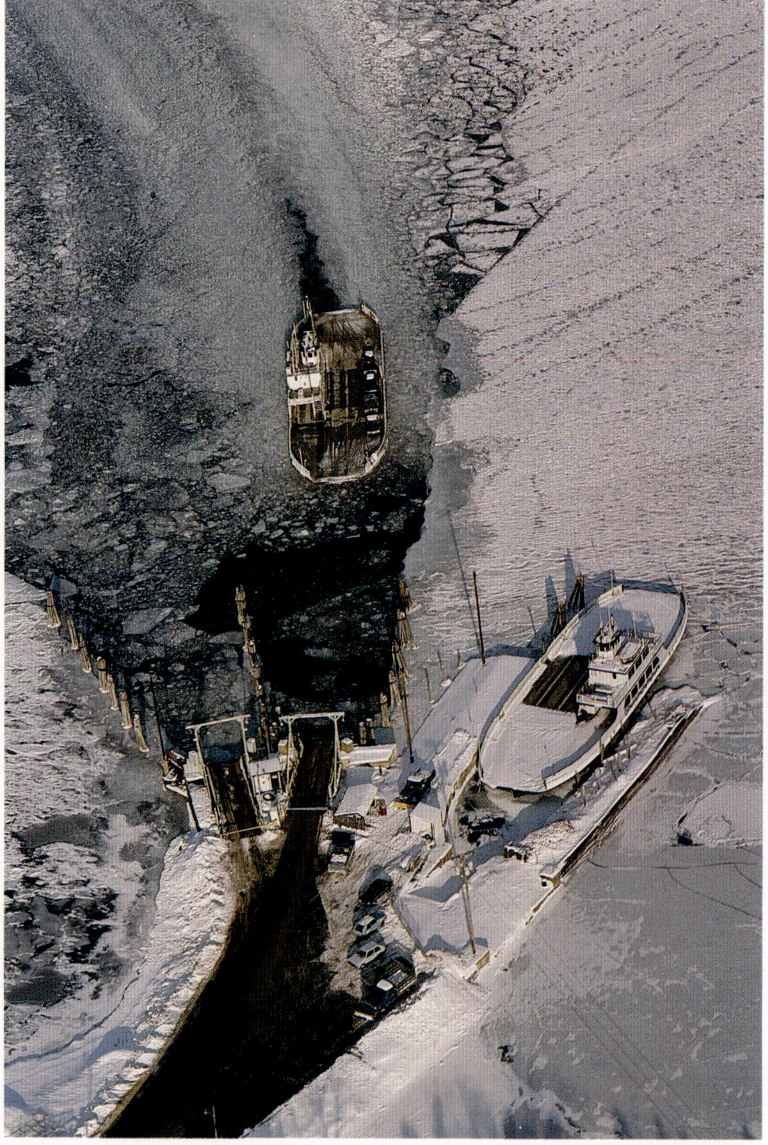

Grand Isle Ferry, Lake Champlain

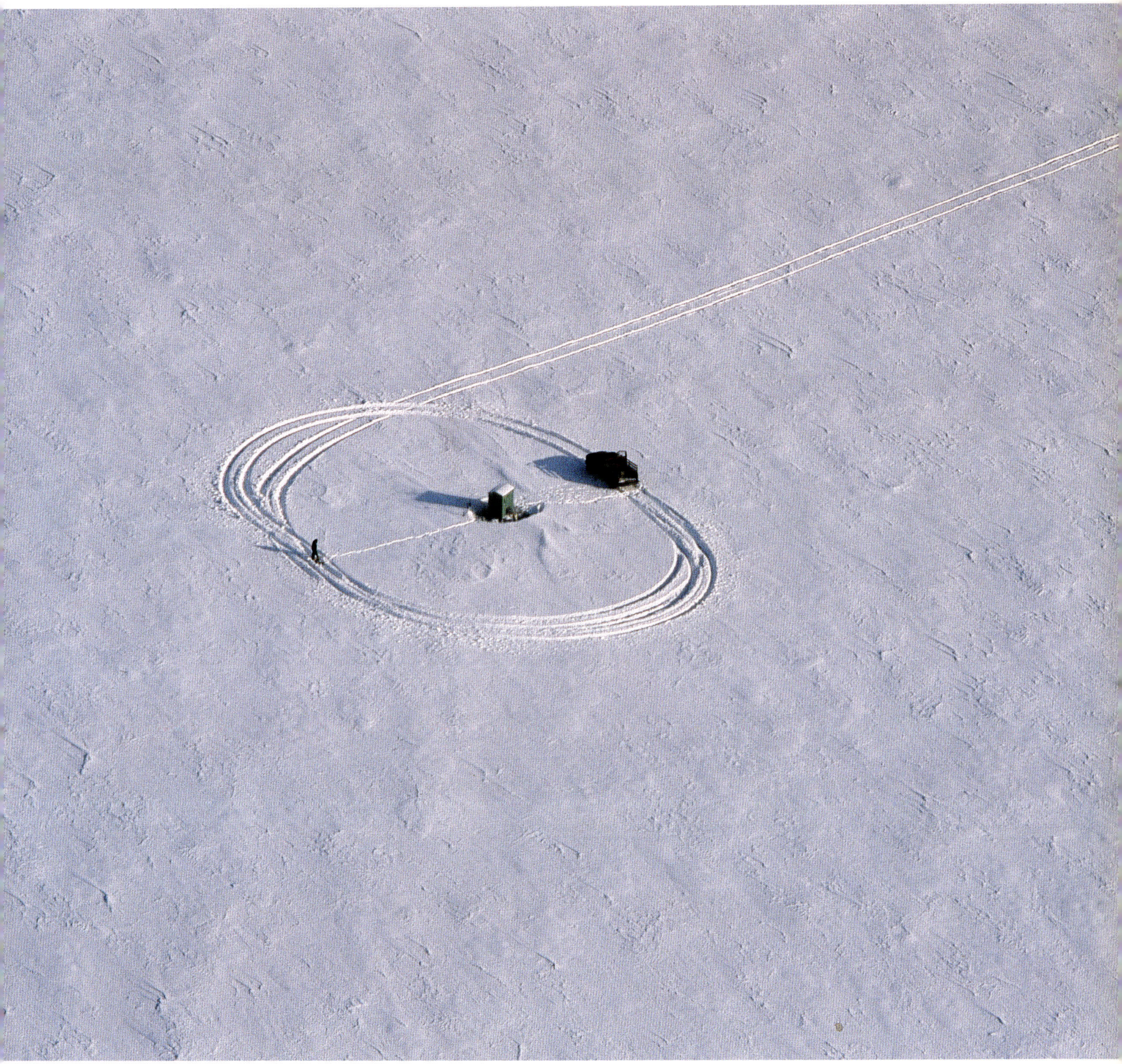

Ice fishing, Lake Champlain

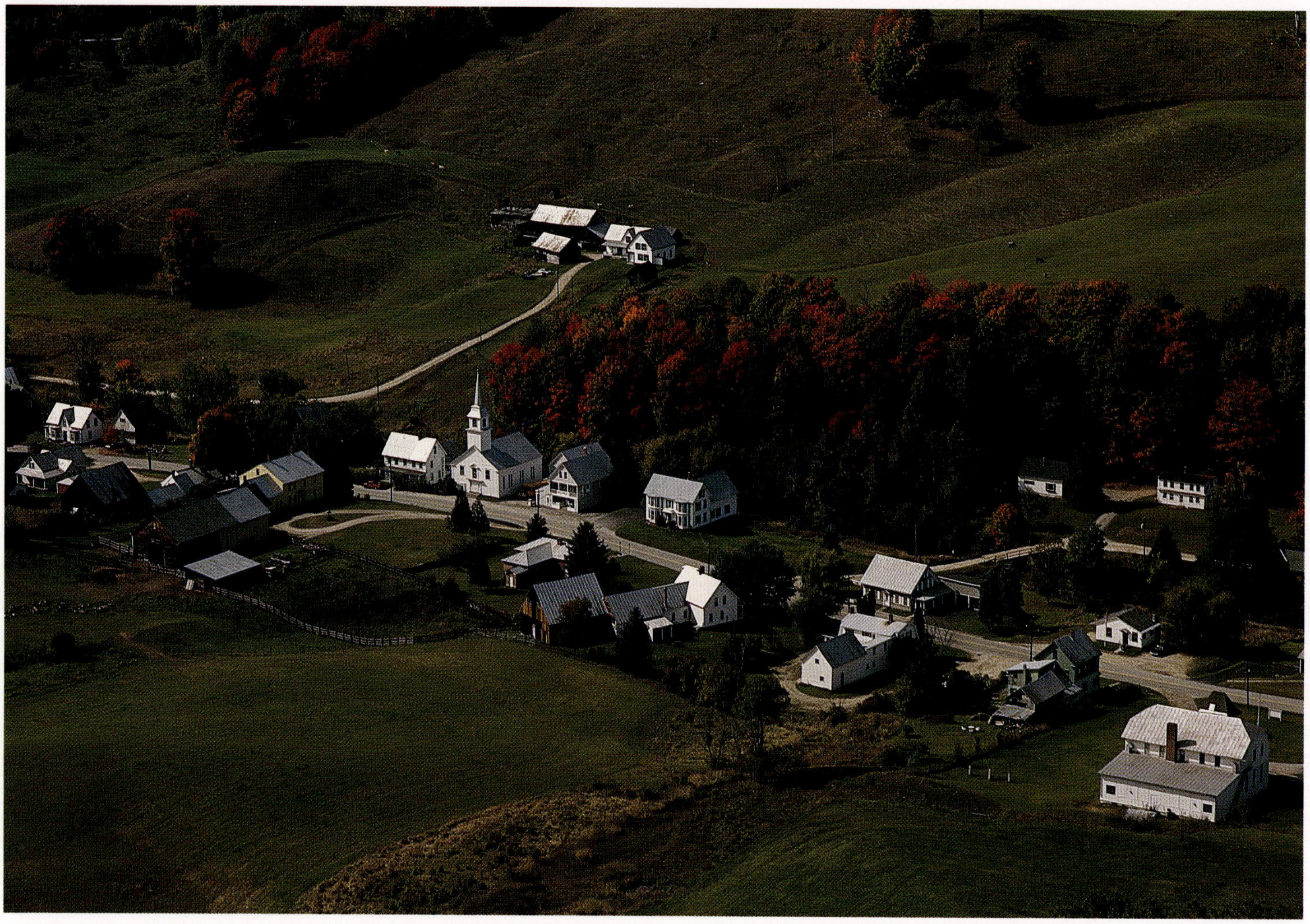

East Corinth

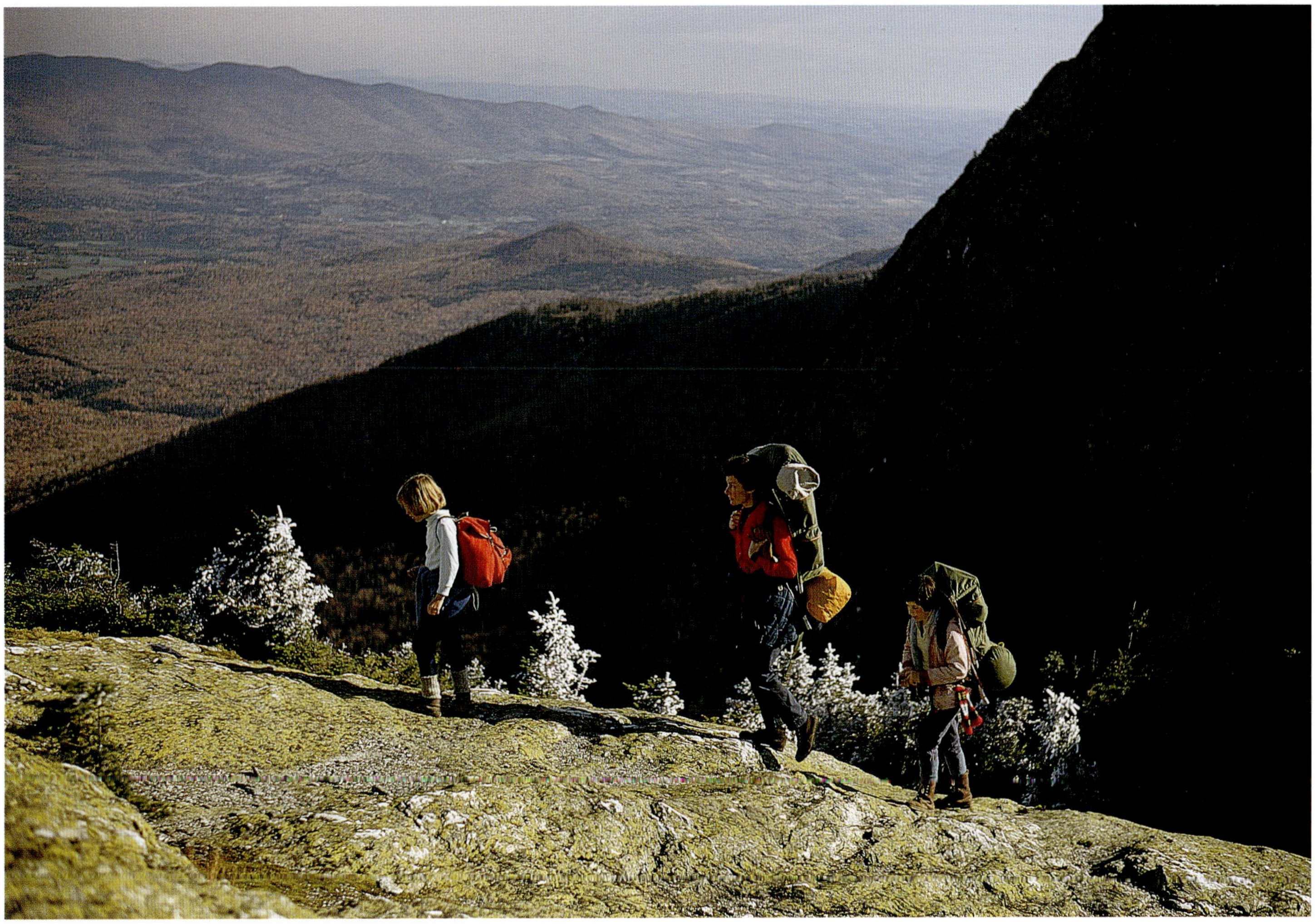

Long Trail hikers

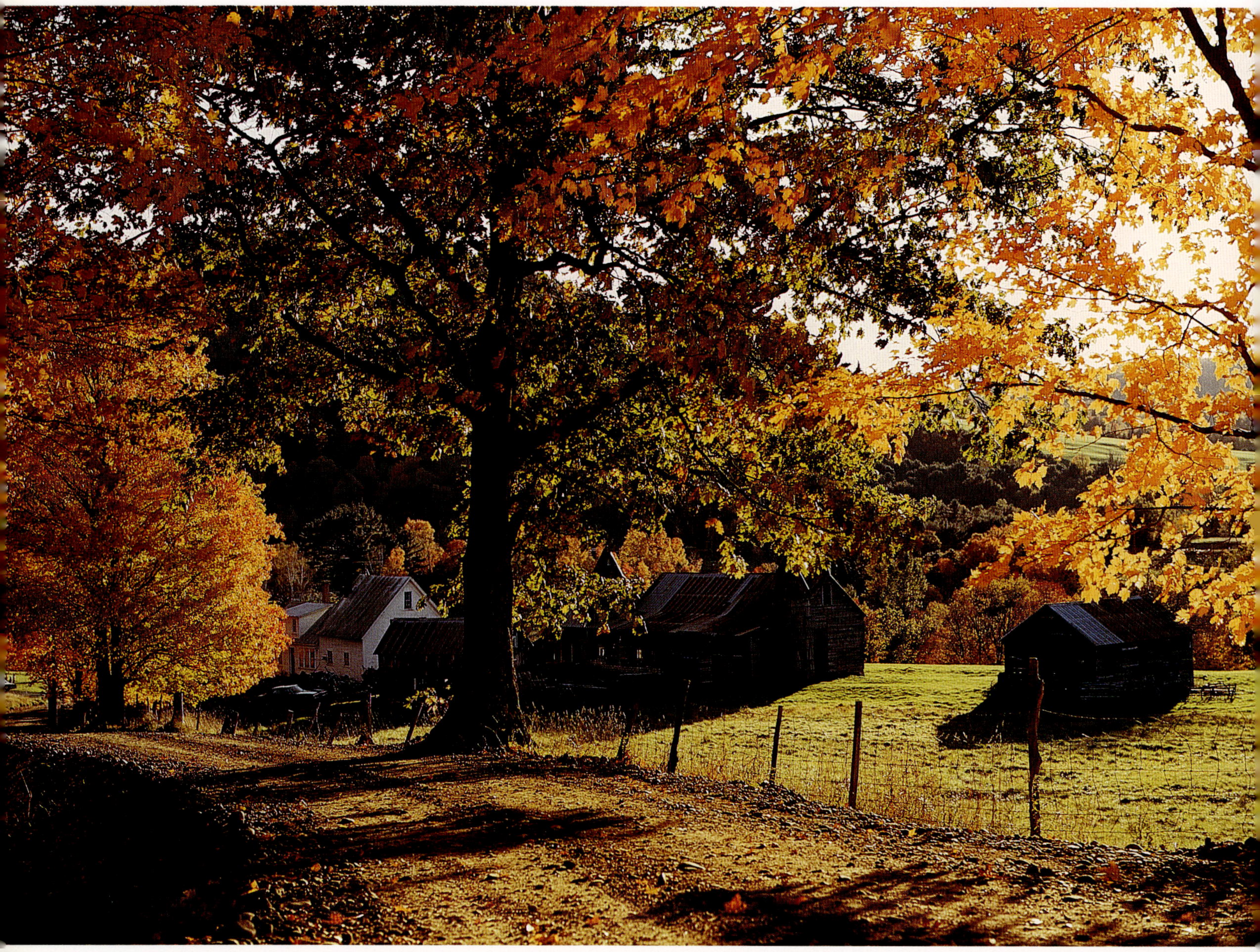

South Woodstock

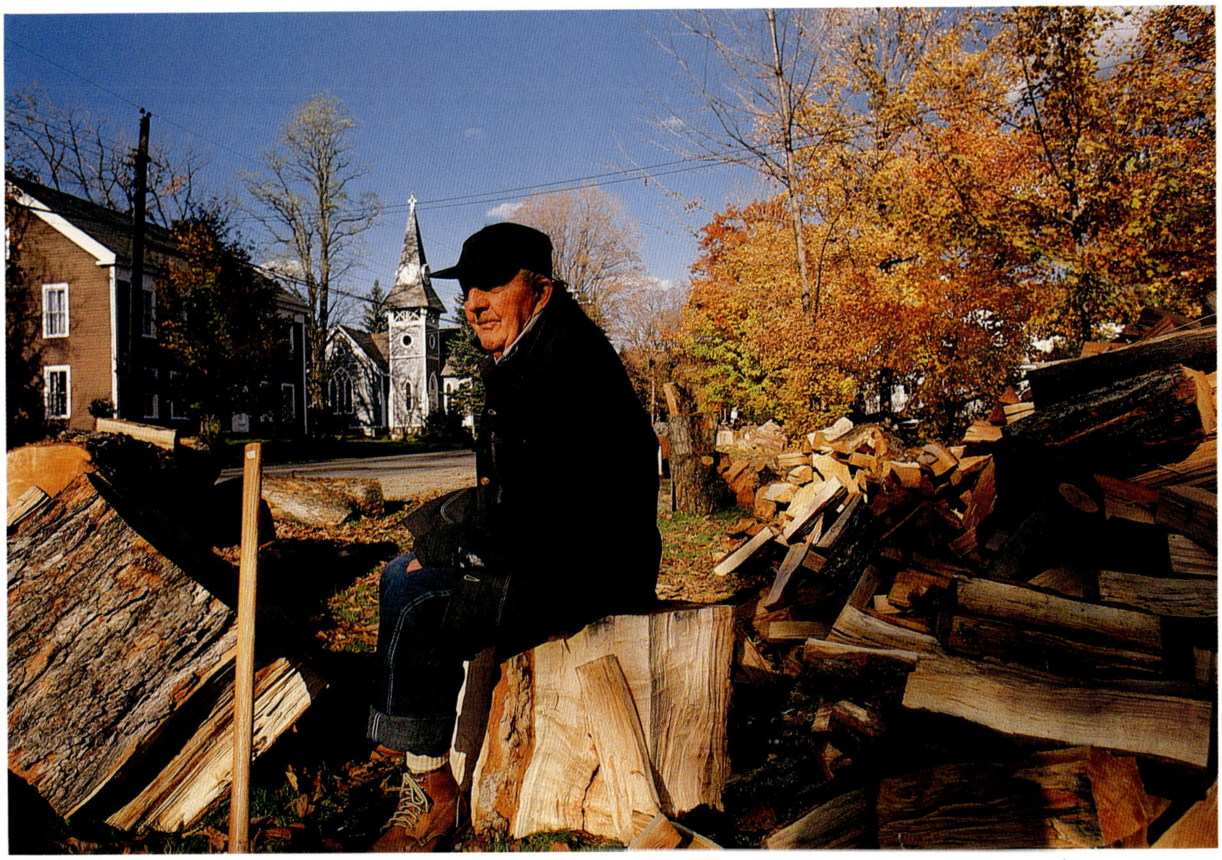

Taking a break in Rupert

Overleaf: Green Mountains, Mt. Dewey center

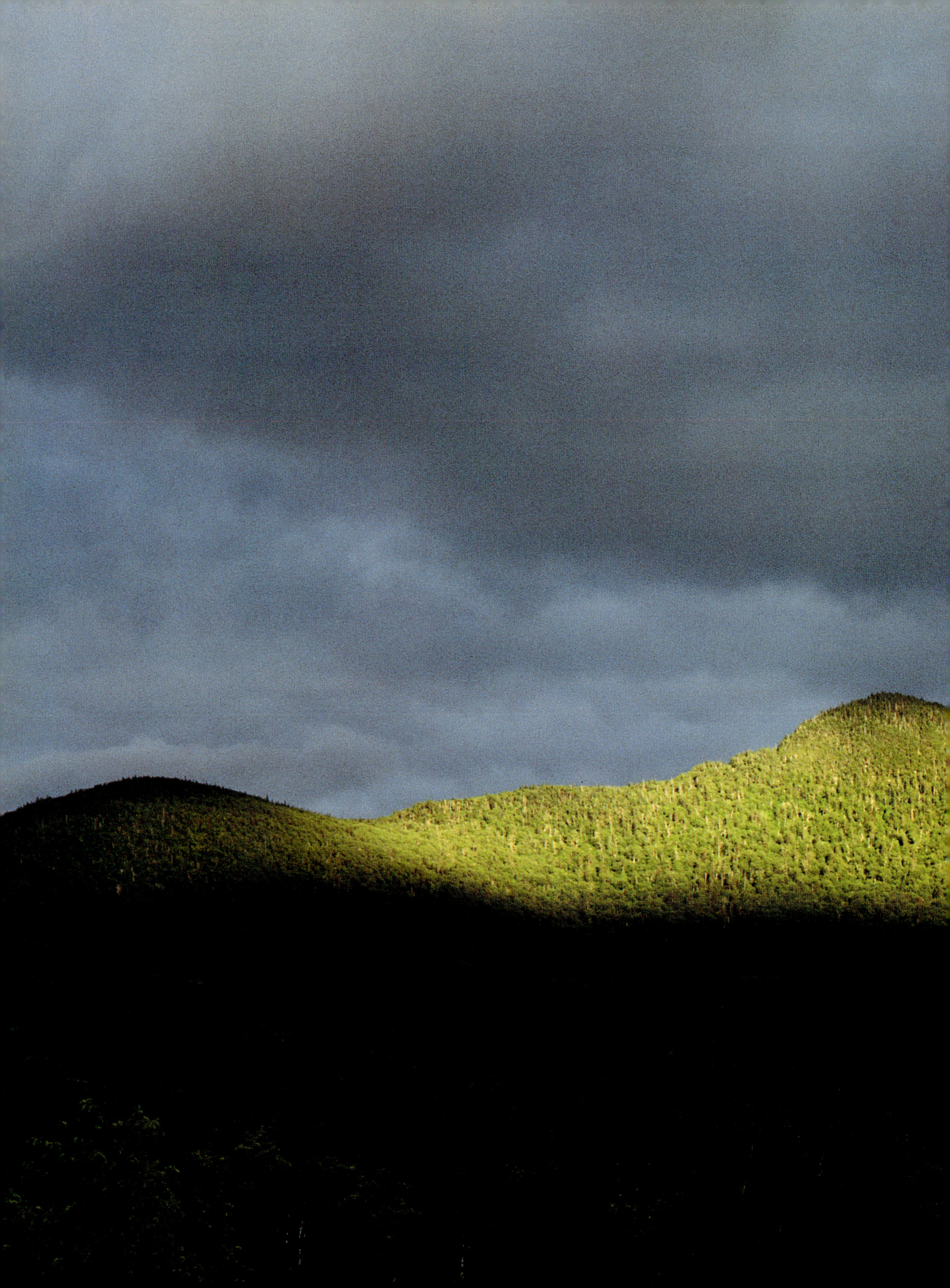

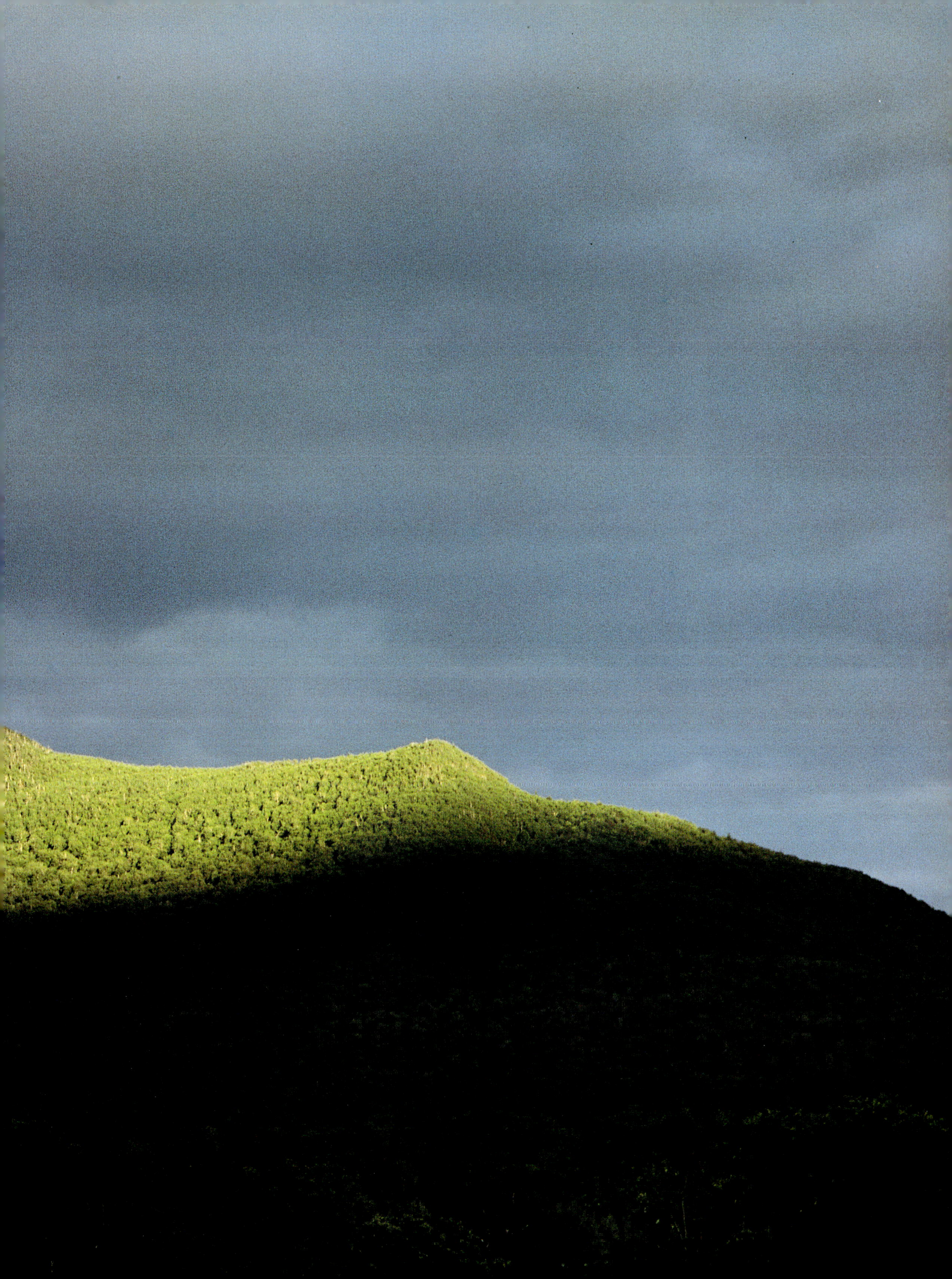

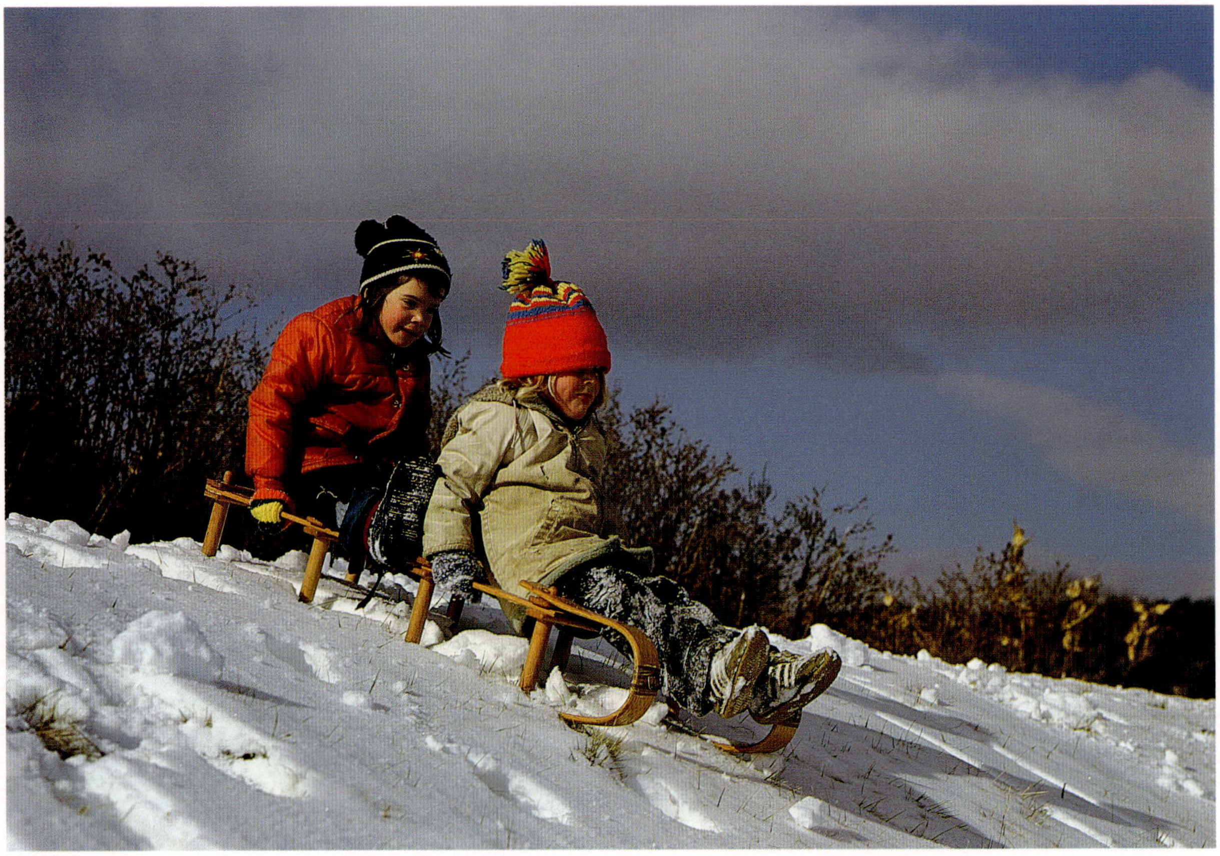

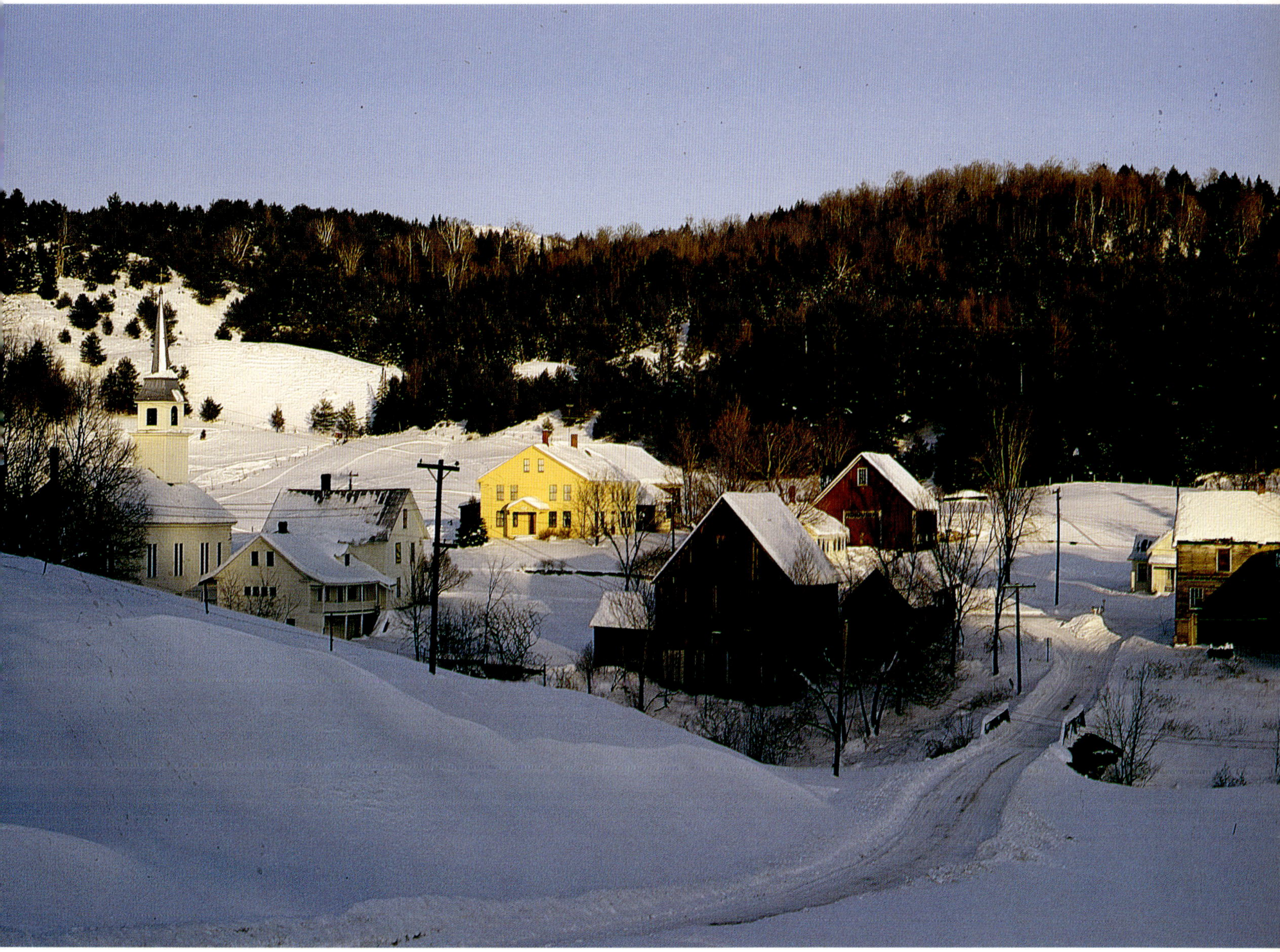

East Corinth

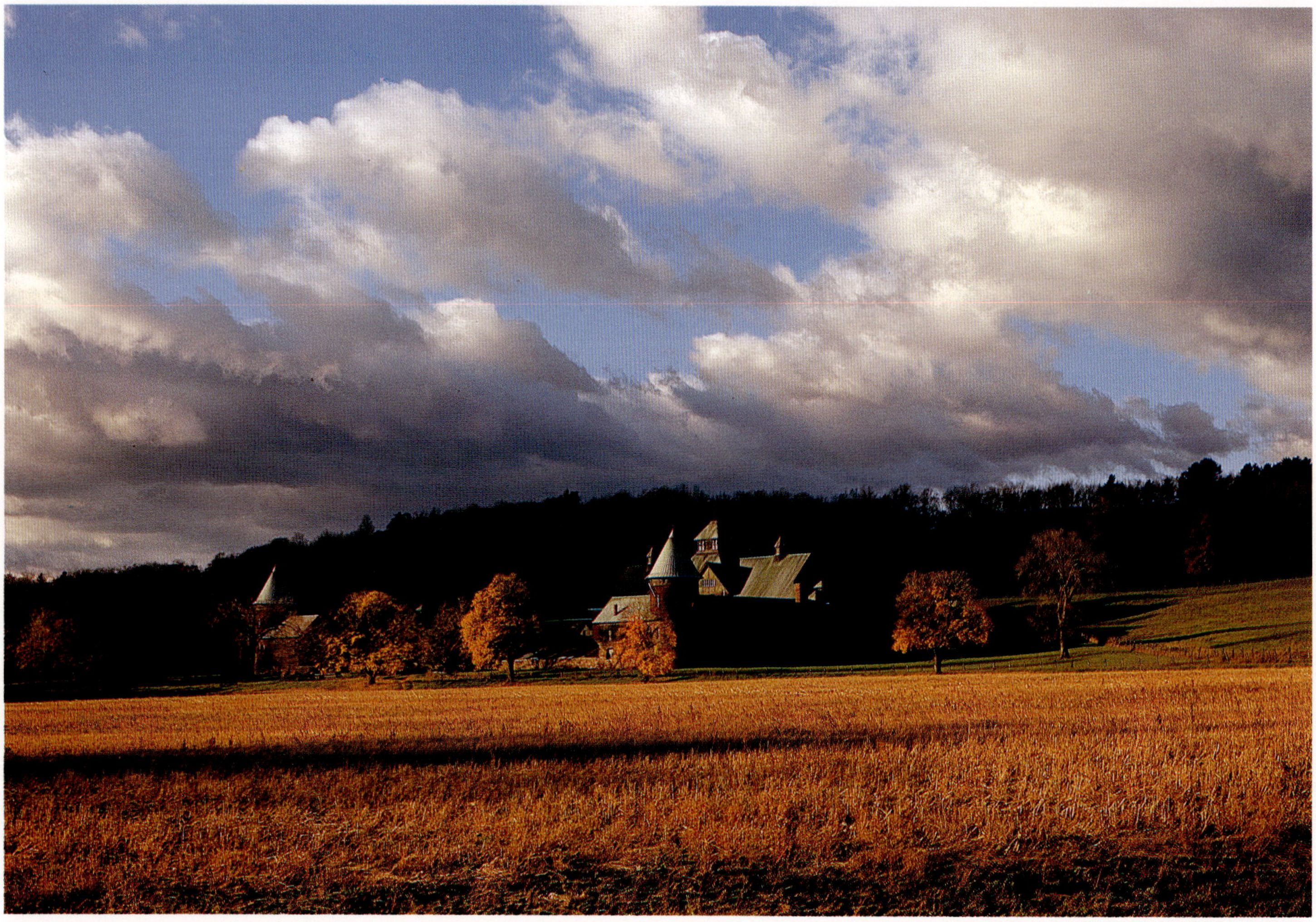

Shelburne Farms

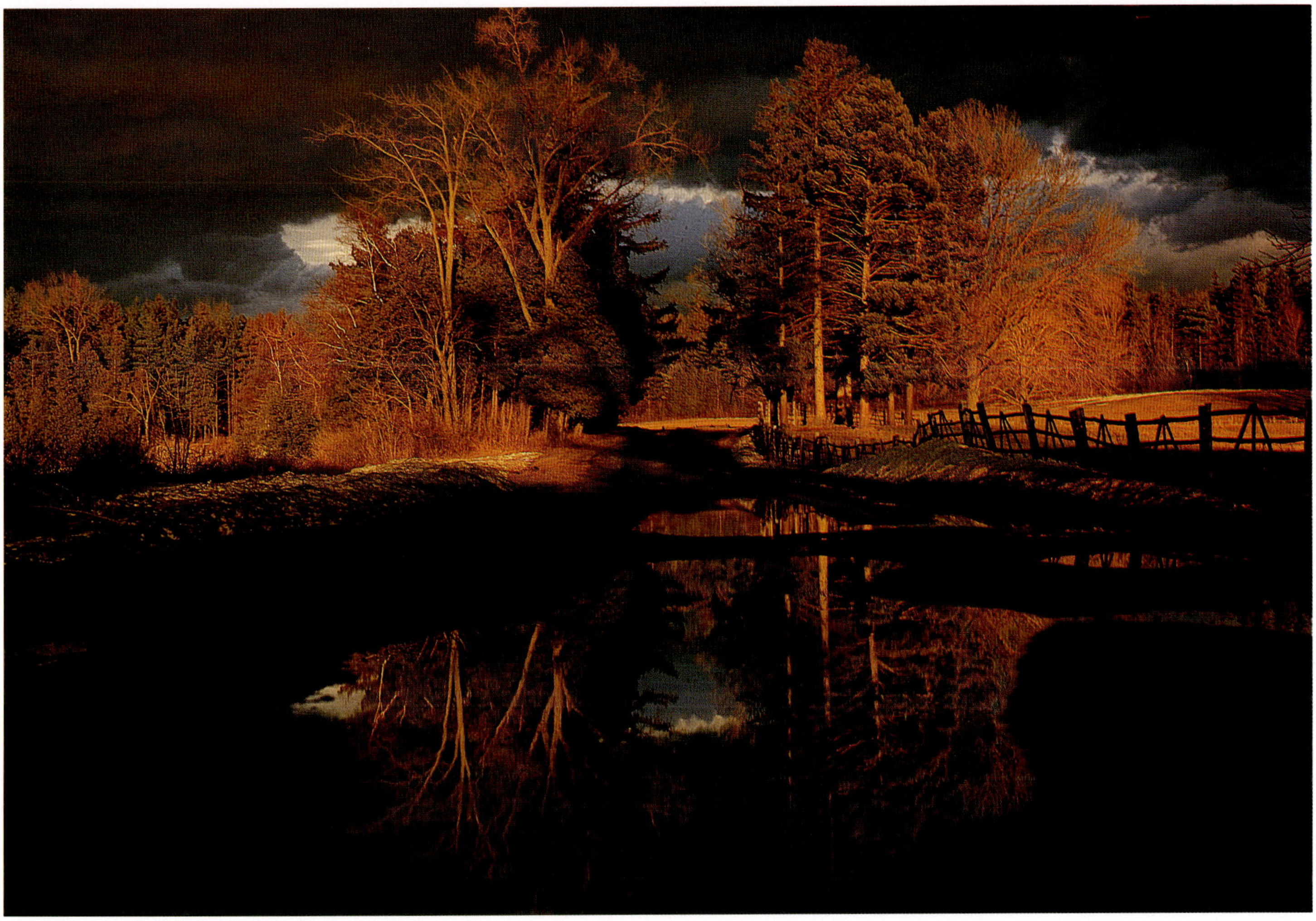

After an Autumn rain

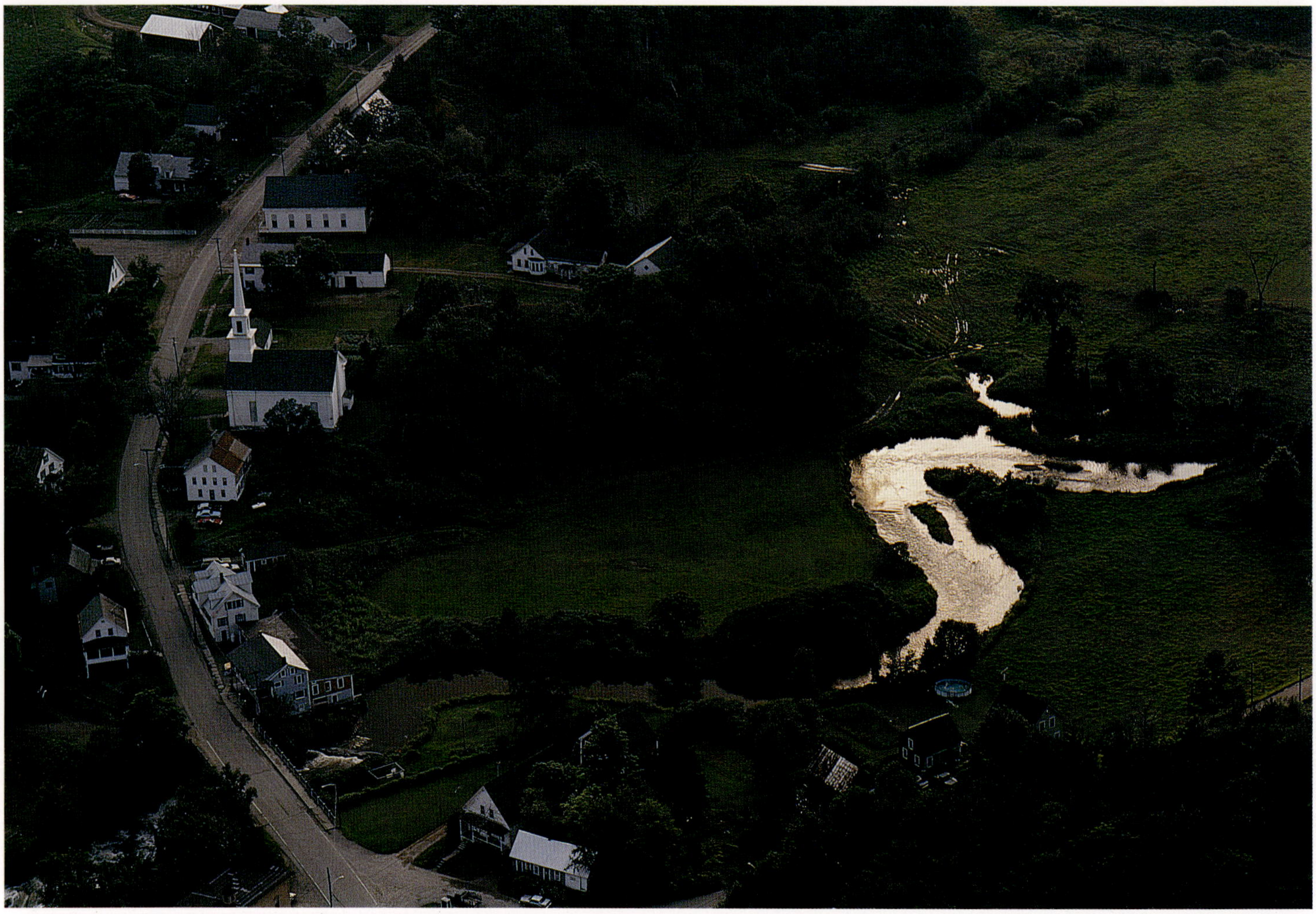

Barnet

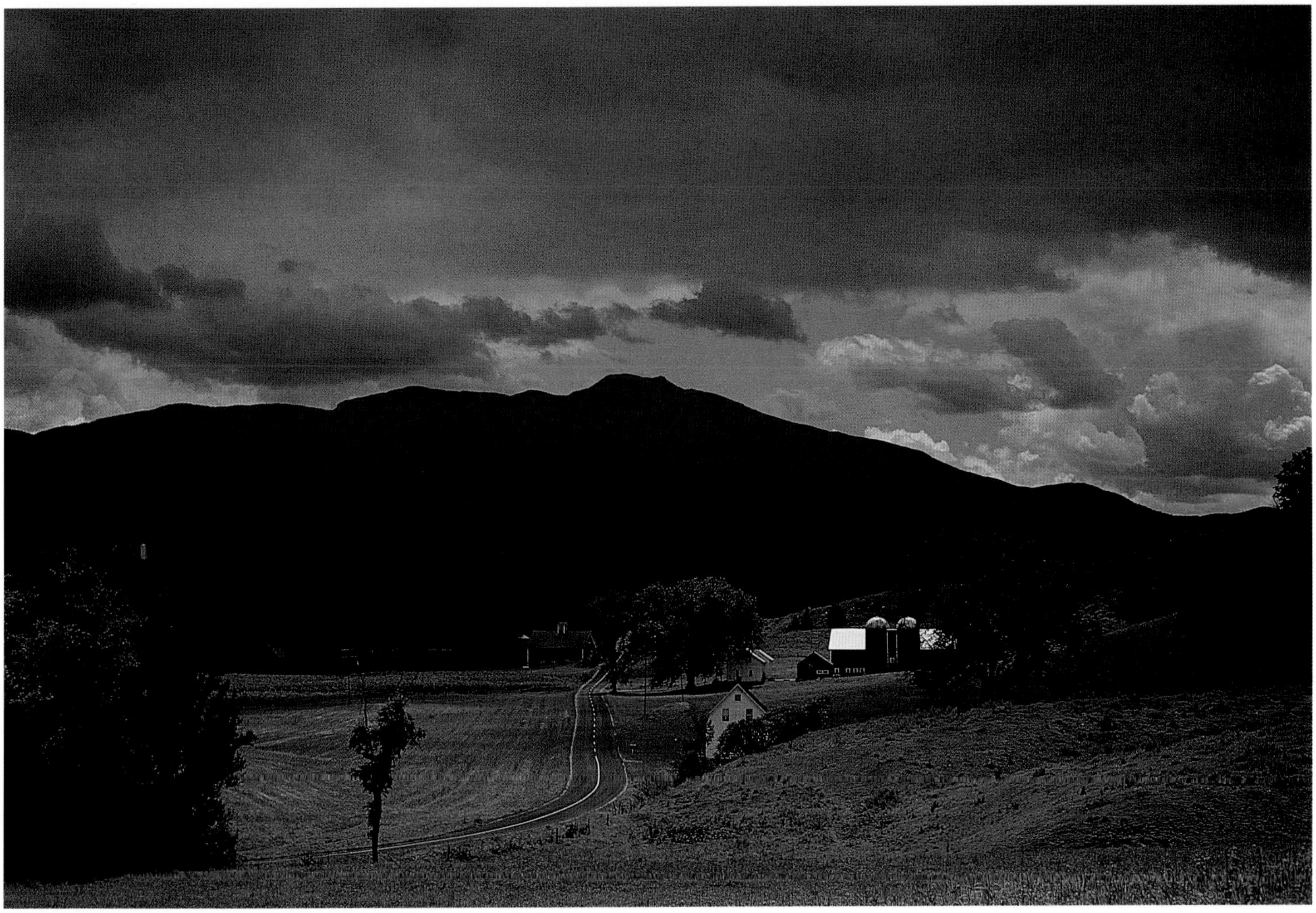

Pleasant Valley

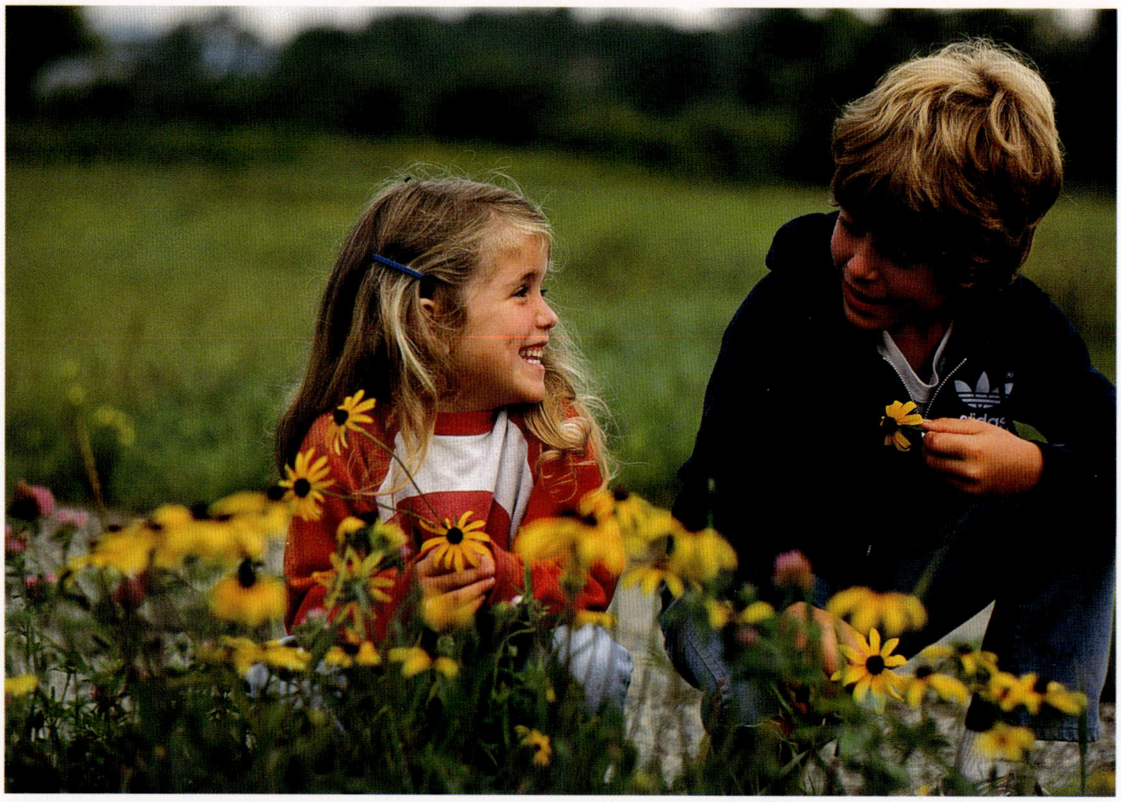

Mettawee Valley near Pawlet

Overleaf: Camels Hump and Lake Champlain

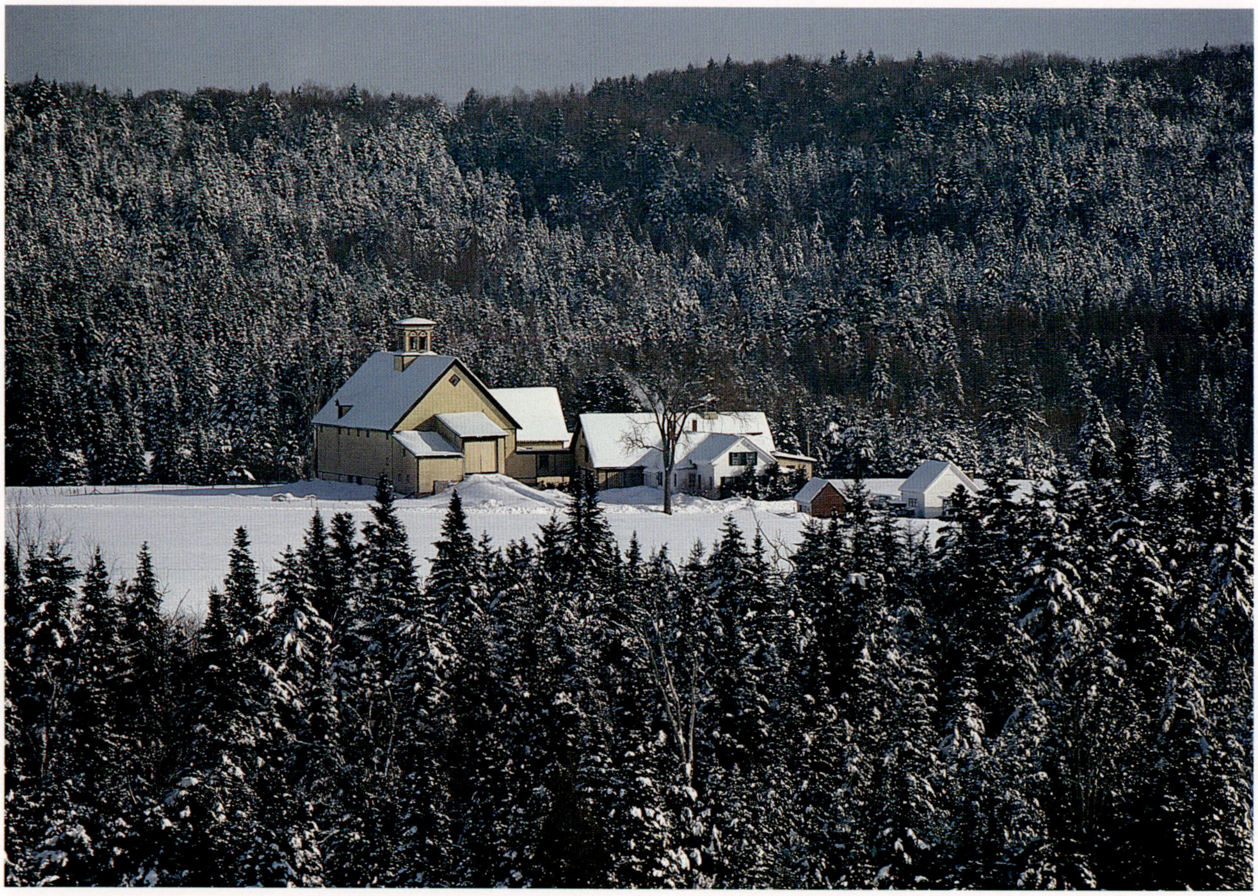

East Montpelier

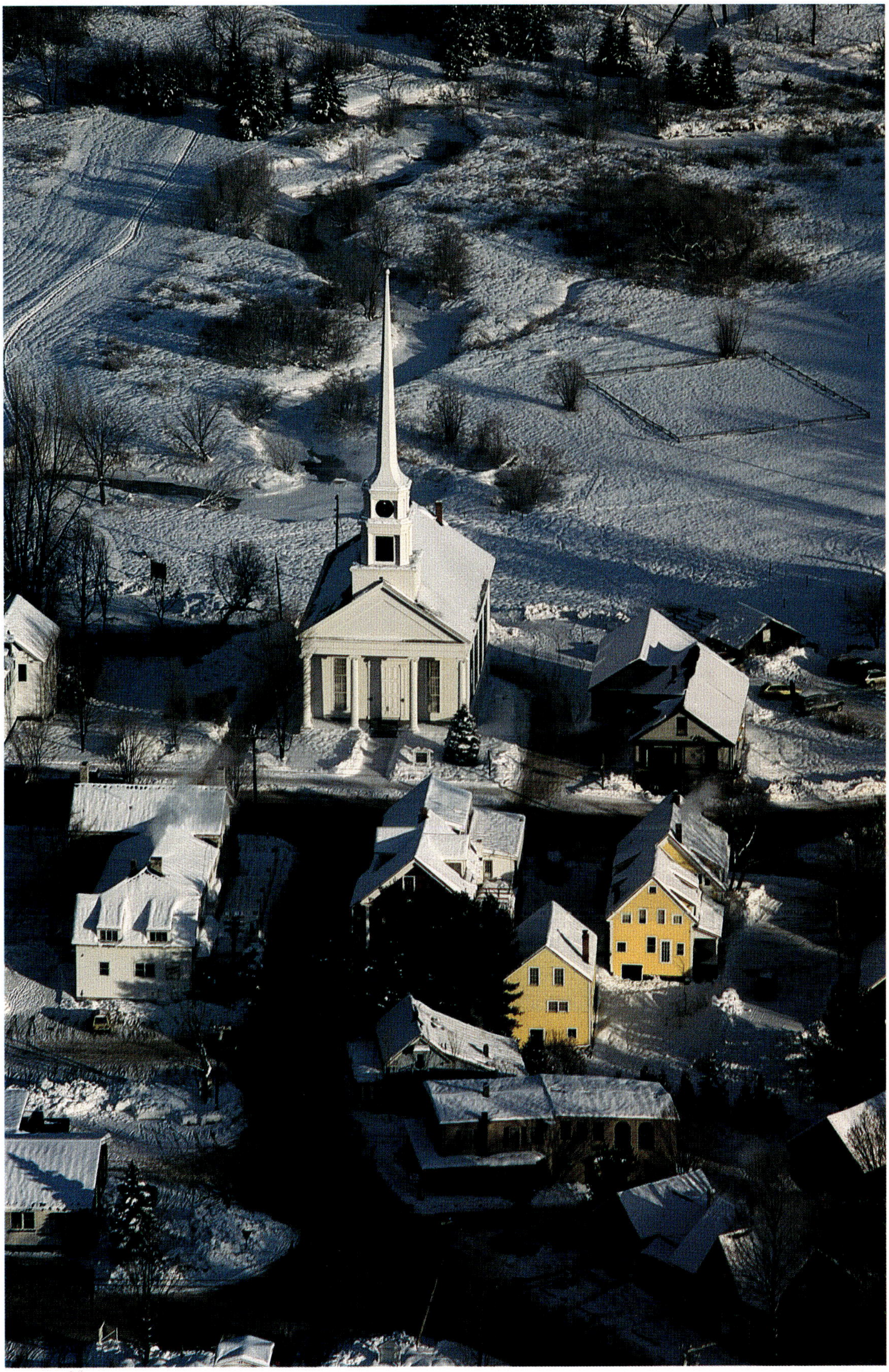

Stowe

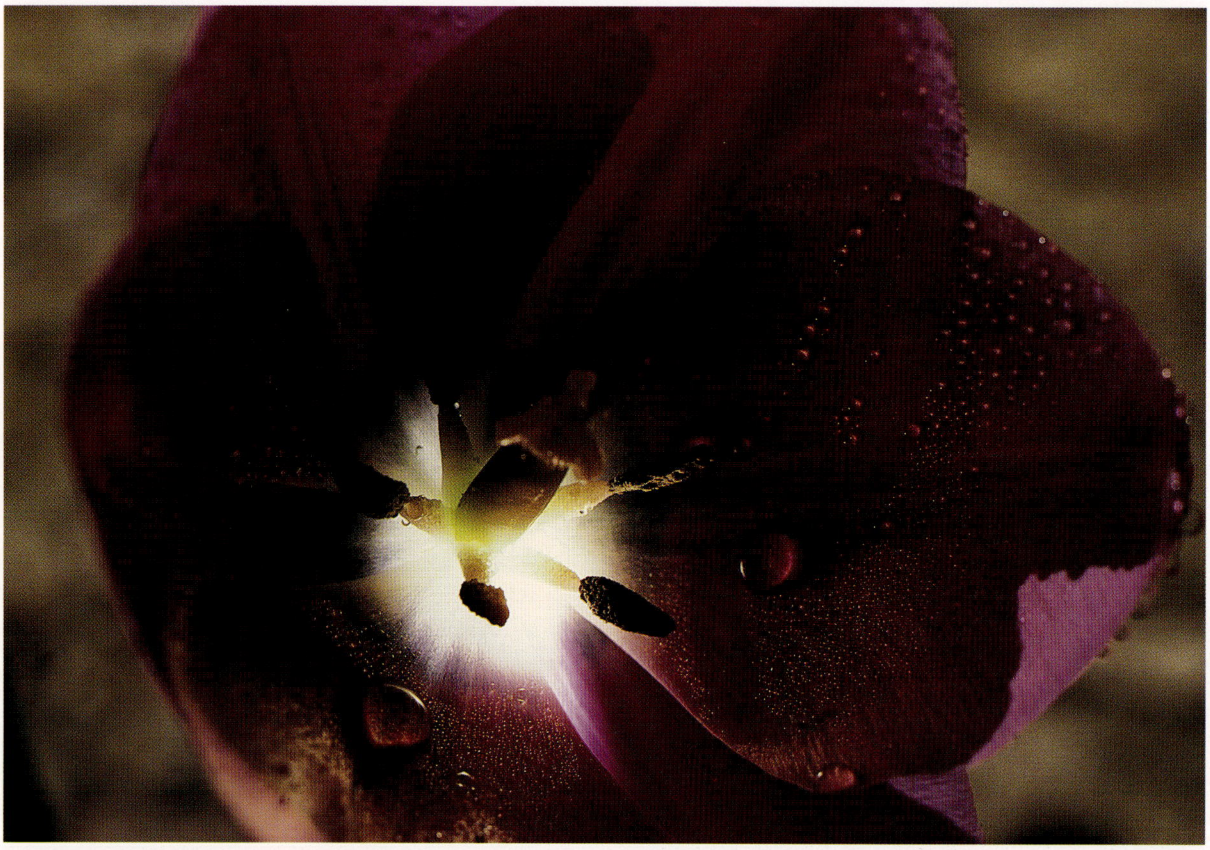

Tulip

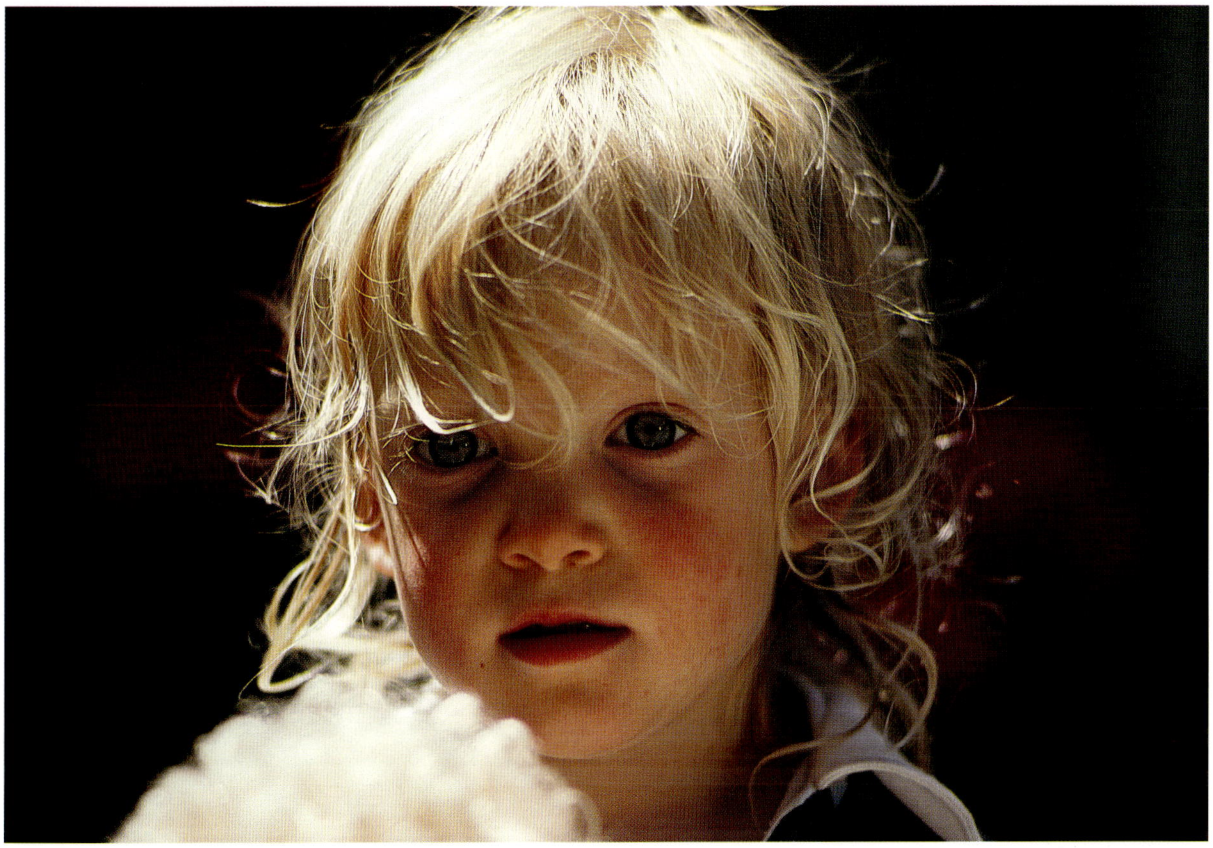

Heather Roberts

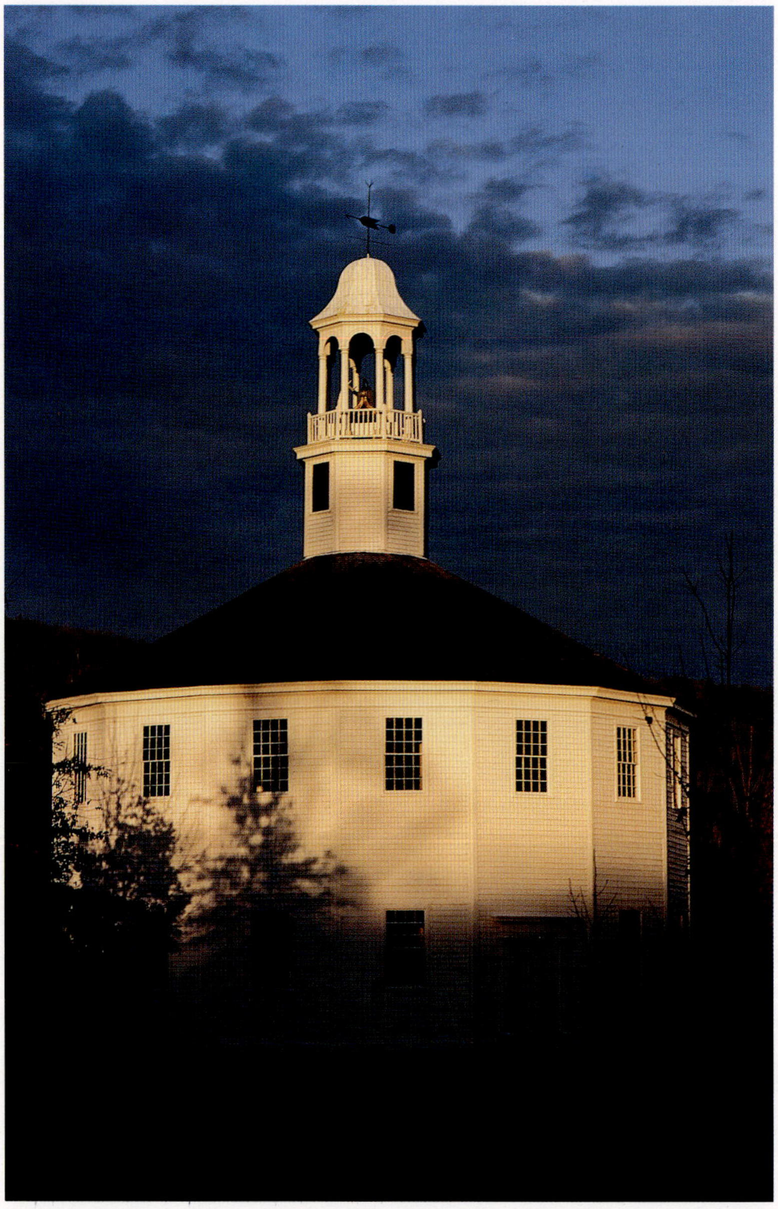

Round Church in Richmond

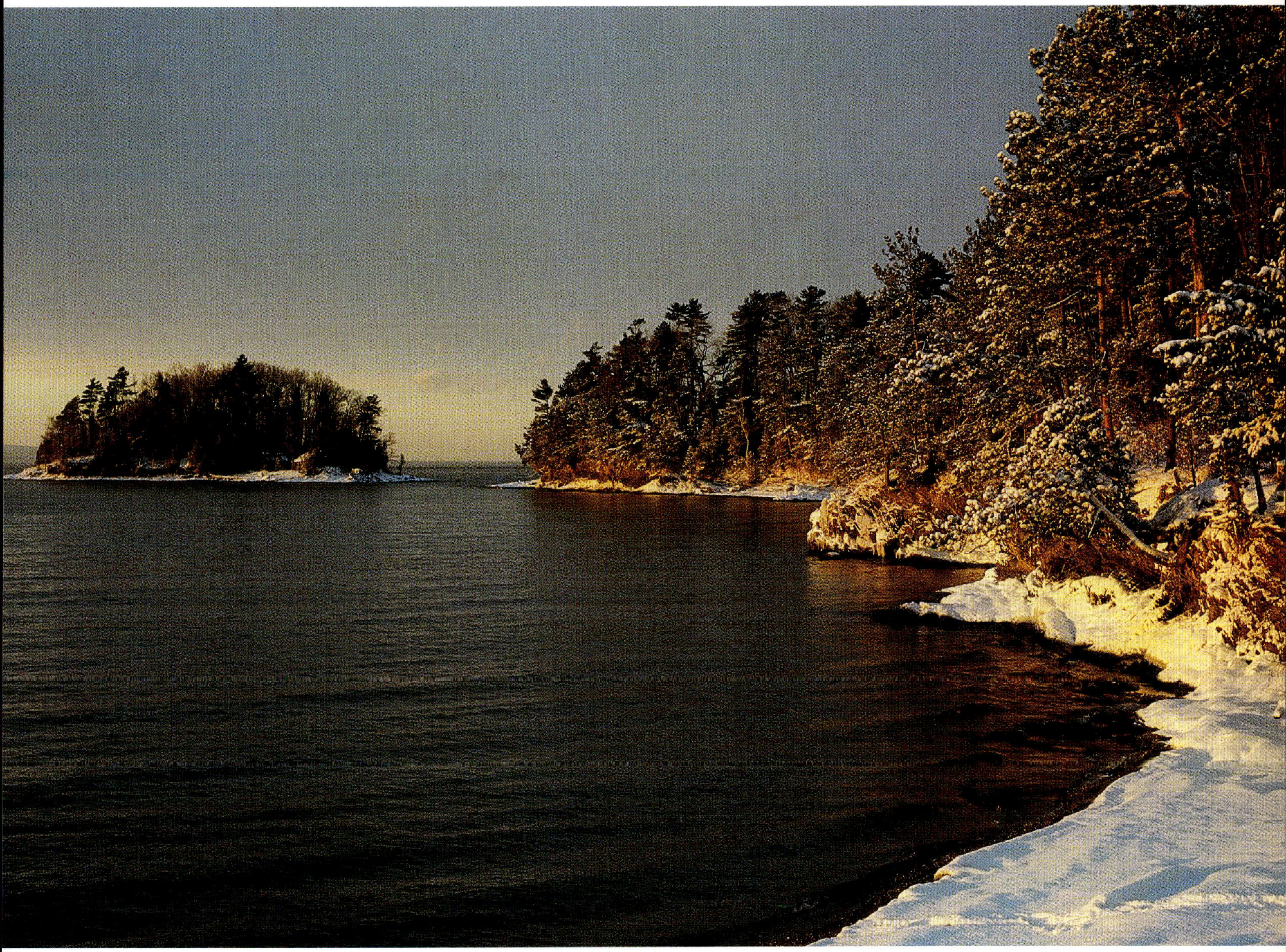

Queneska Island off Shelburne Point

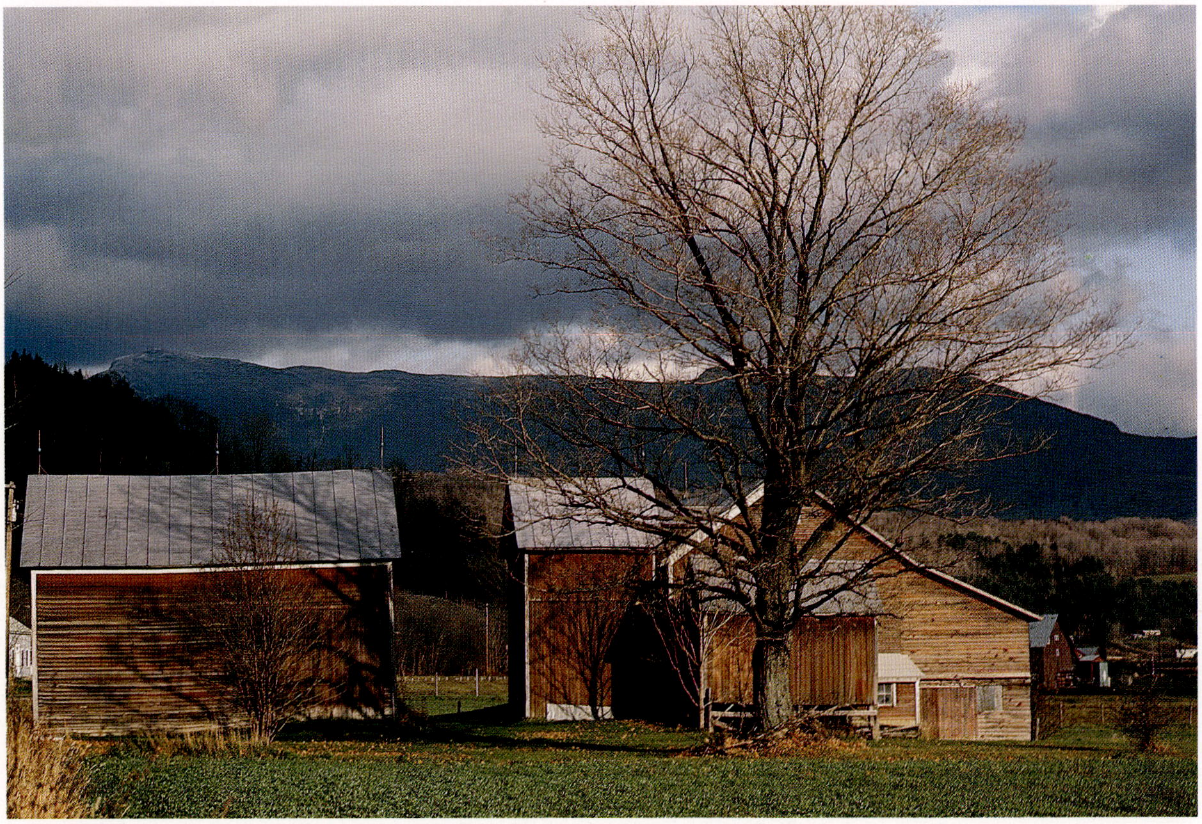

Underhill

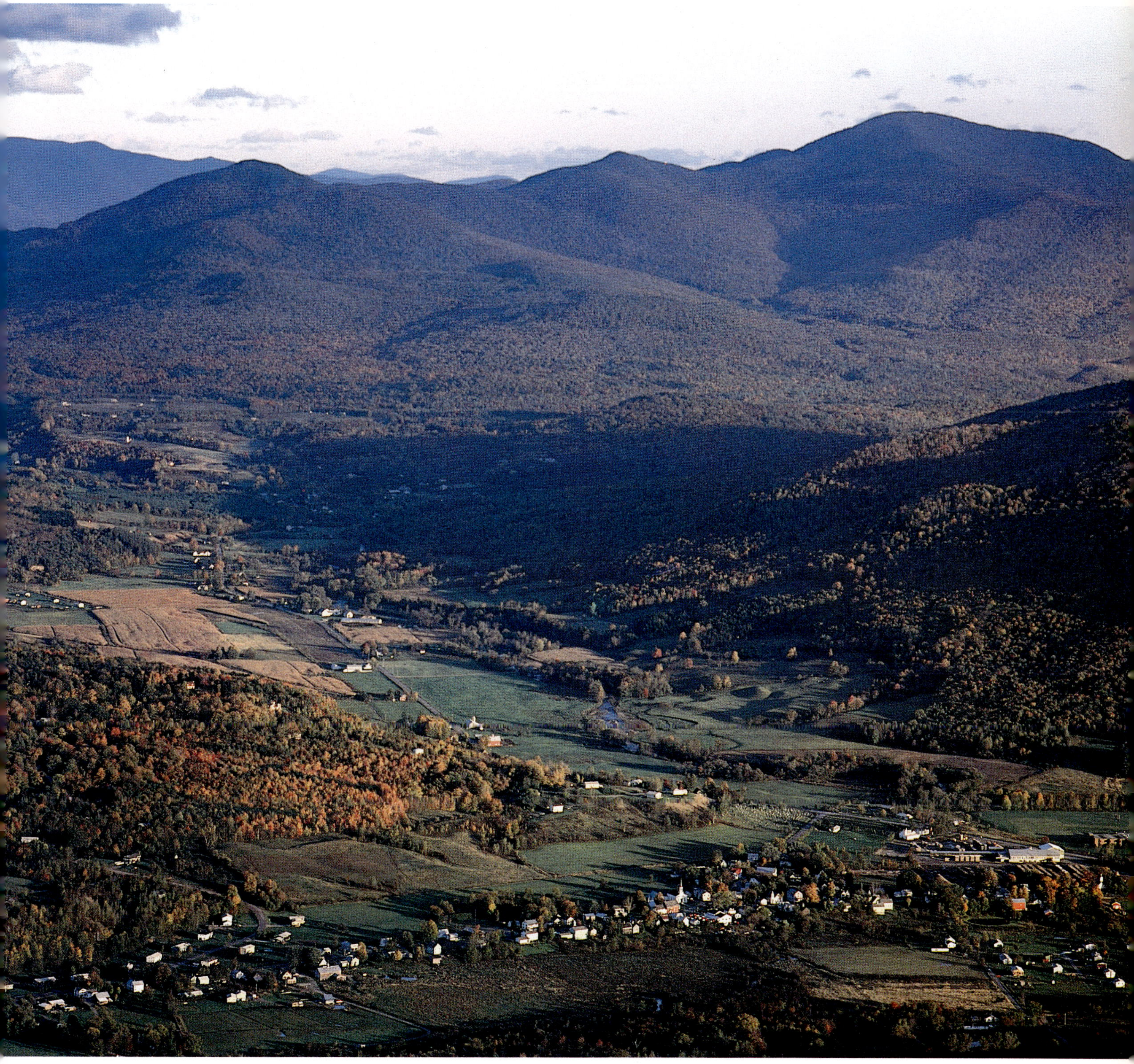

Underhill and Mt. Mansfield

Overleaf: The Capstone "Chin," highest point in Vermont

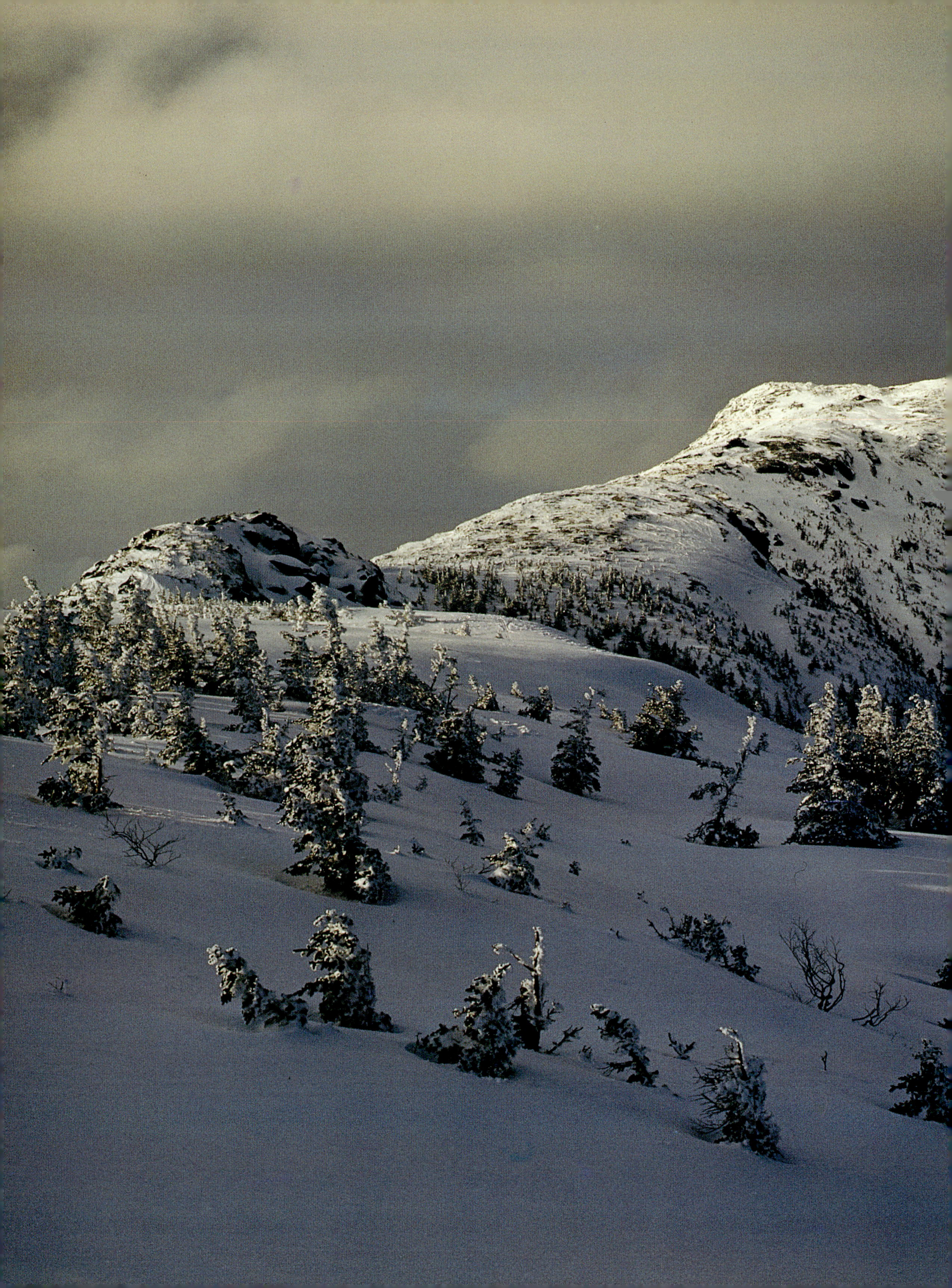

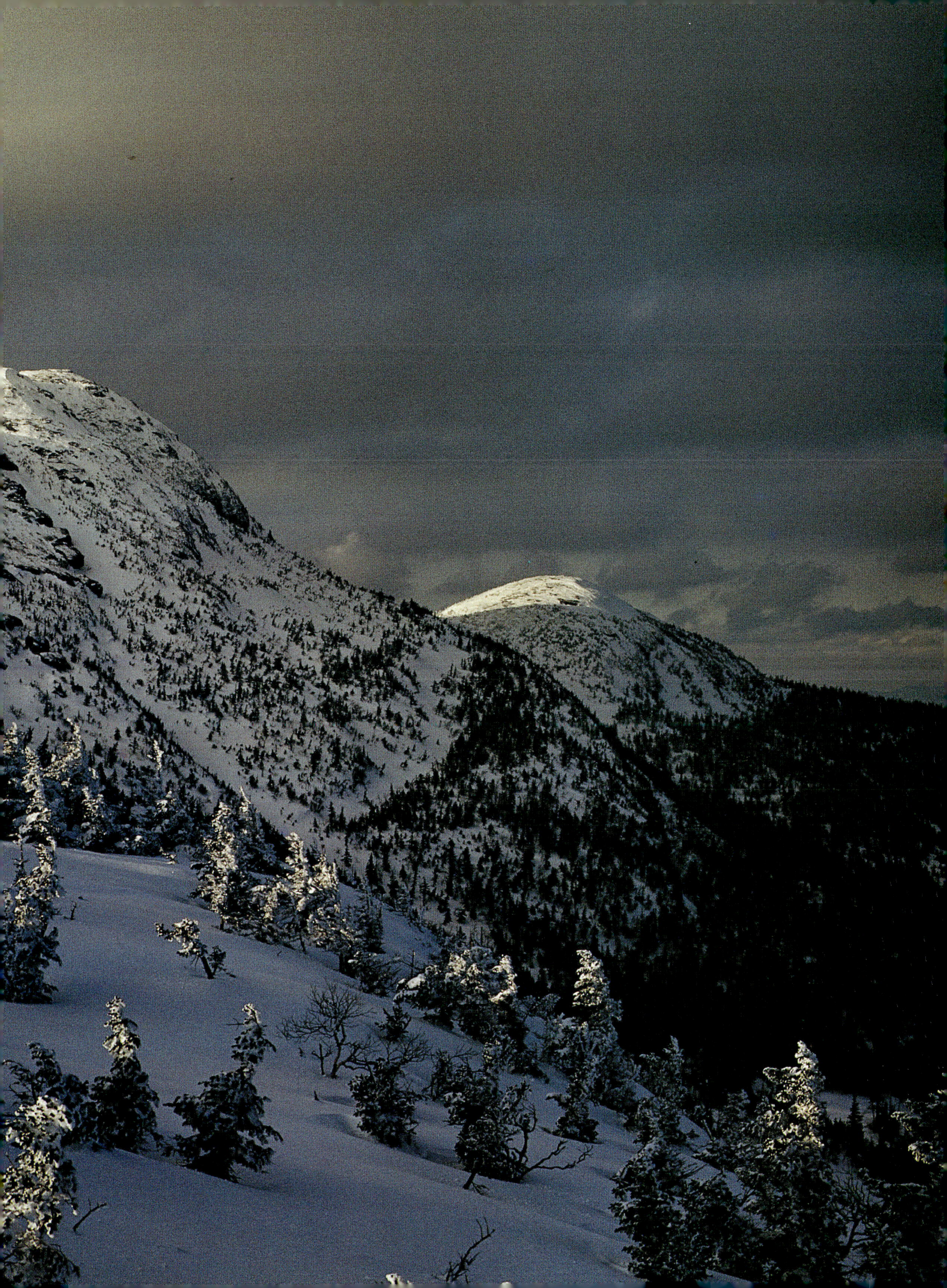

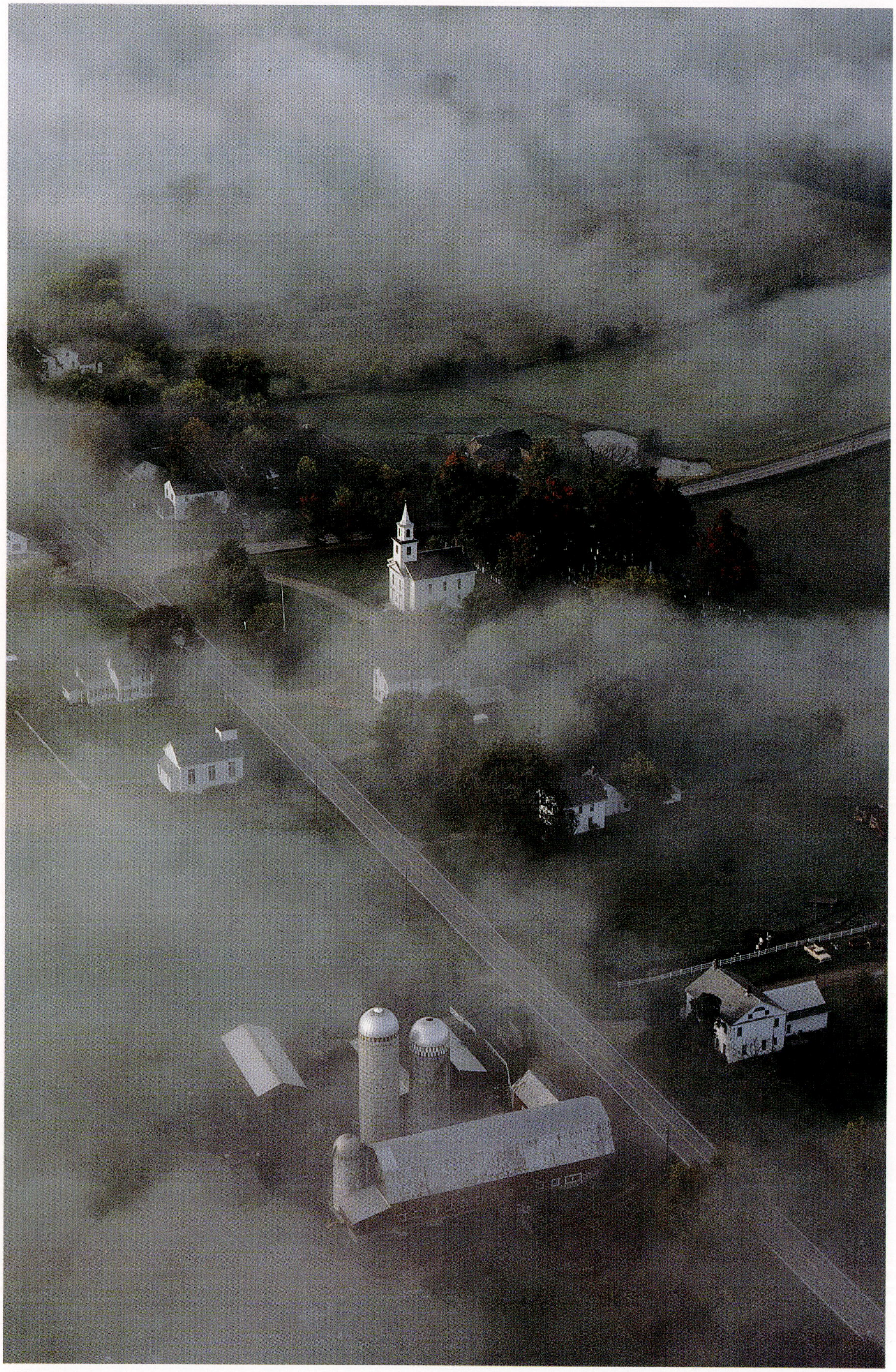

Whiting

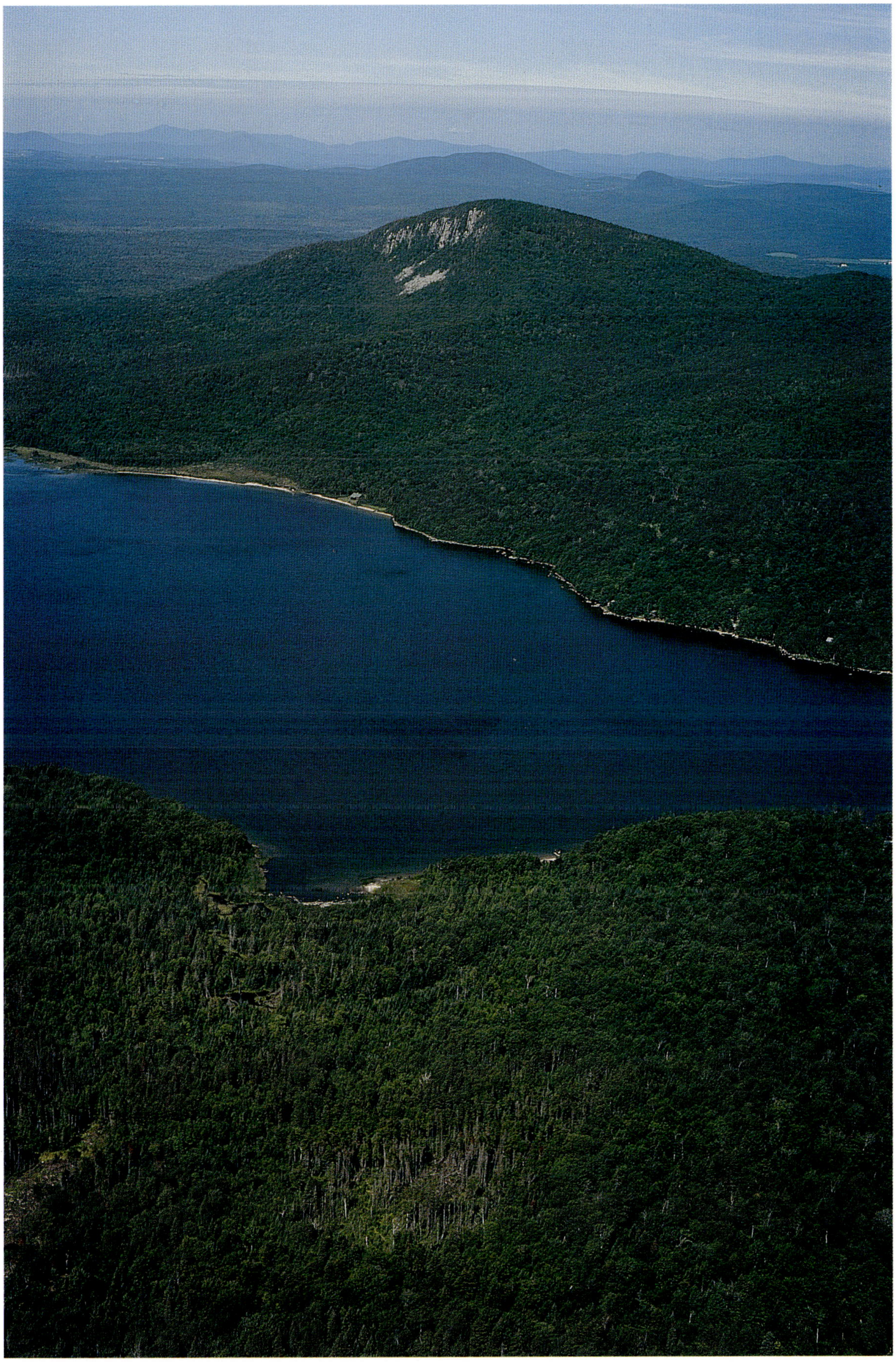

Little Averill Lake, Mt. Brousseau

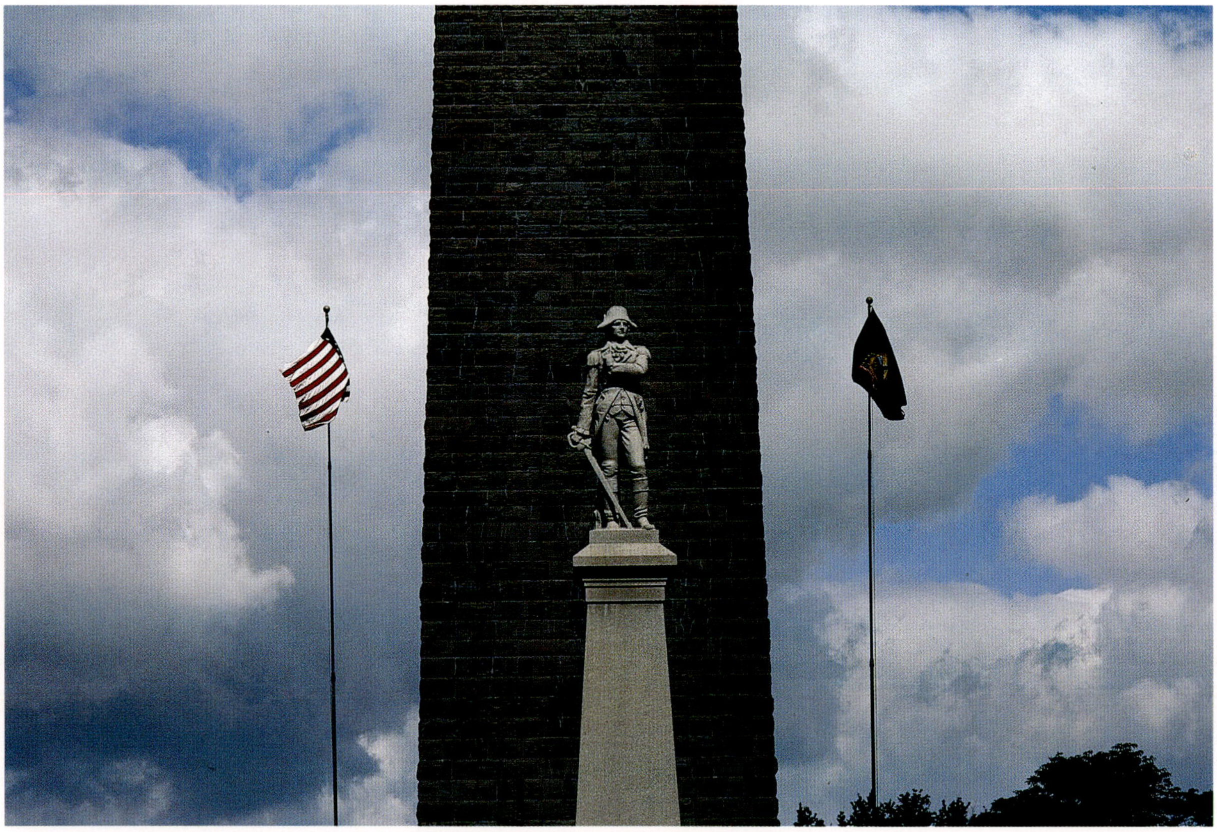

Bennington Battle Monument

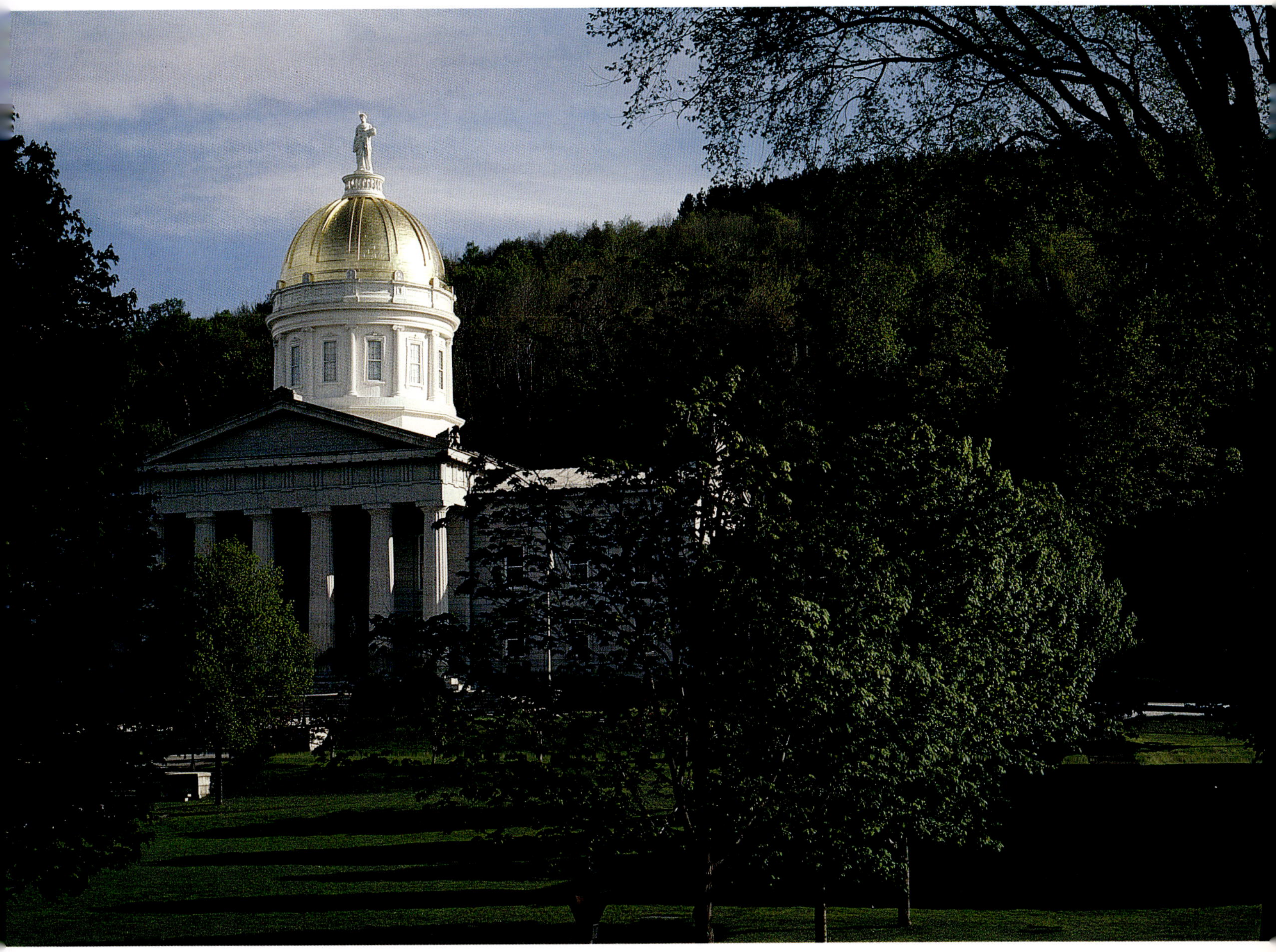

Capitol in Montpelier

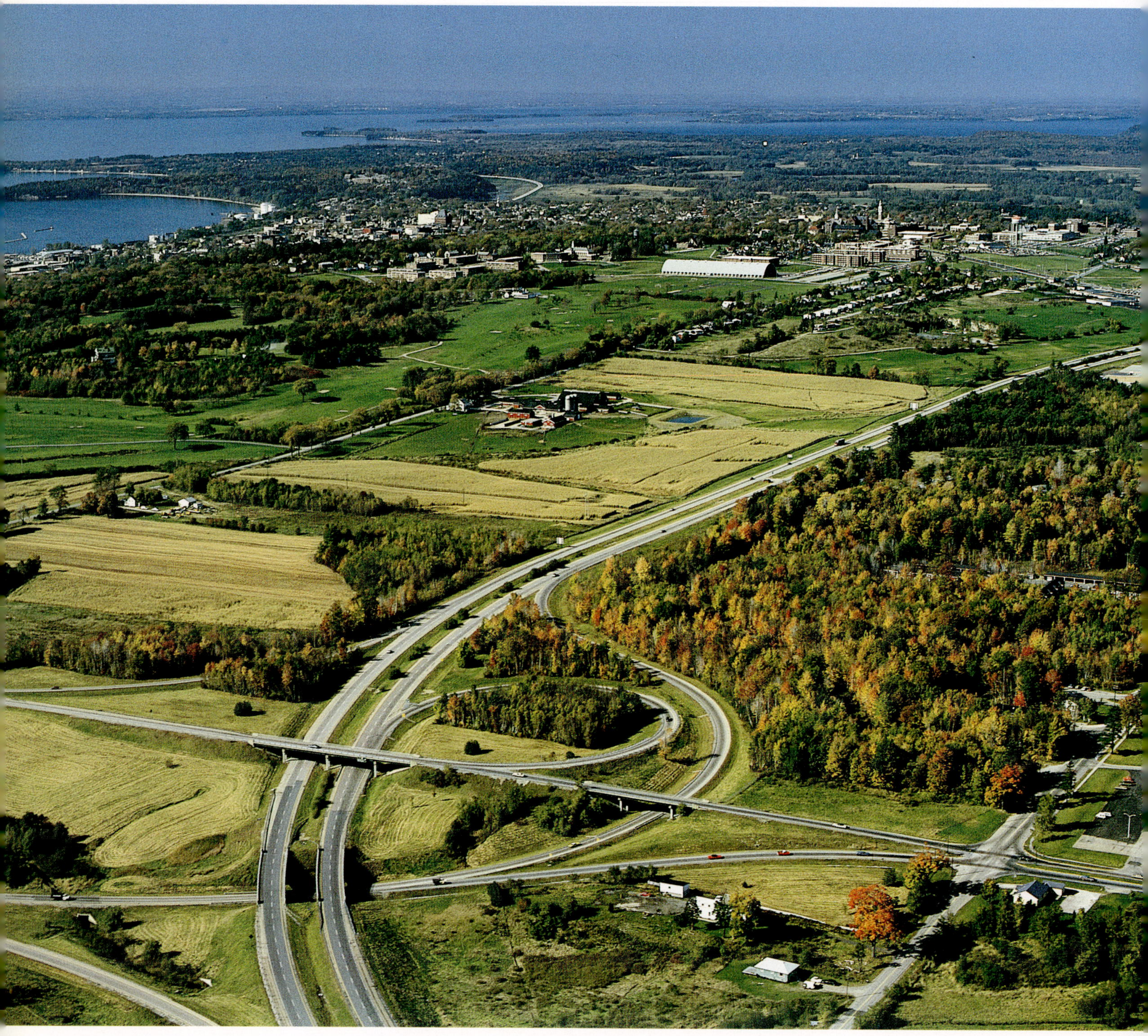

South Burlington

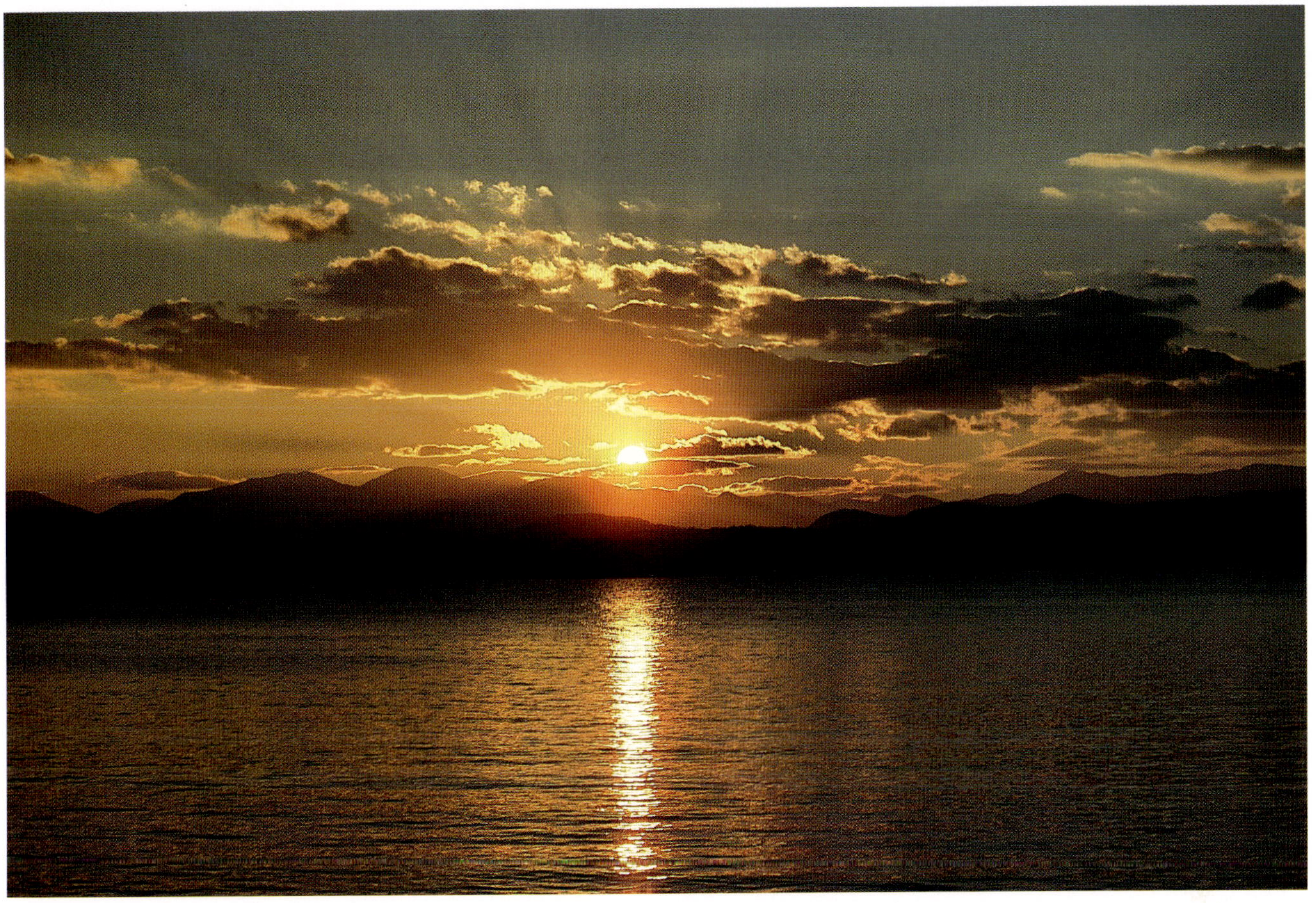

Lake Champlain and the Adirondacks

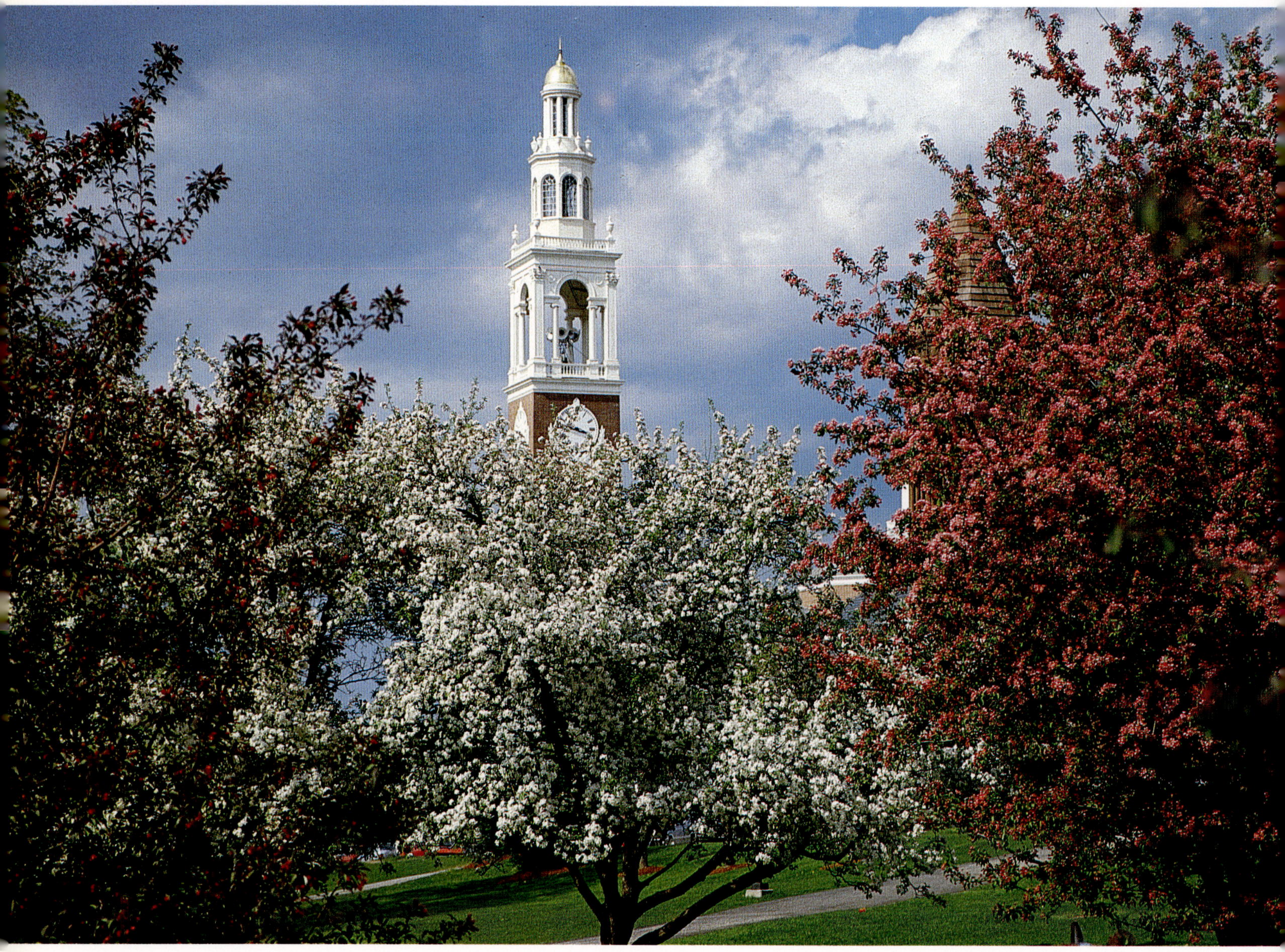

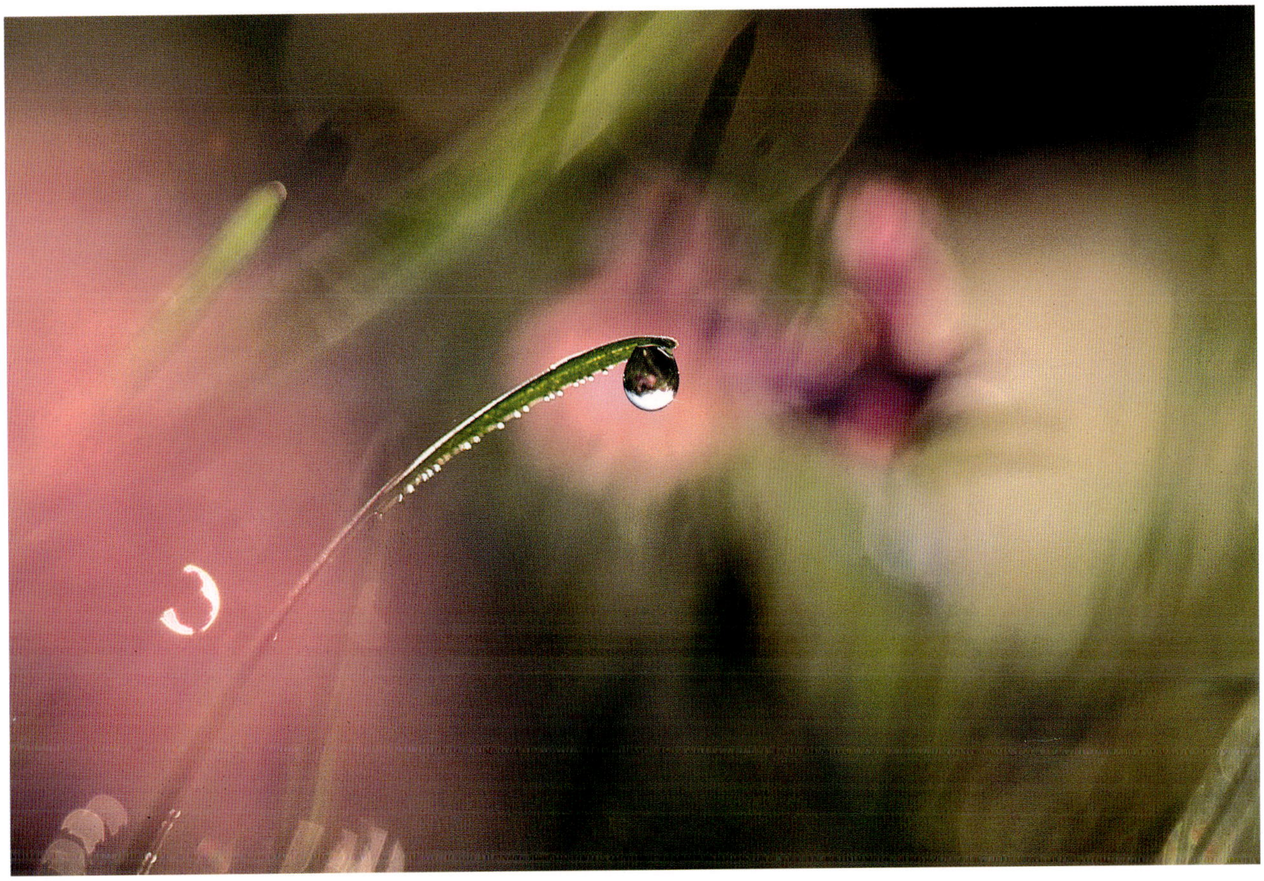

Spring detail

Overleaf: Connecticut River, Windsor

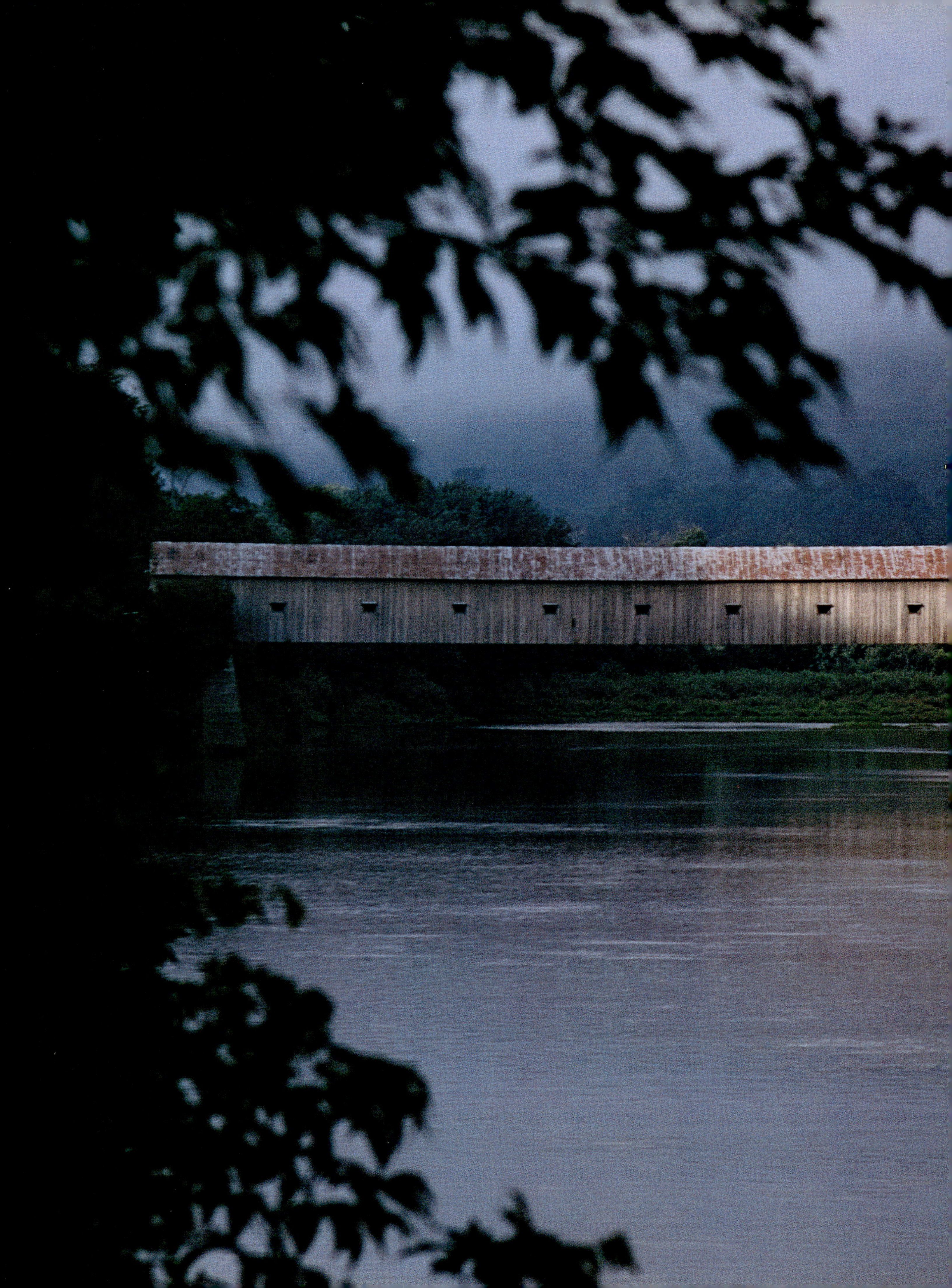

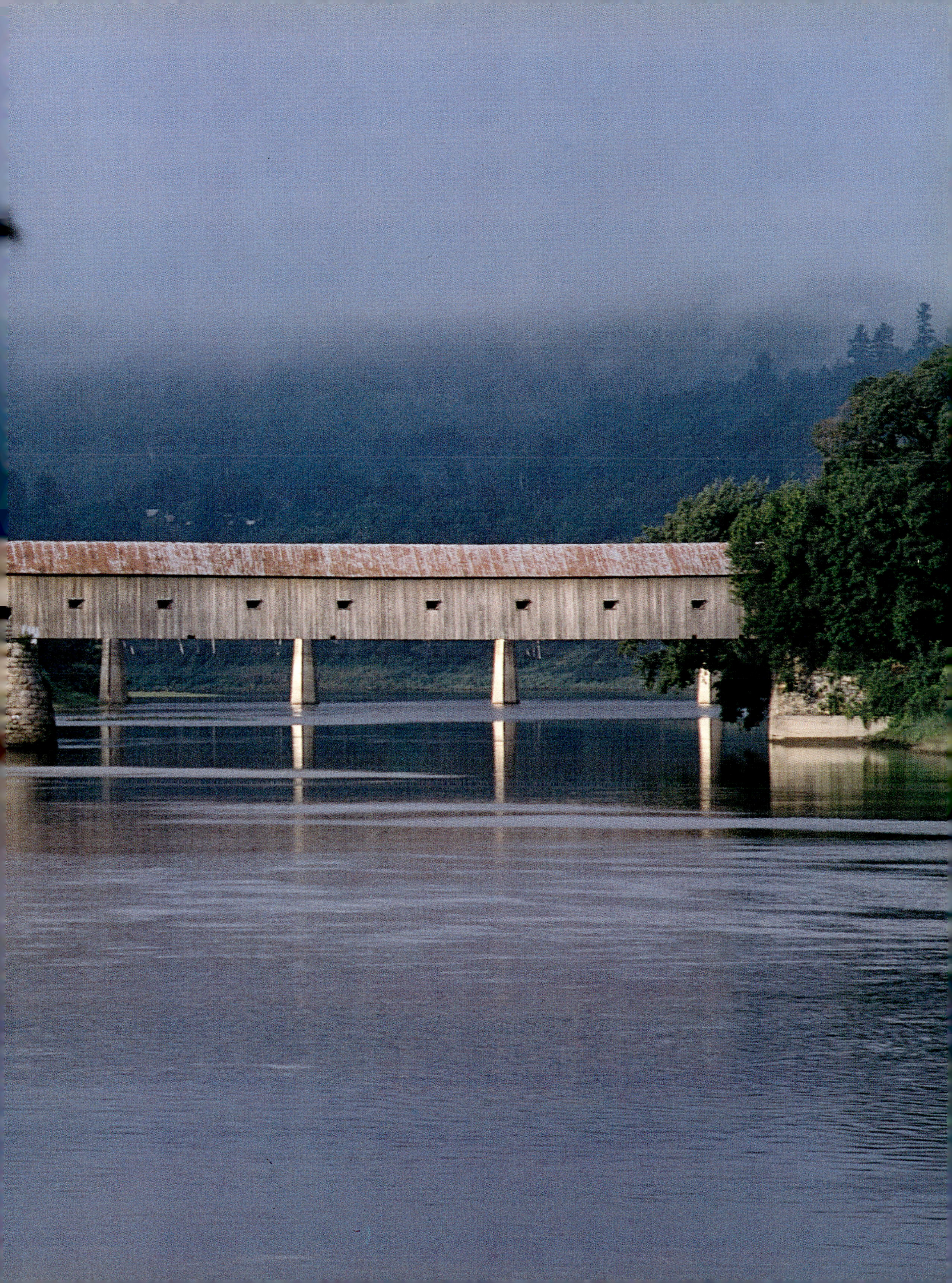

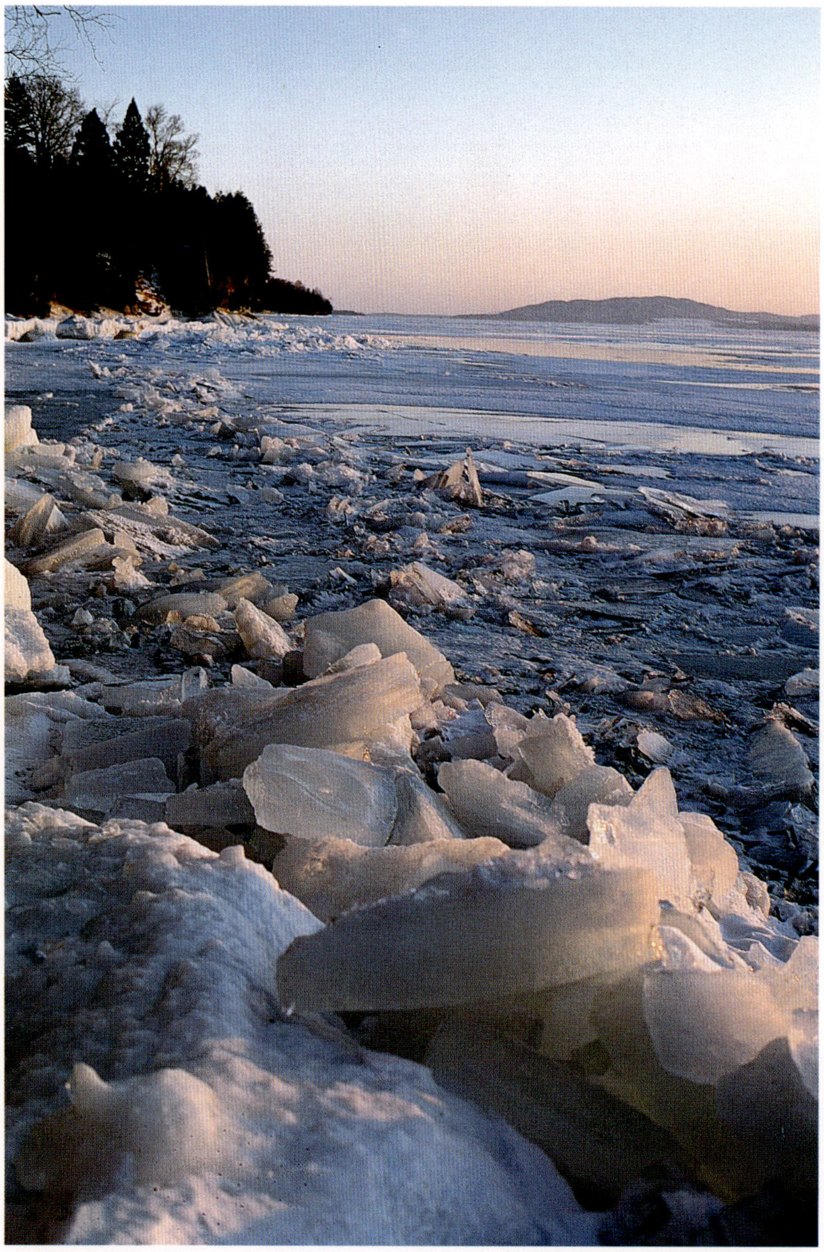

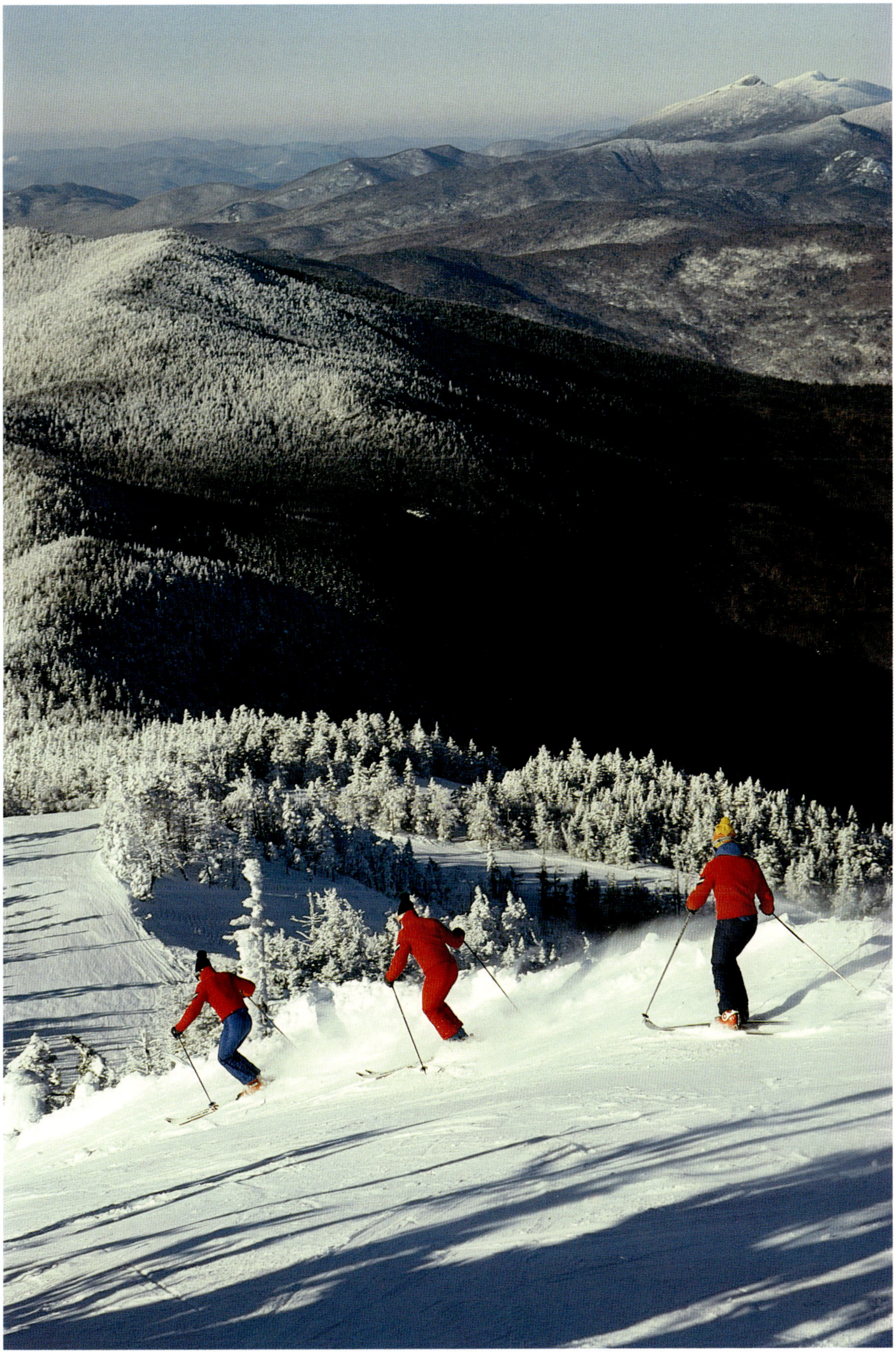

Sugarbush

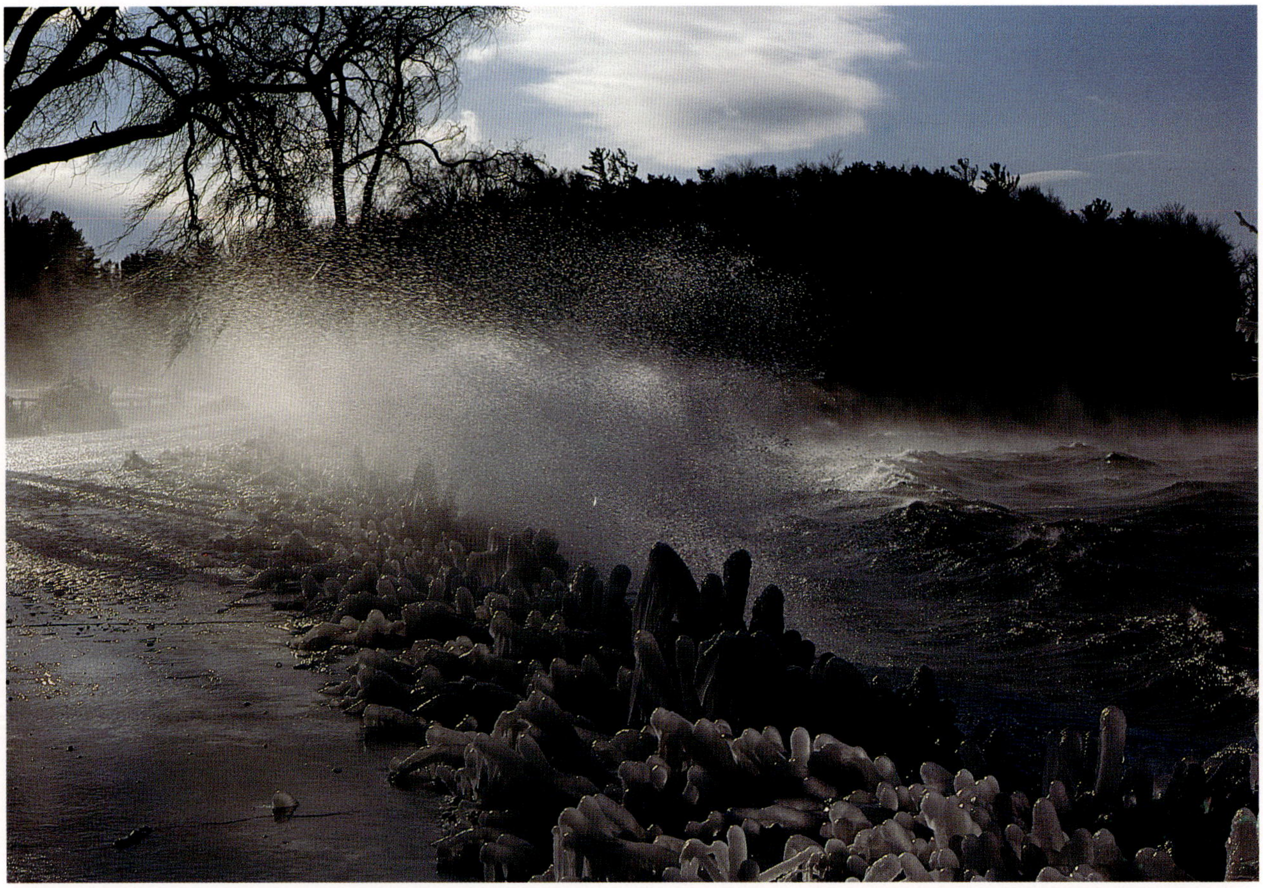

Lake Champlain, Shelburne

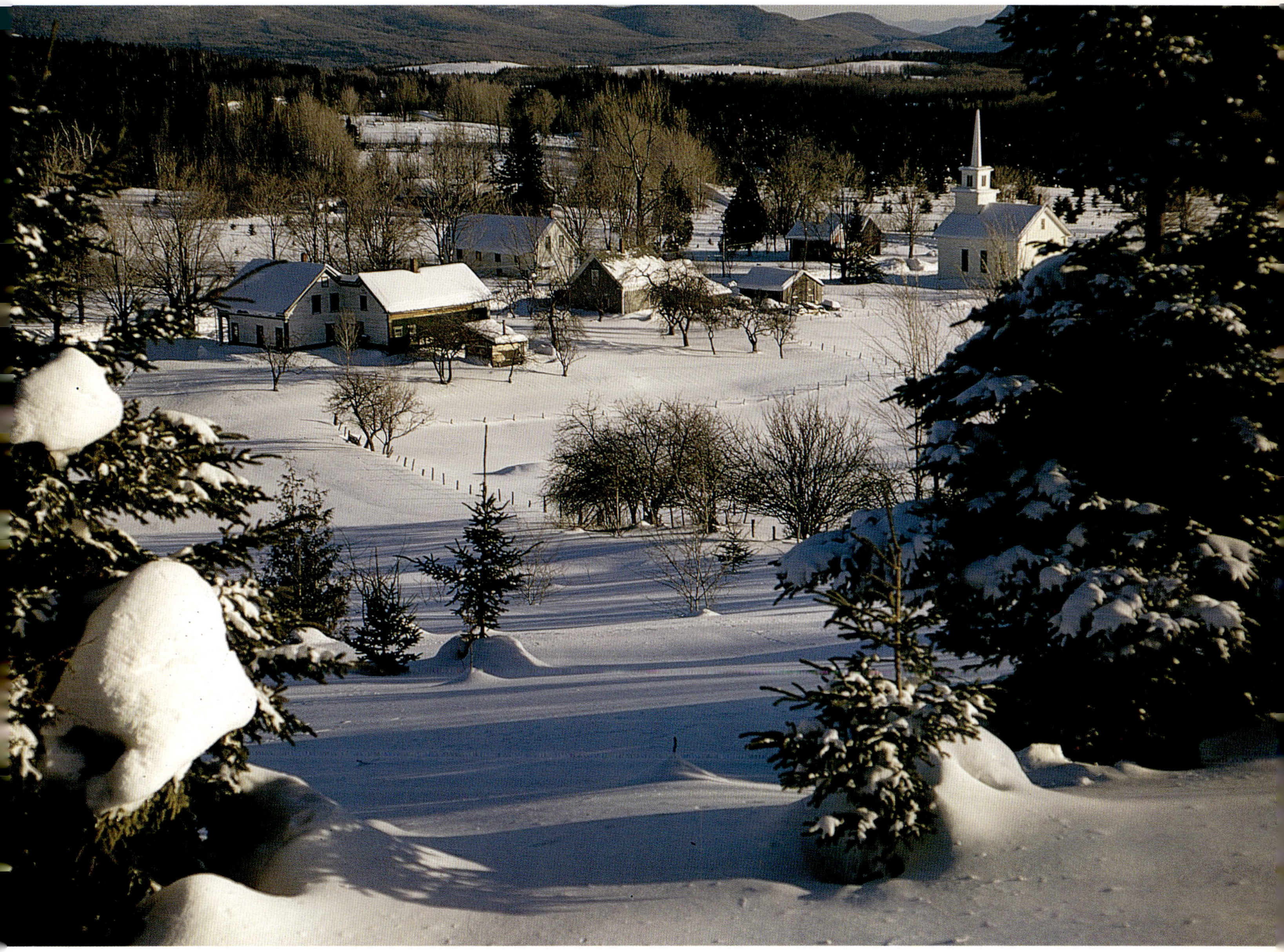

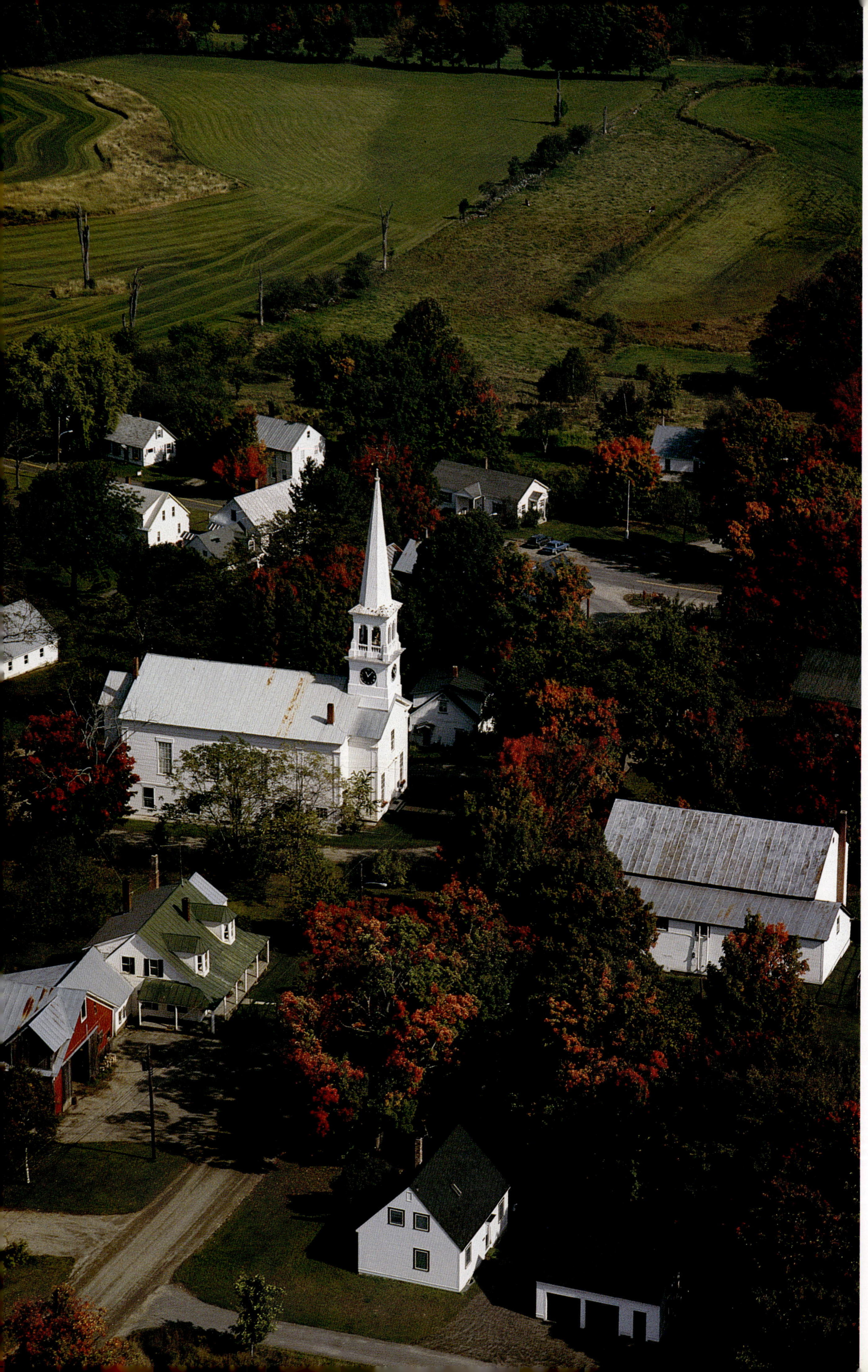

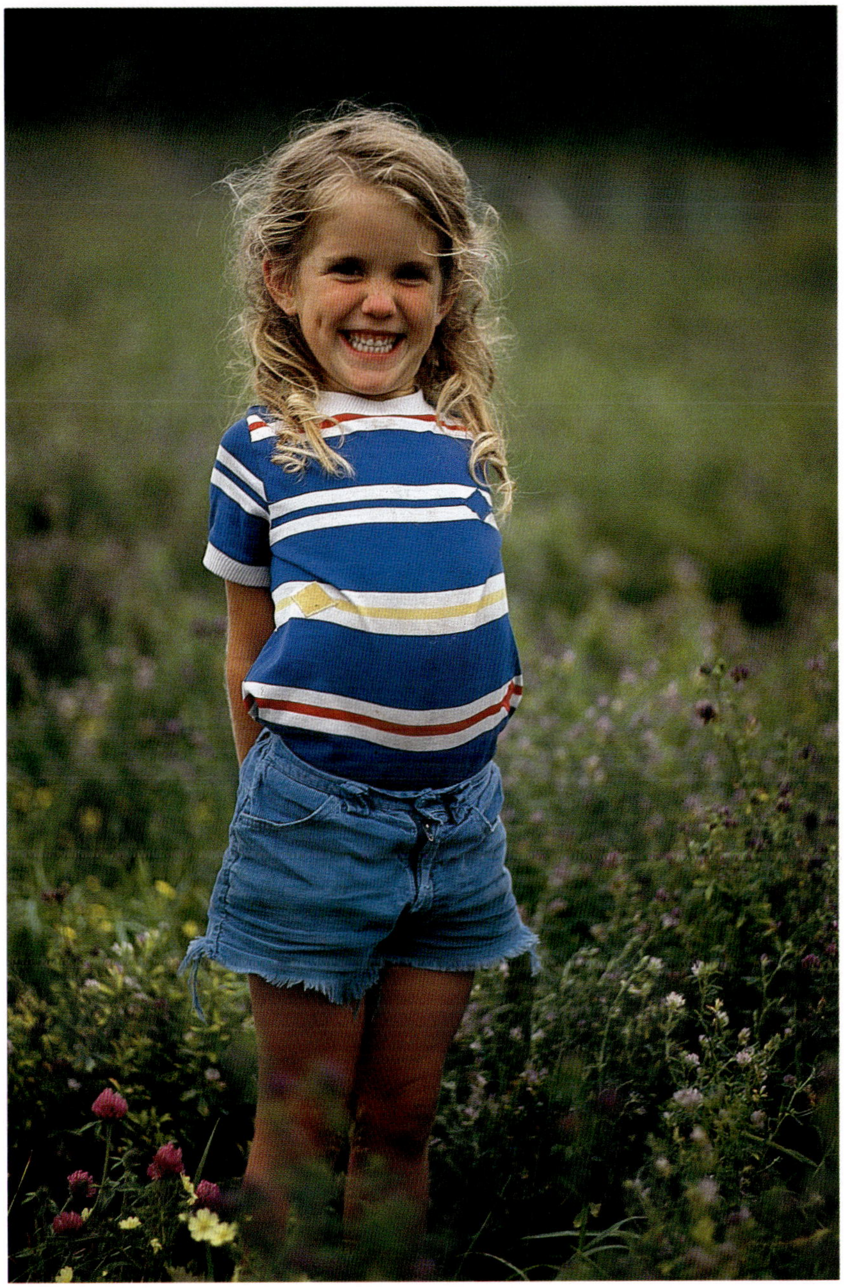

Peacham Linnea Phillips

Overleaf: South Londonderry

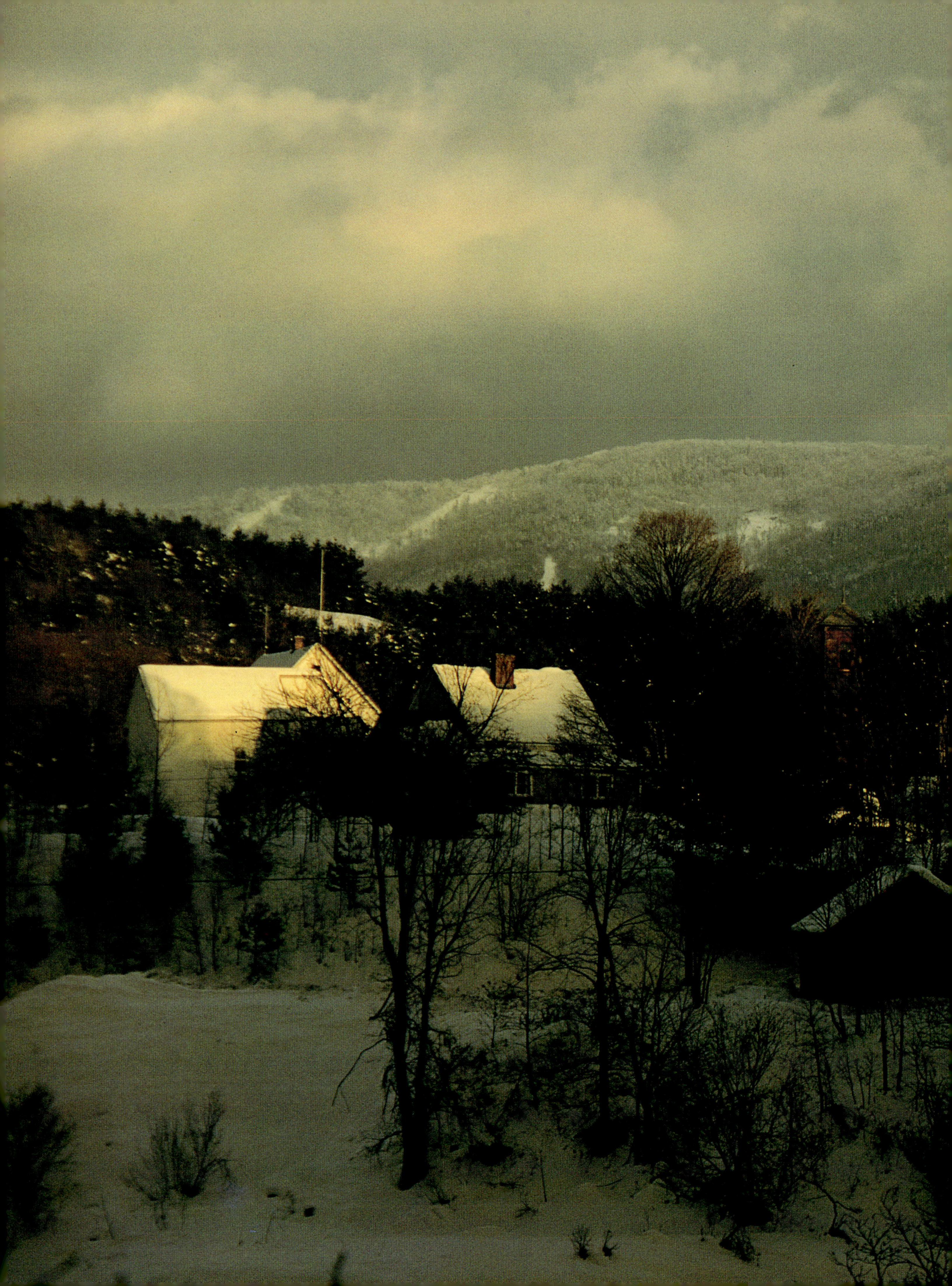

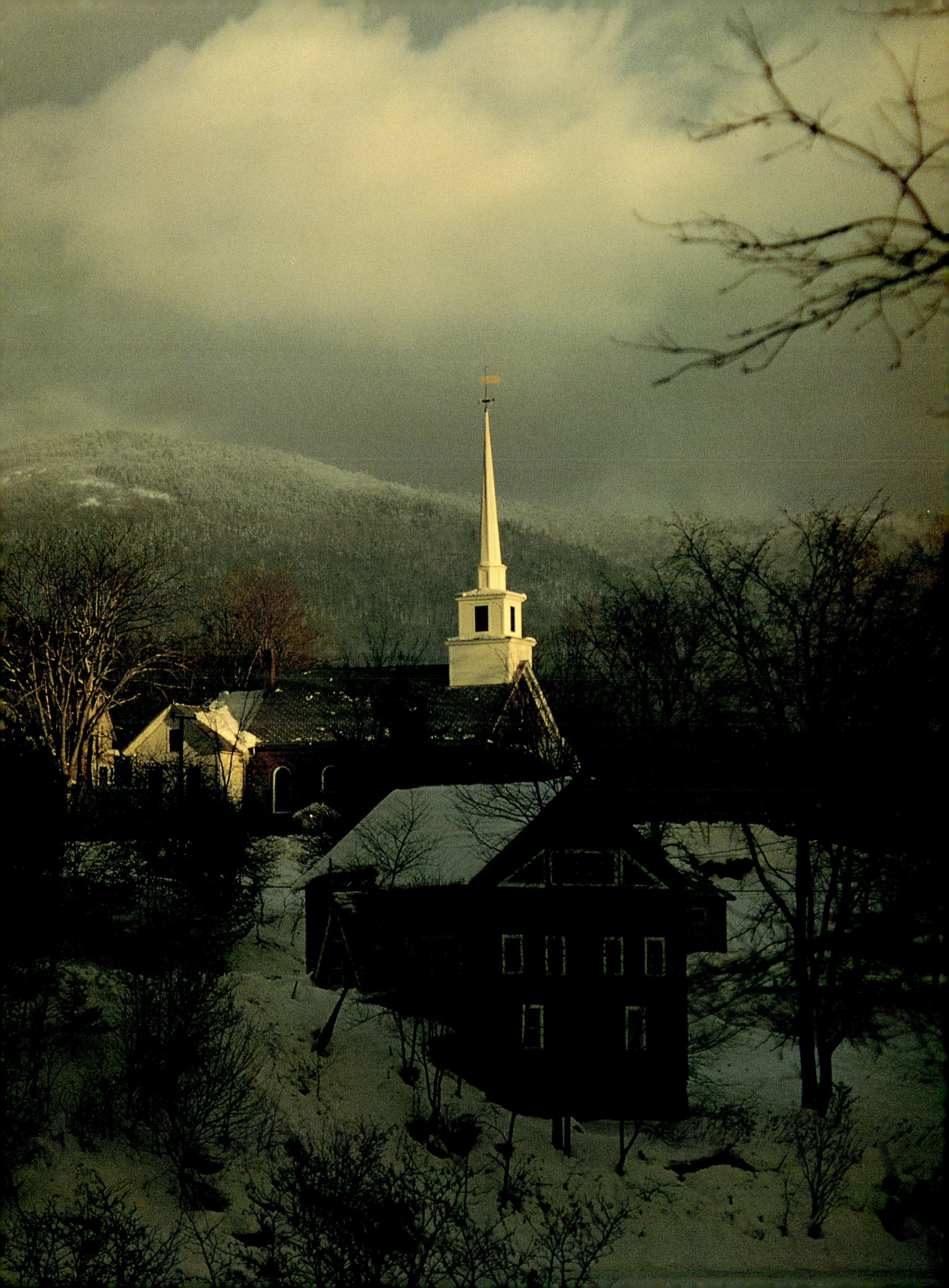

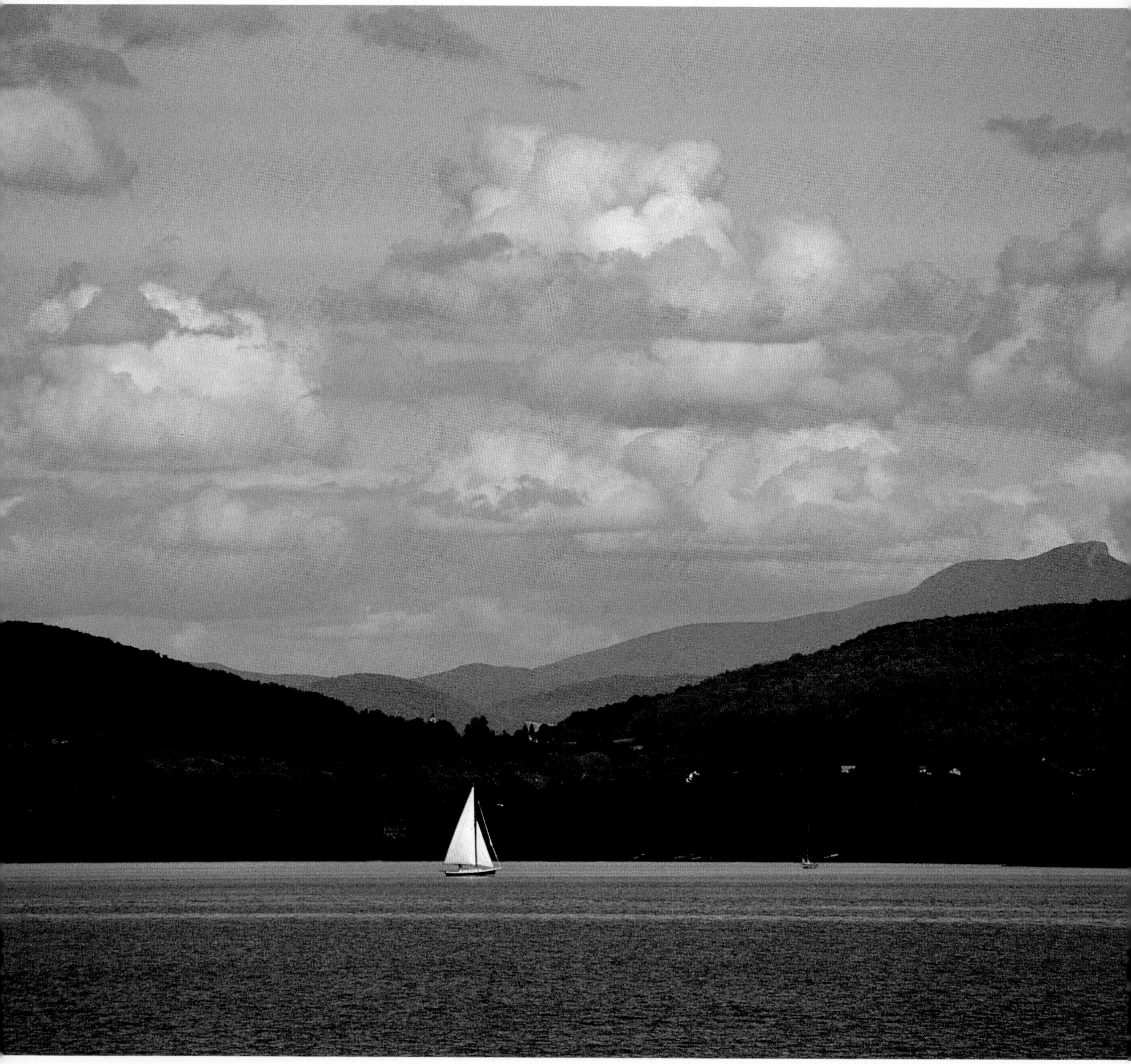

Lake Champlain, Charlotte

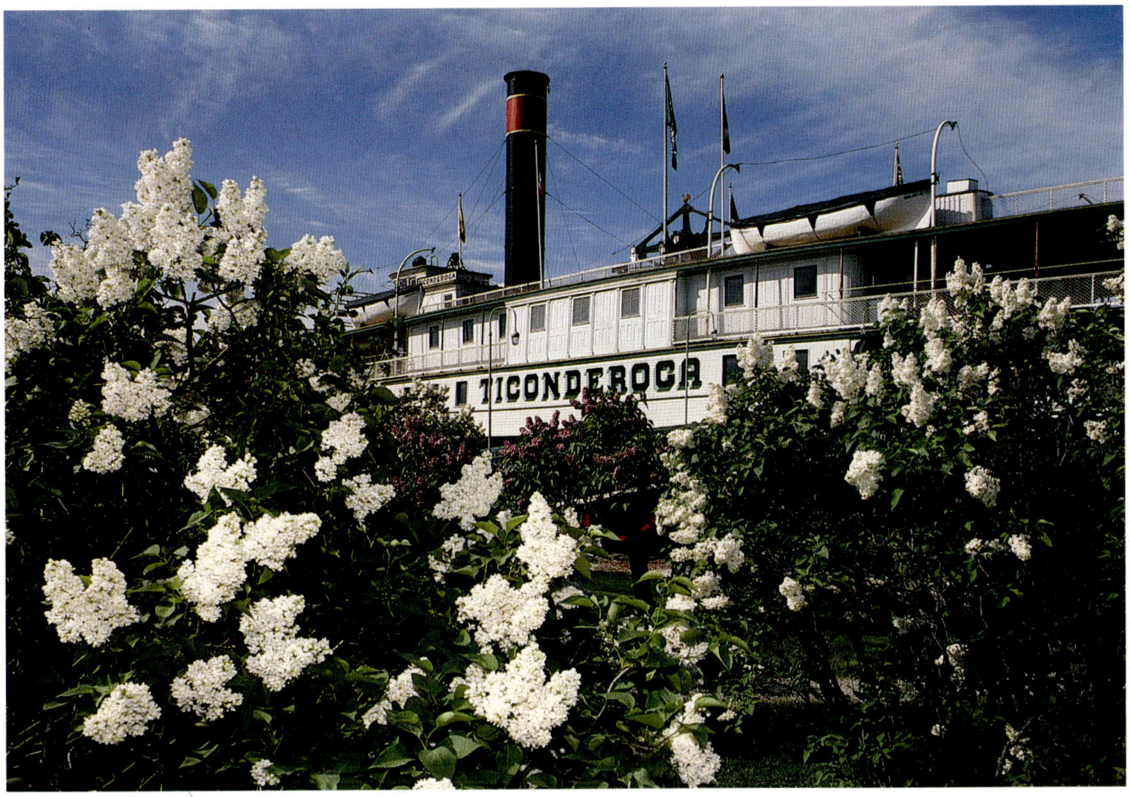
TICONDEROGA

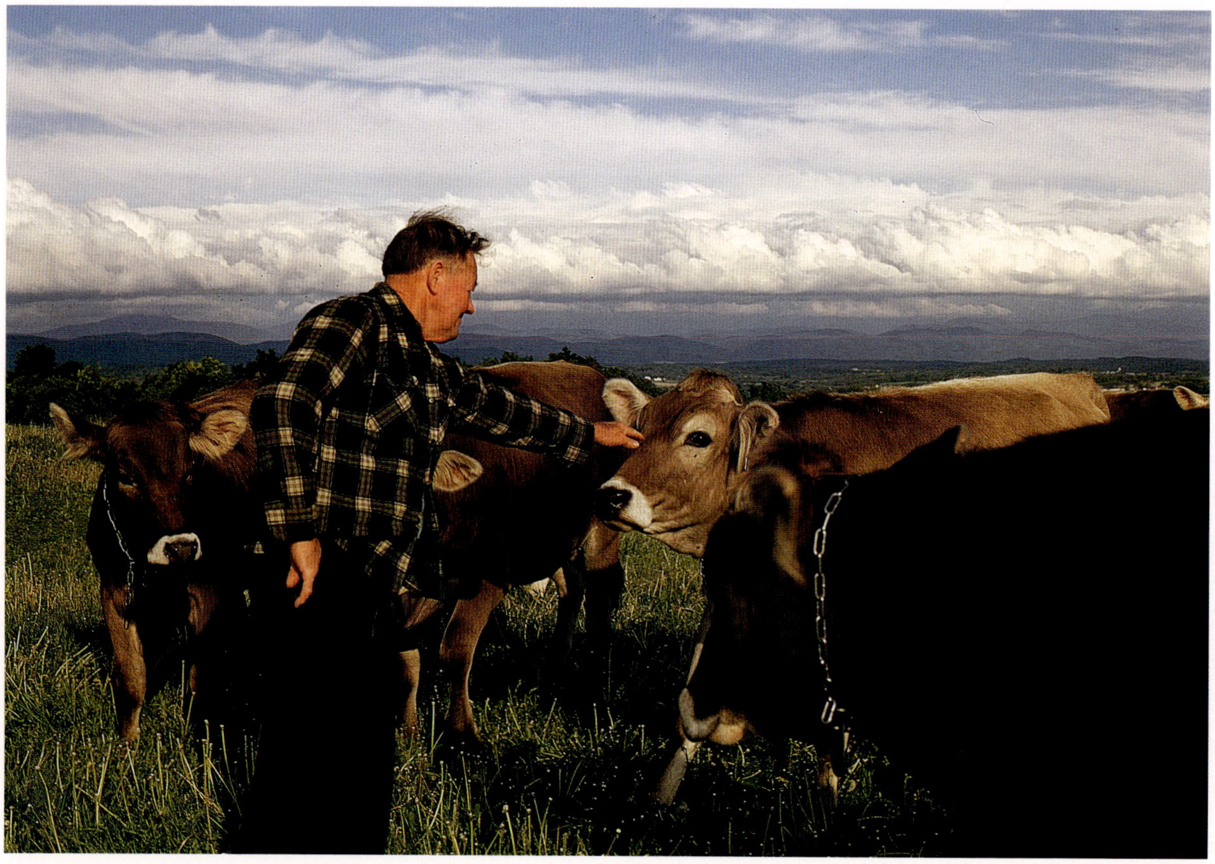

Shelburne Farms, Shelburne

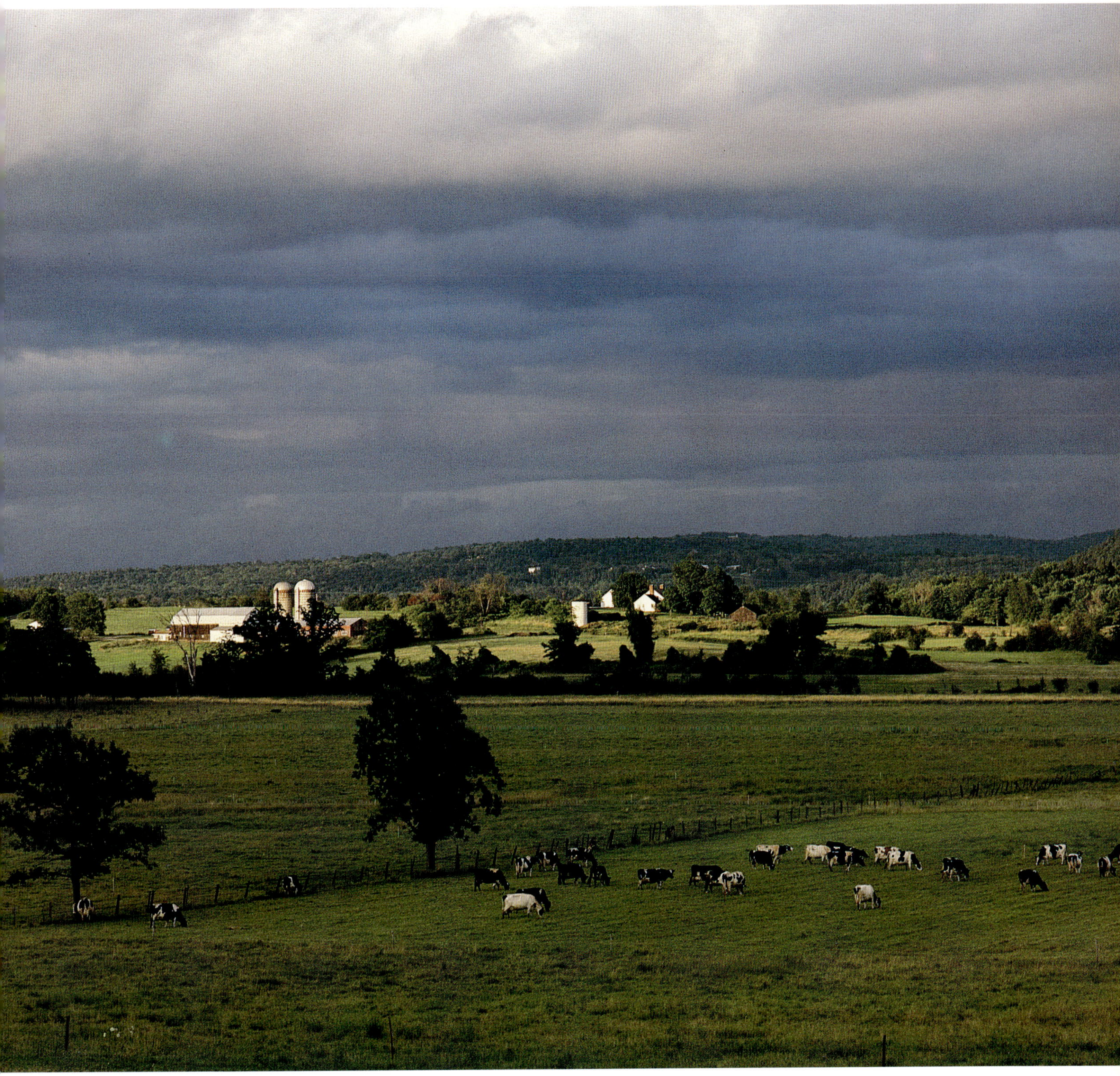

Williston

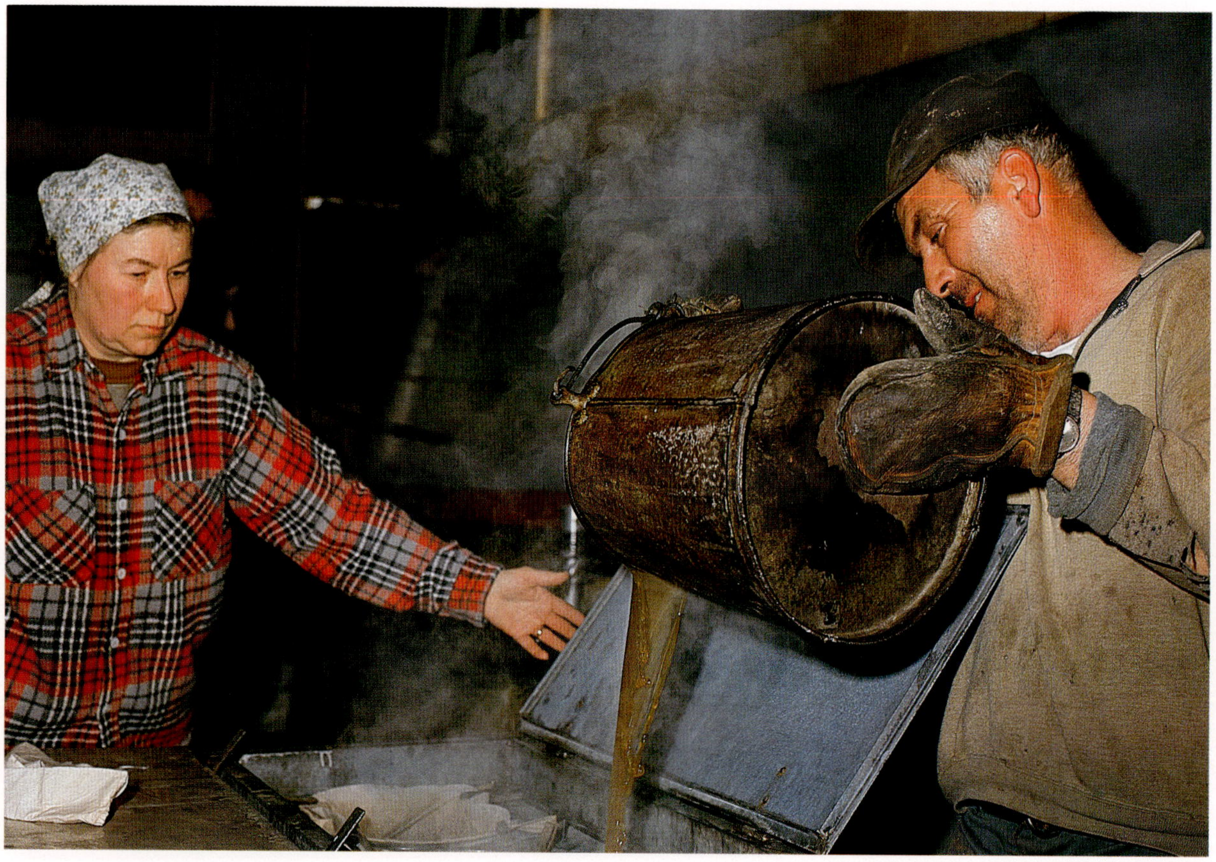

Jeffersonville

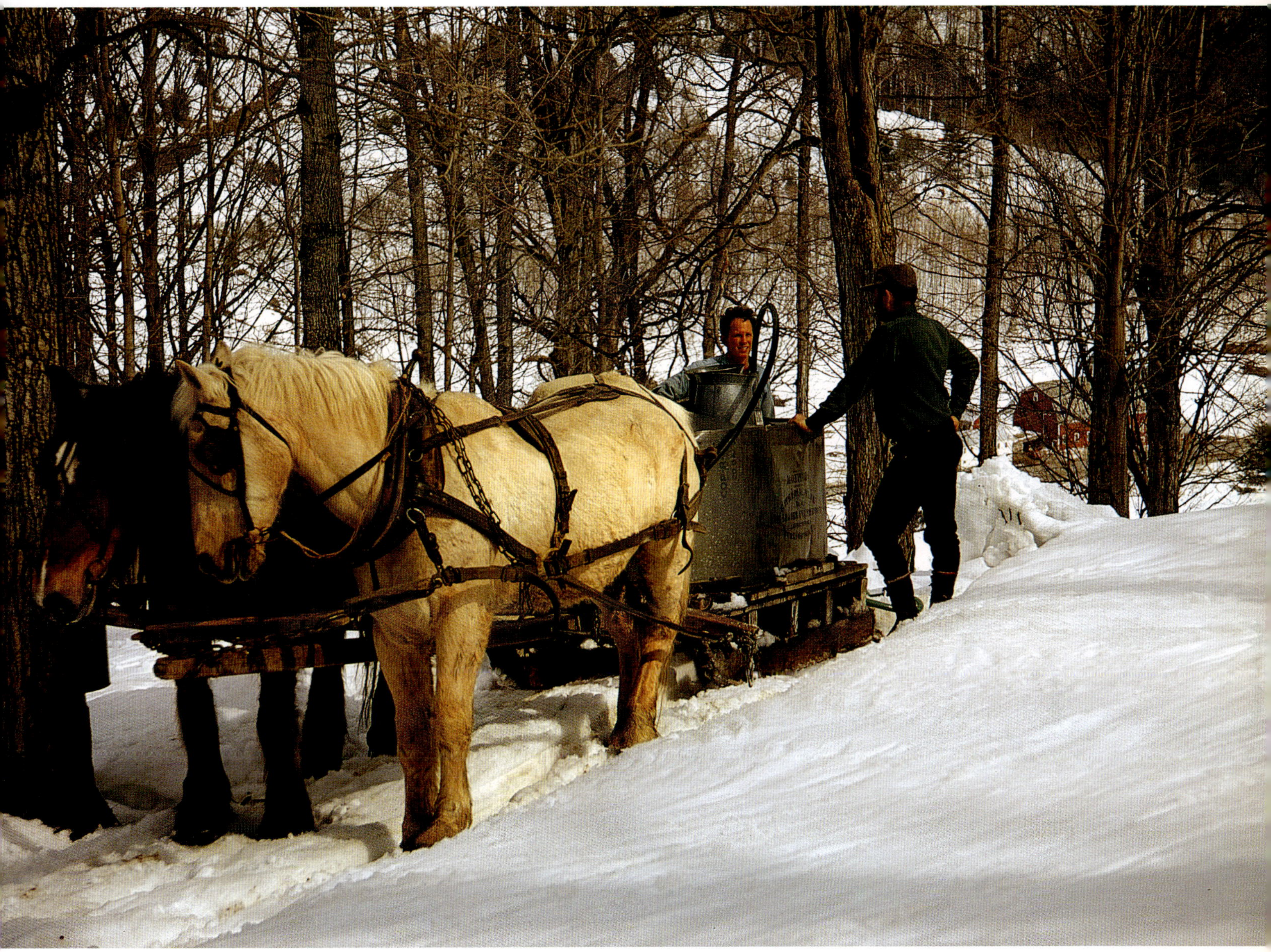

Woodstock

Overleaf: North Ferrisburg

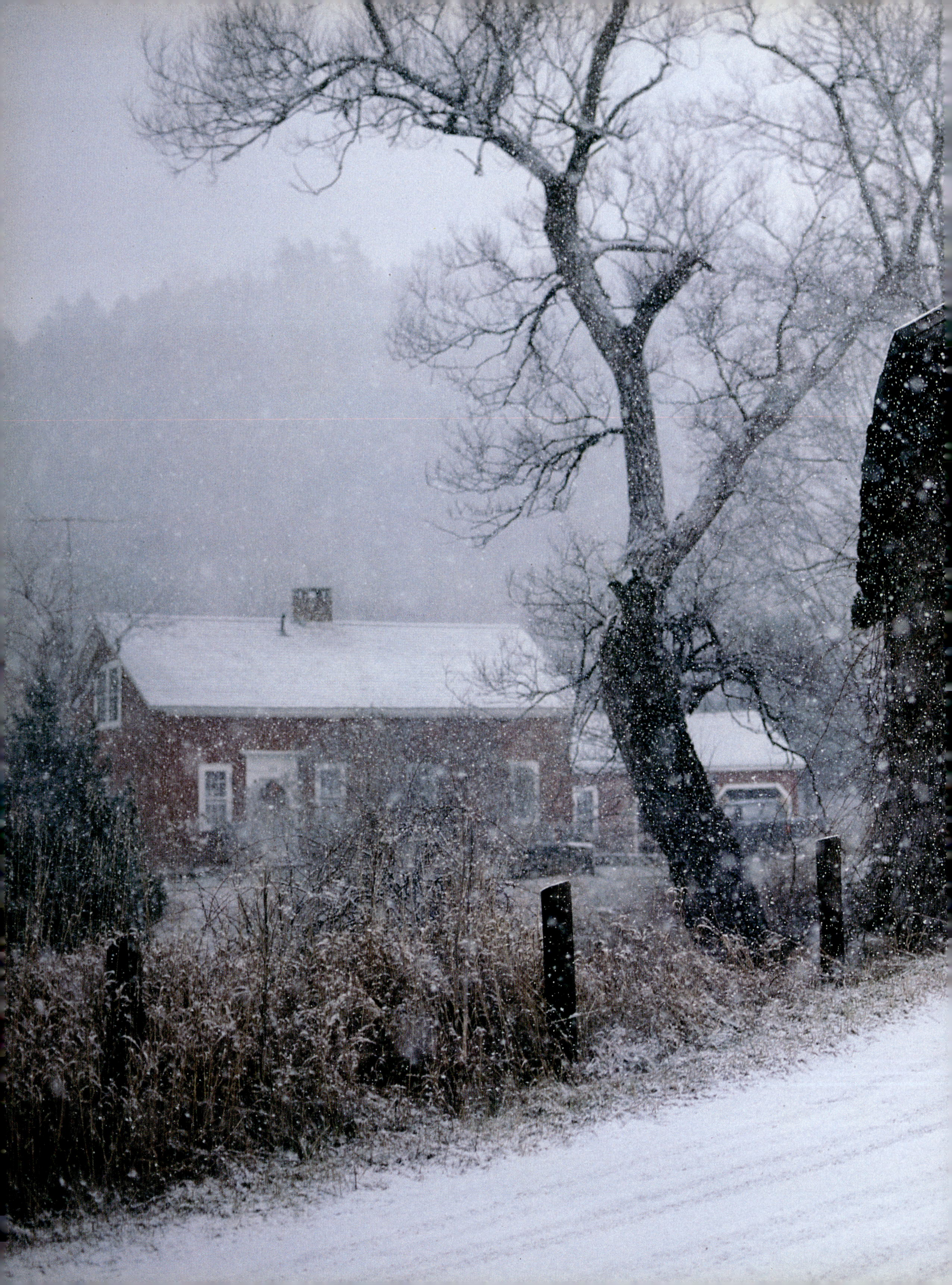

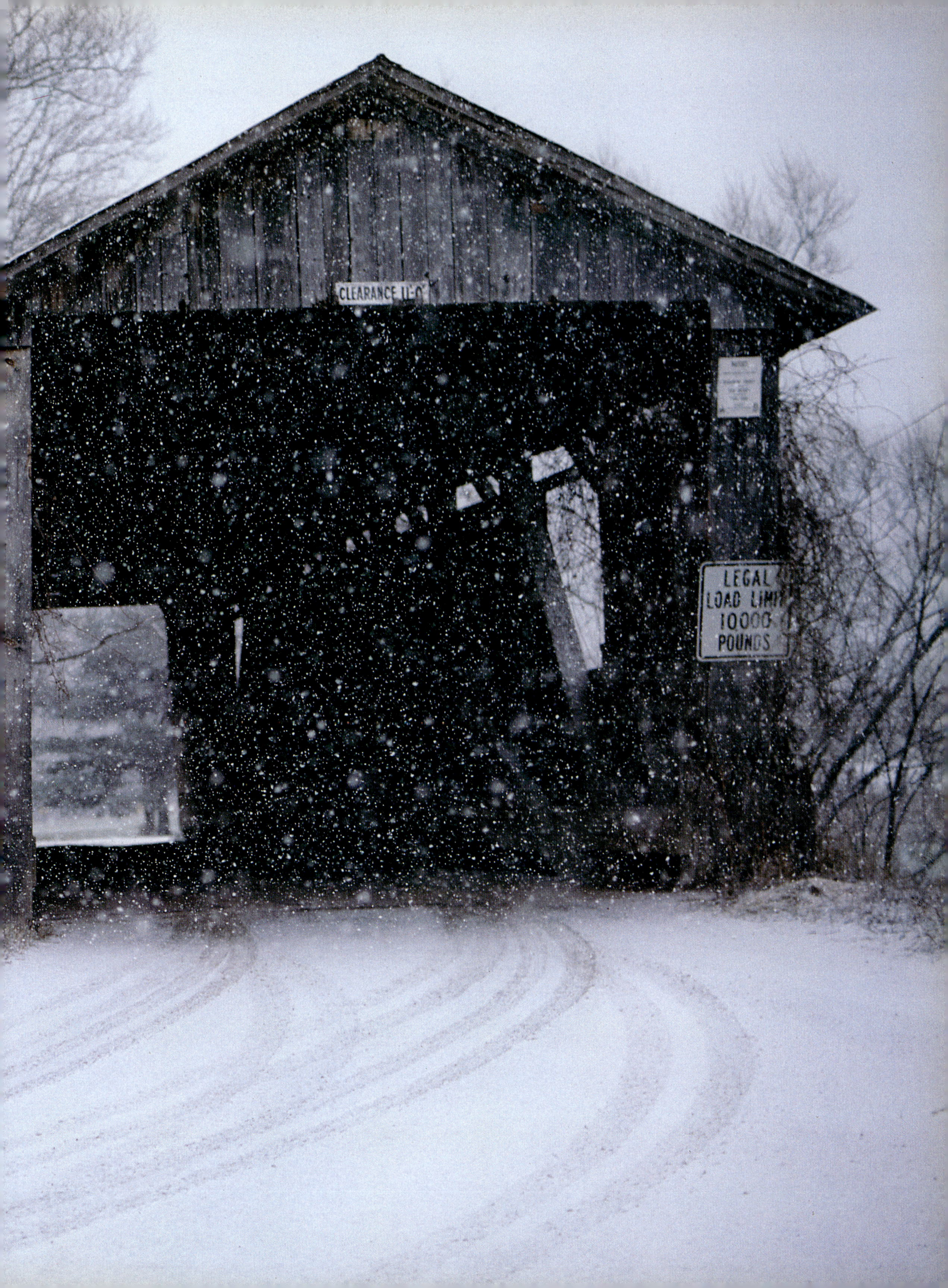
CLEARANCE 11-0
LEGAL
LOAD LIMI
10000
POUNDS

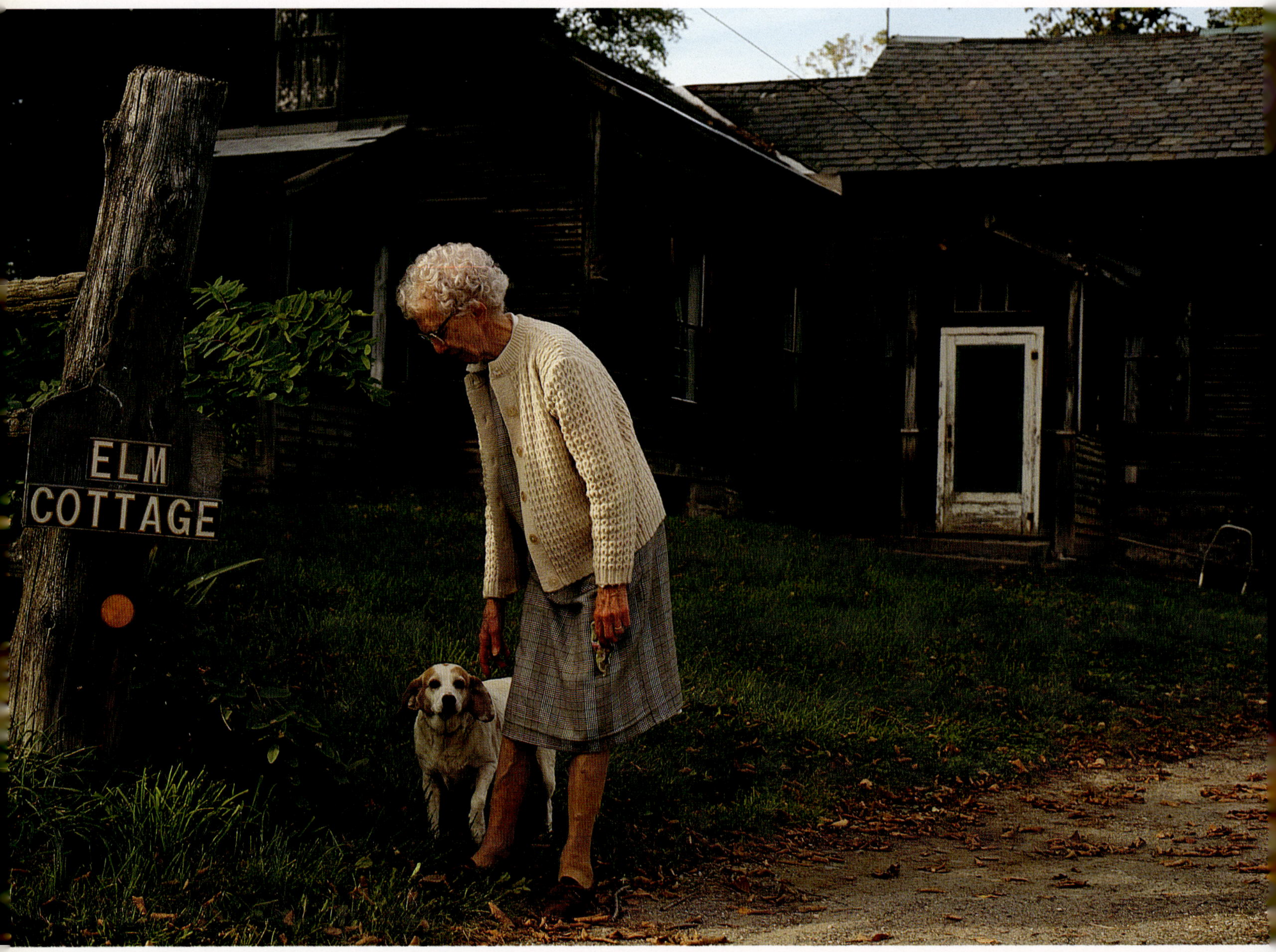

Elm Cottage in Benson

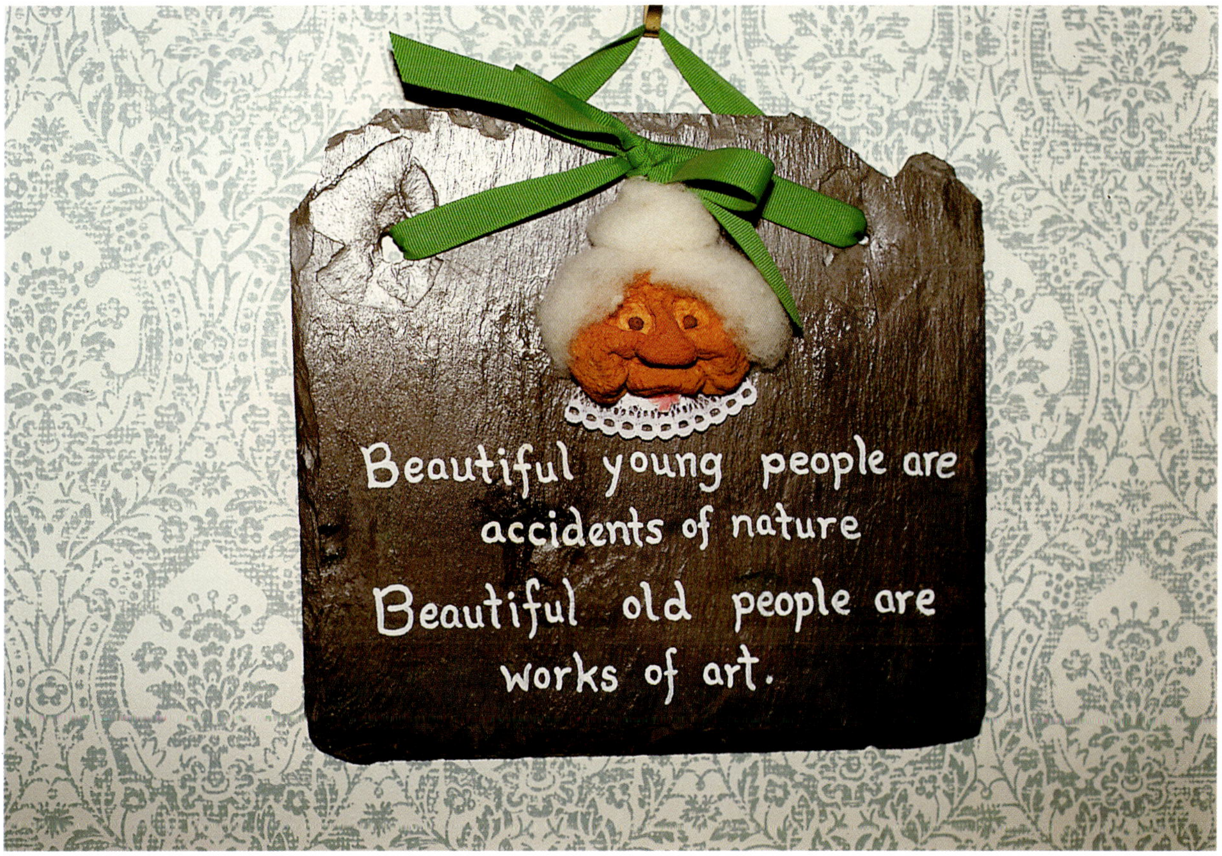

Hanging prose, Elm Cottage

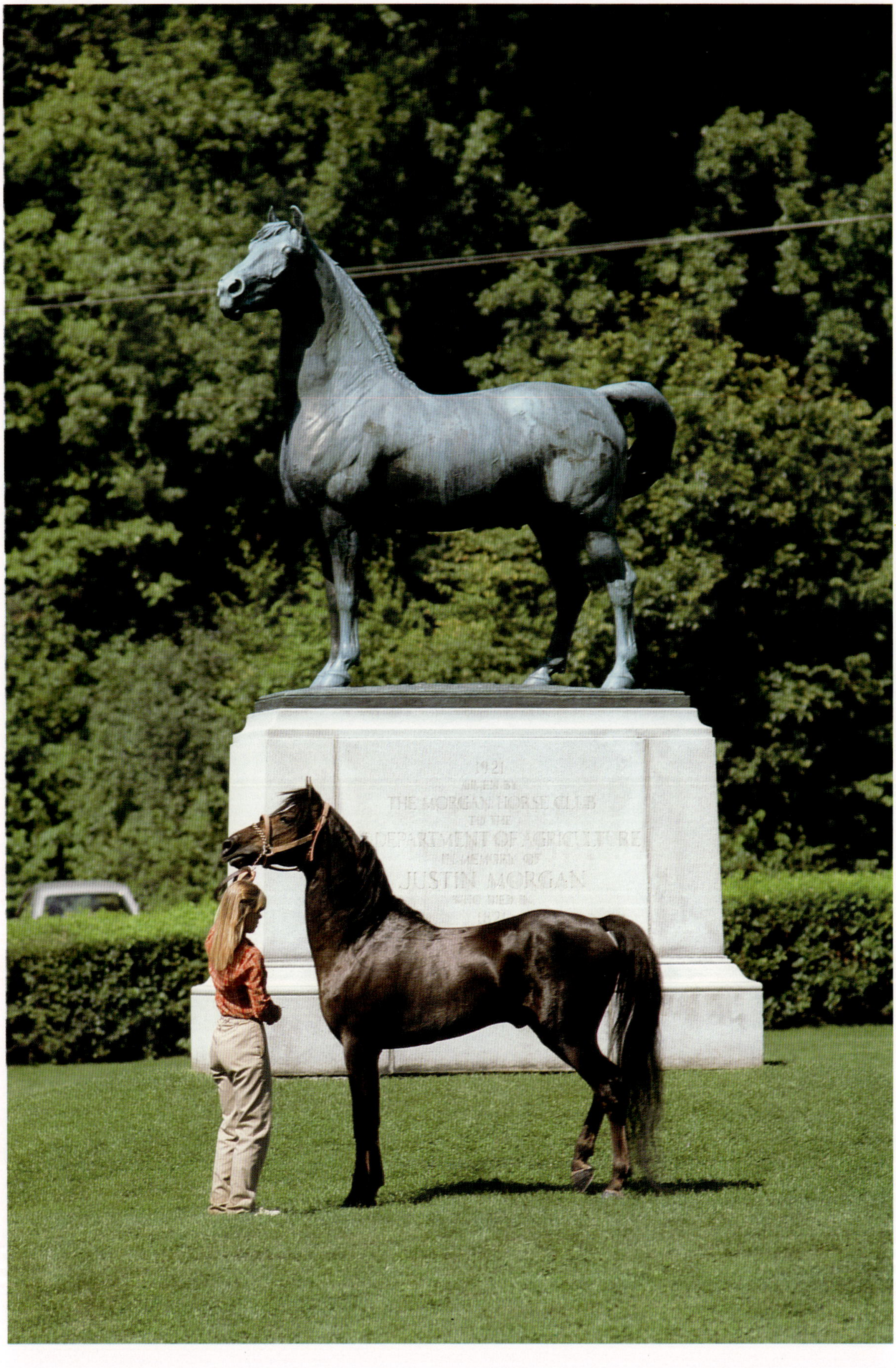

Morgan Horse Farm, Weybridge

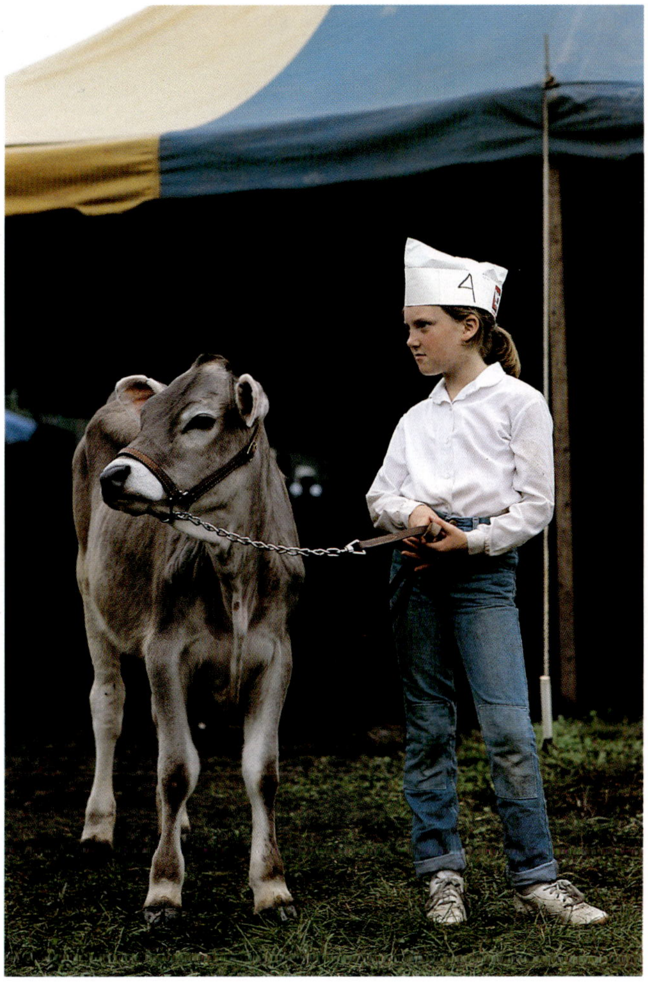

Jennifer and her Brown Swiss calf

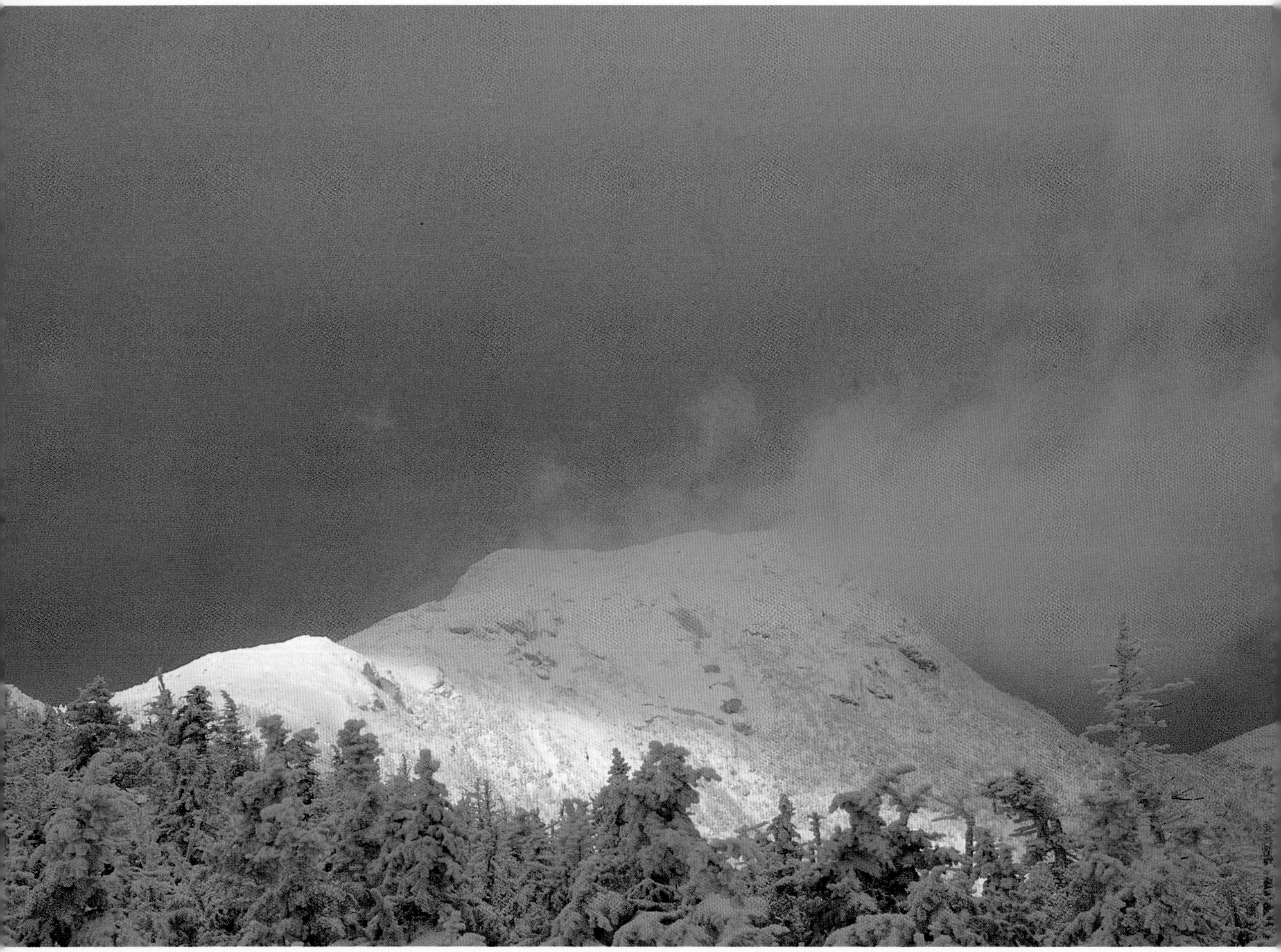

The Capstone of Mt. Mansfield

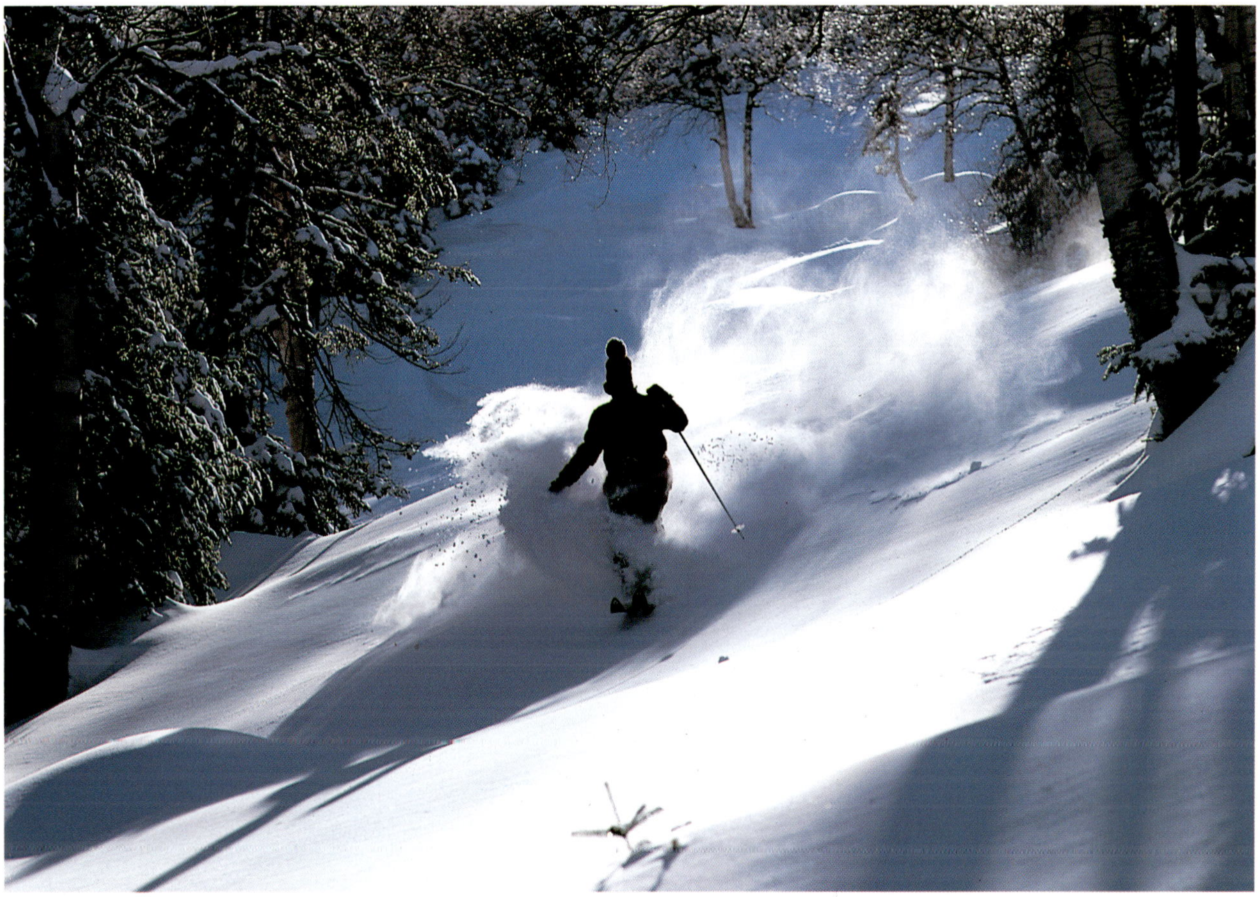

"Paradise Trail," Sugarbush

Overleaf: Village of Derby

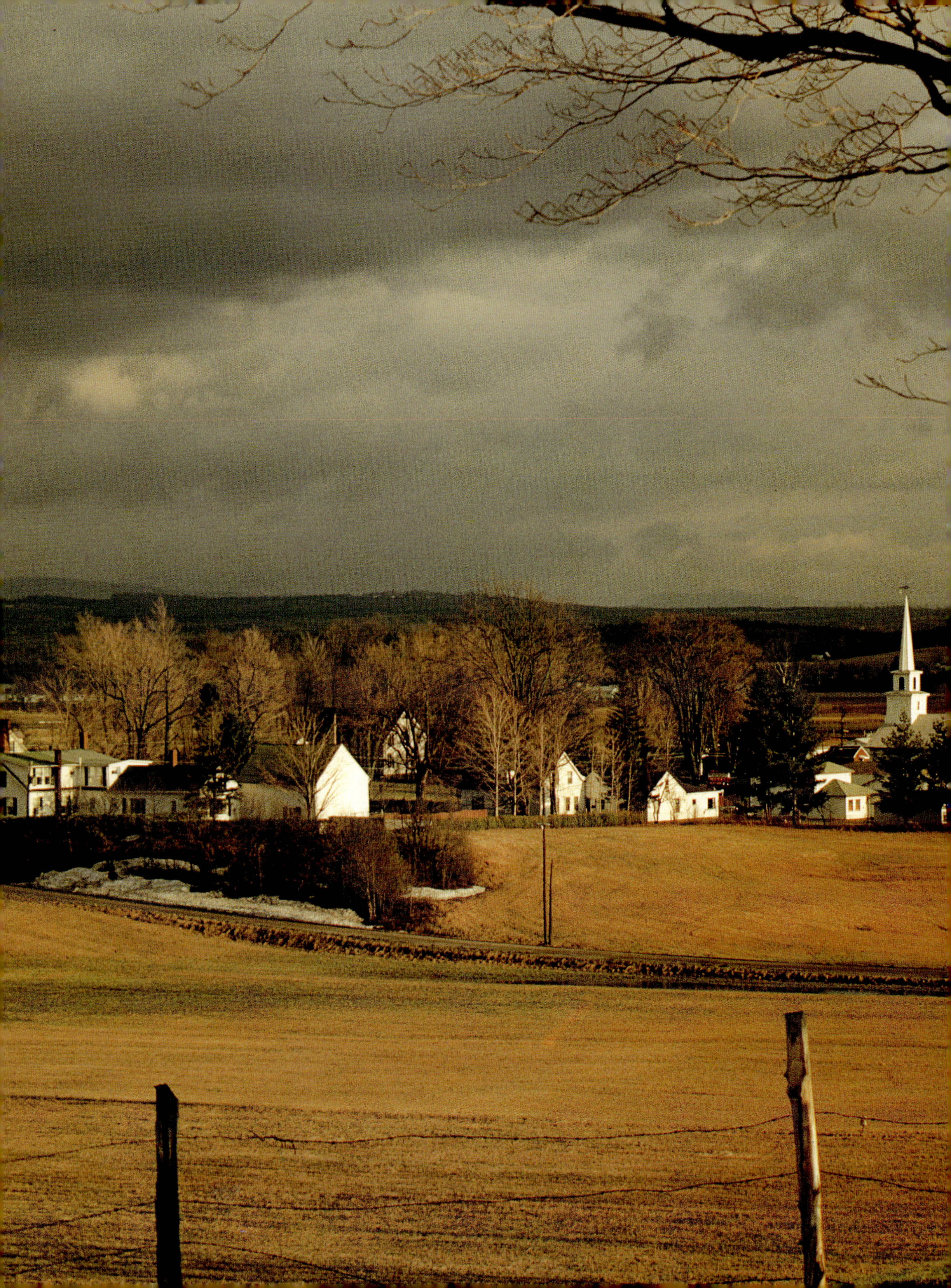

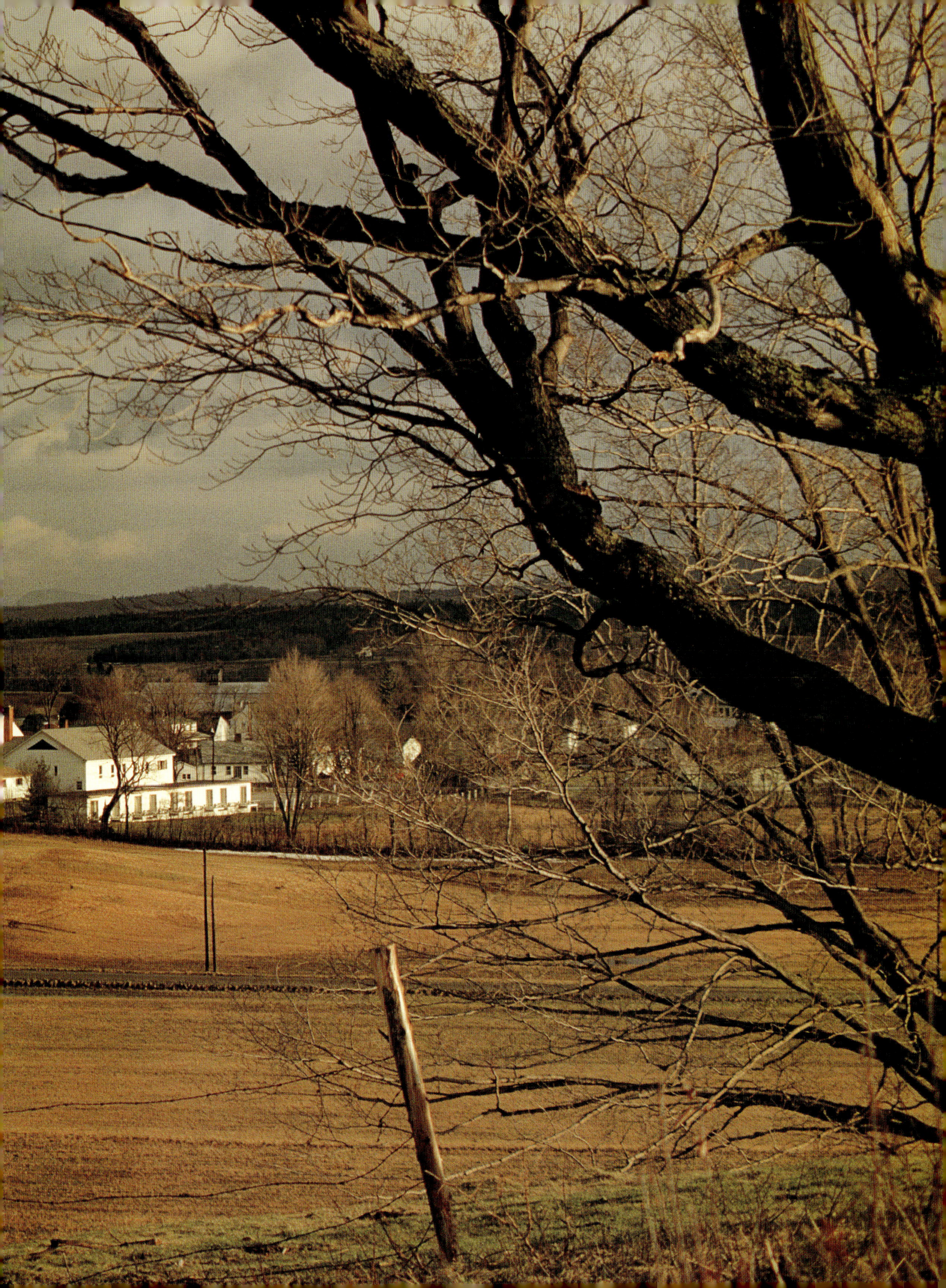

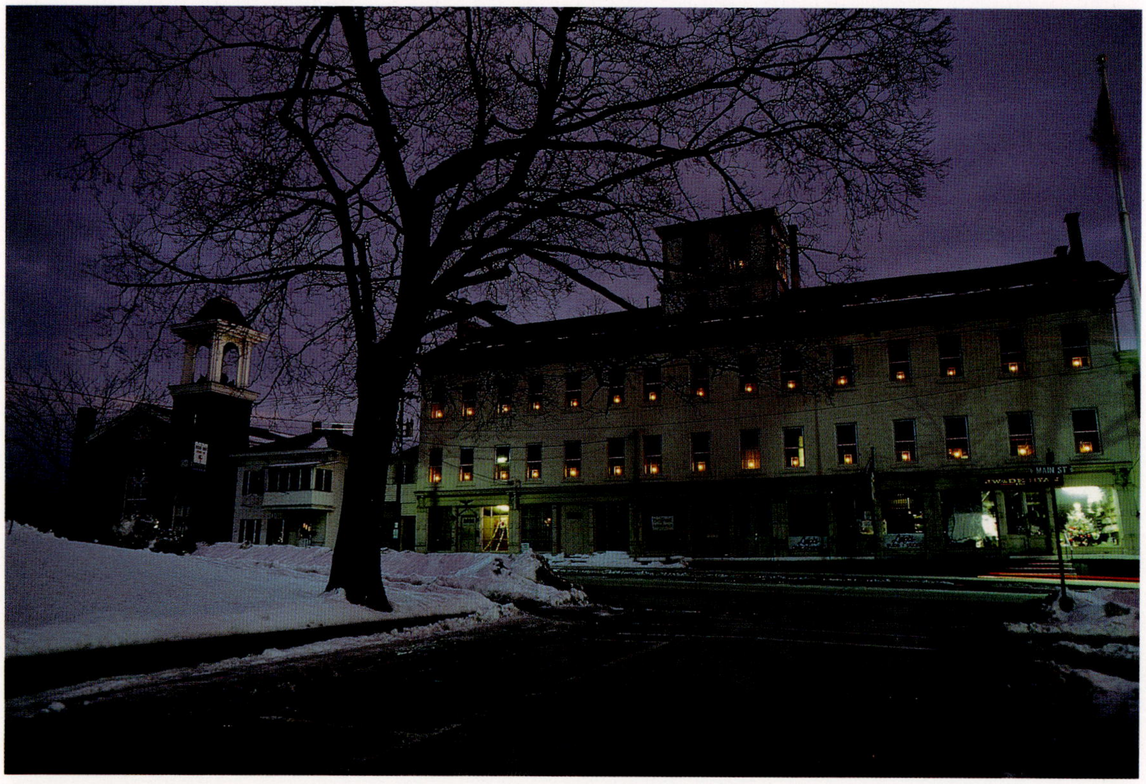

Vergennes

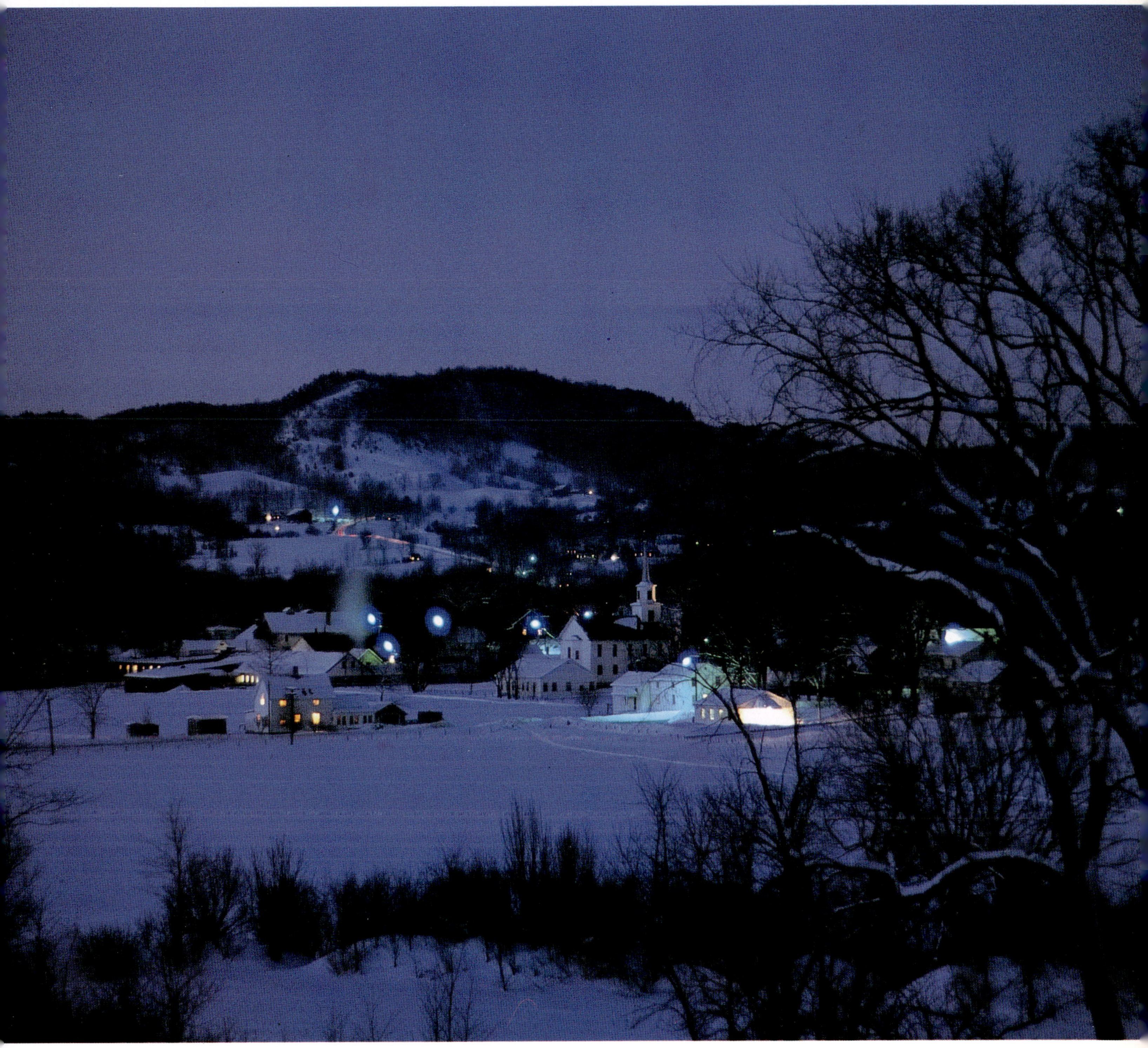

Hinesburg

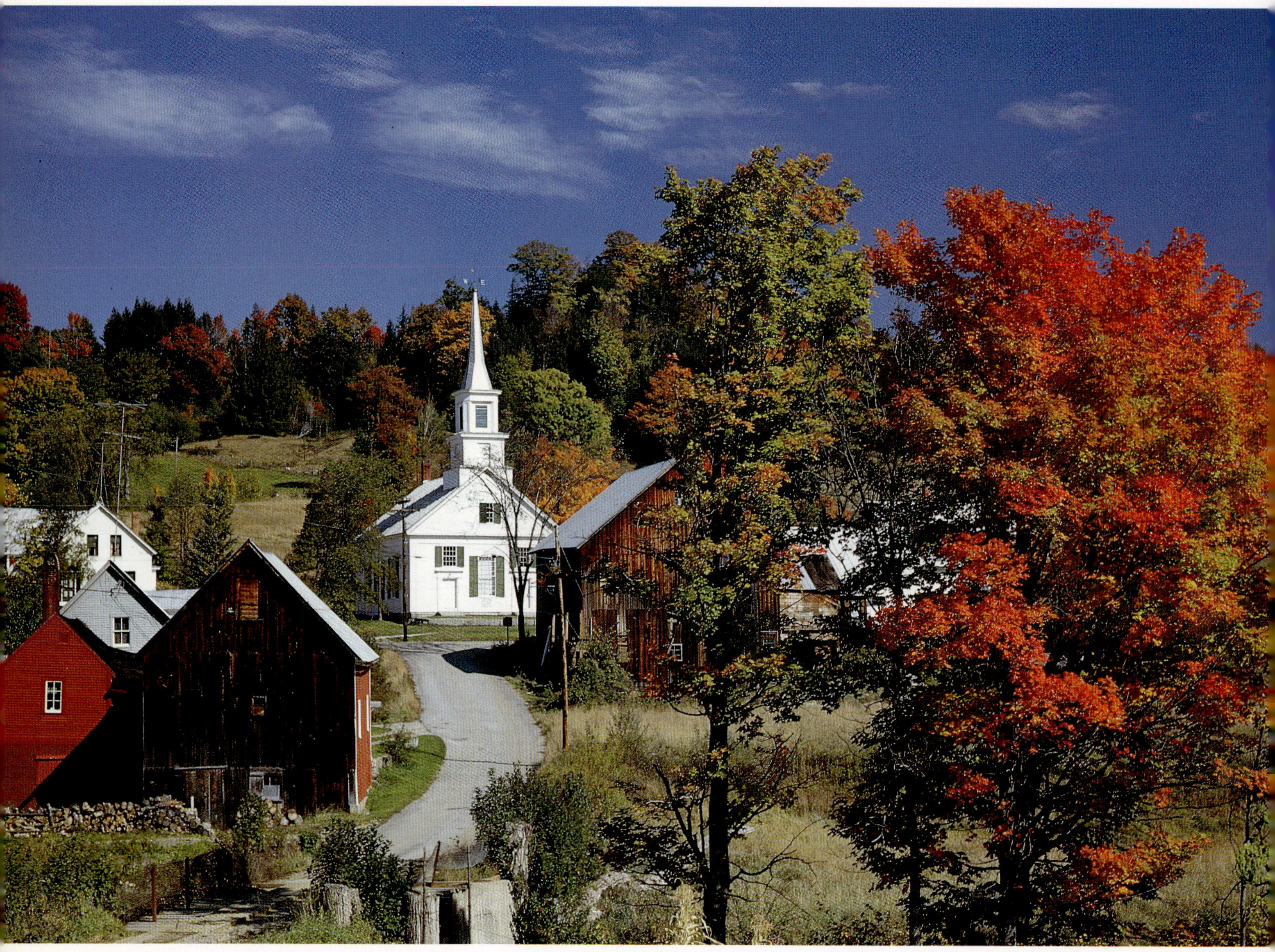

Waits River Village

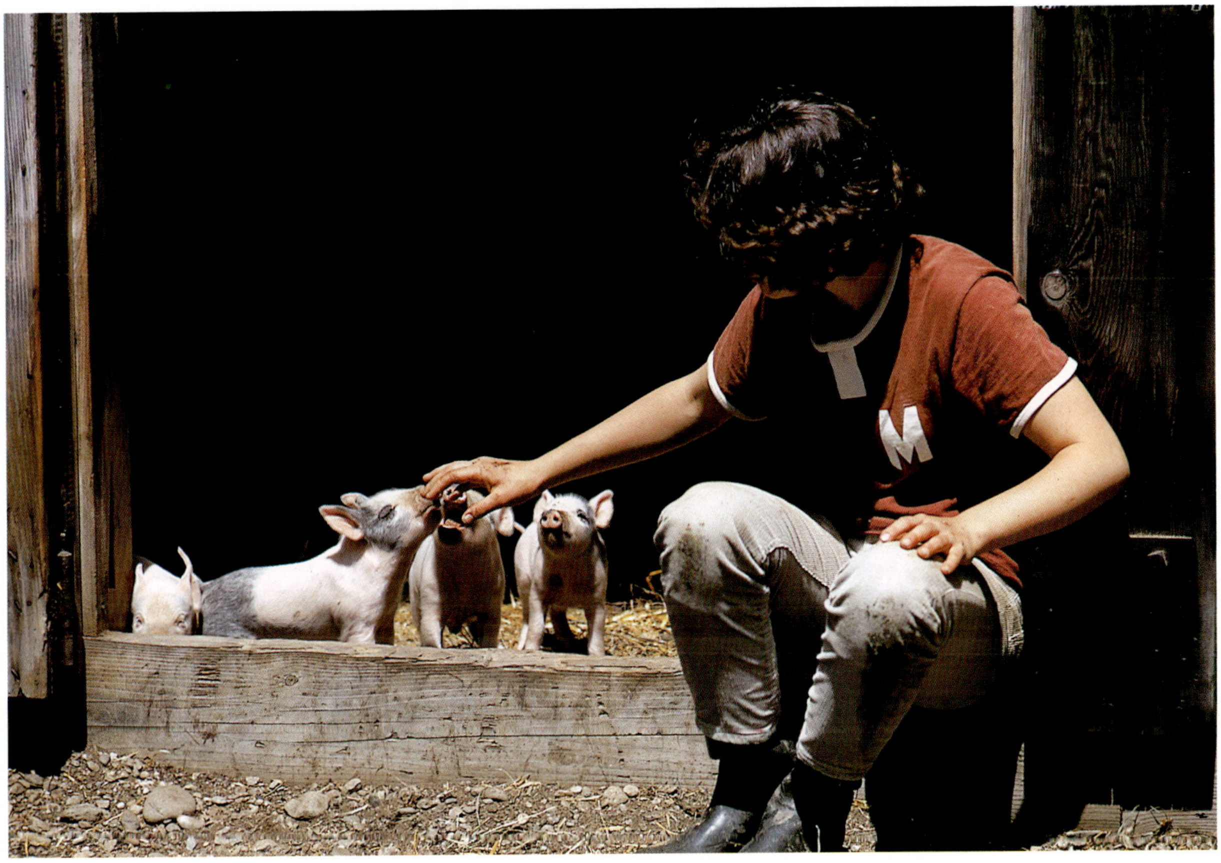

Lisa with piglets

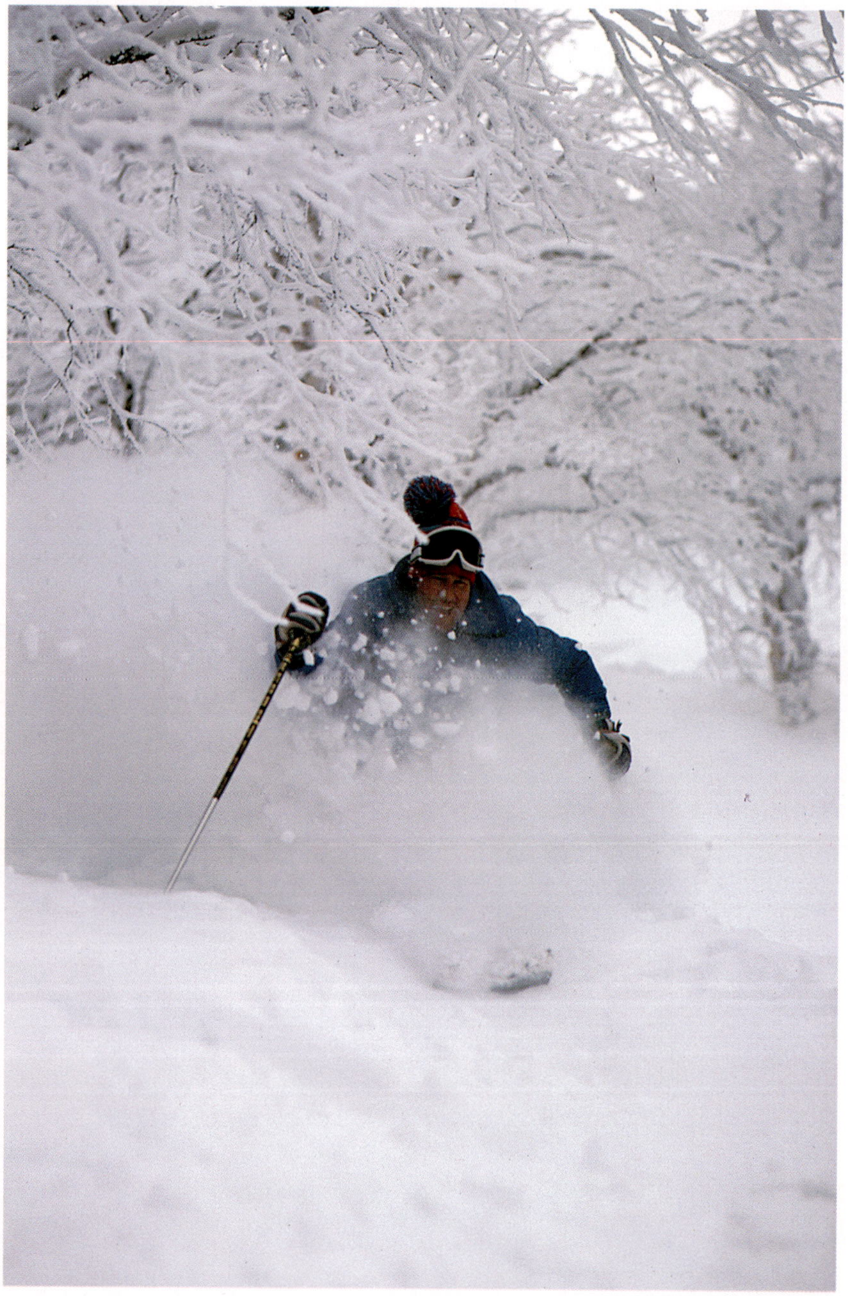

Sugarbush Ski Village, Warren

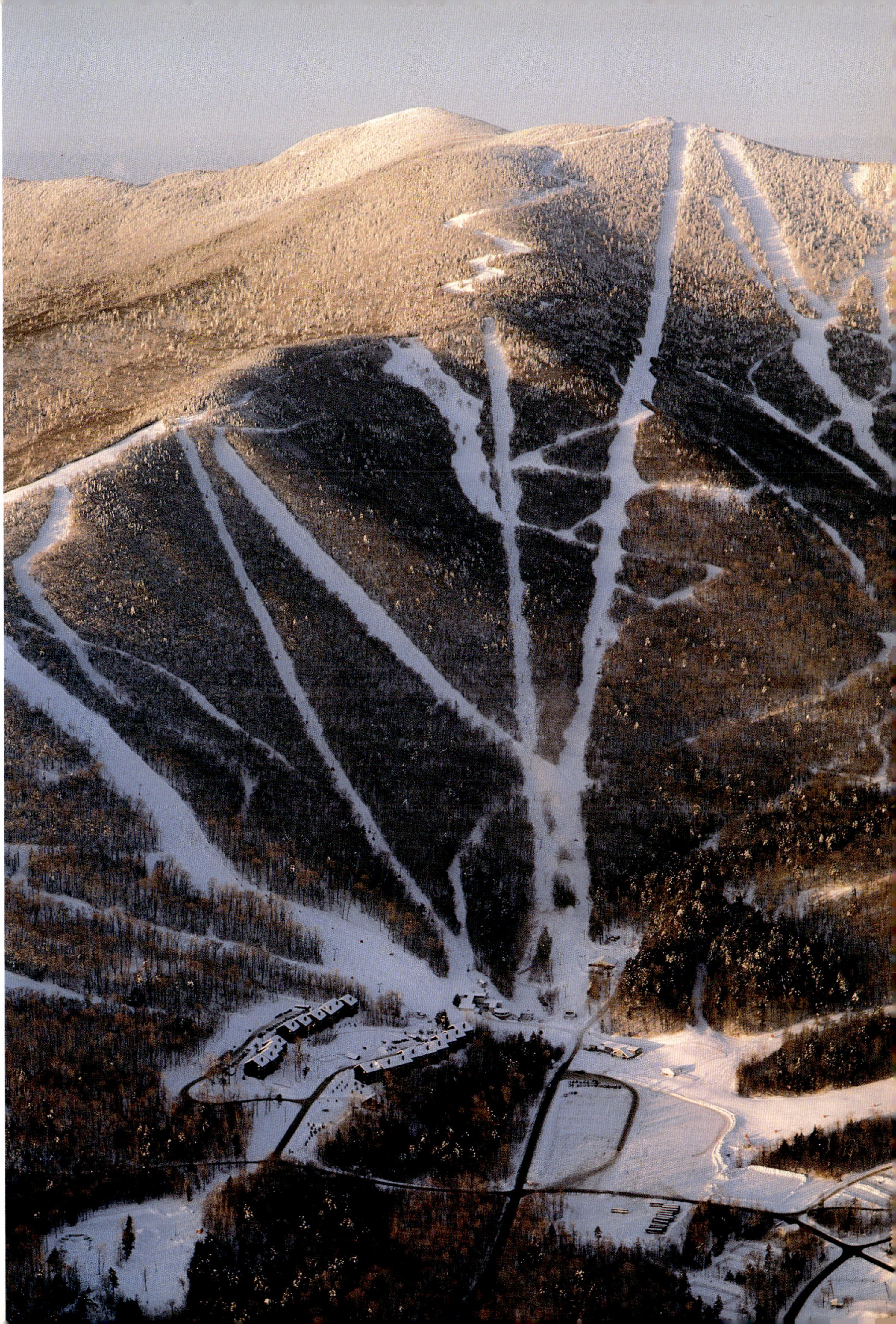

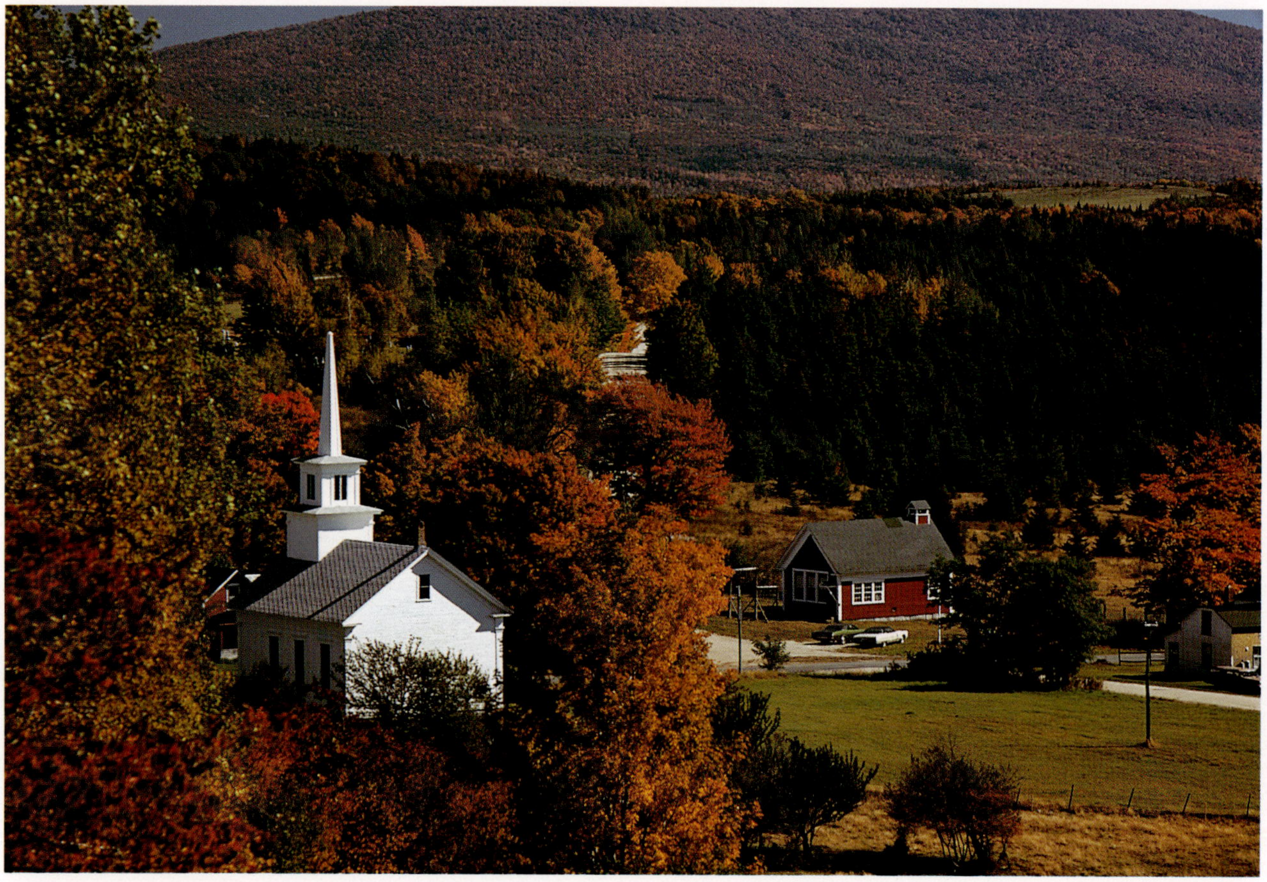

Newark in the Northeast Kingdom

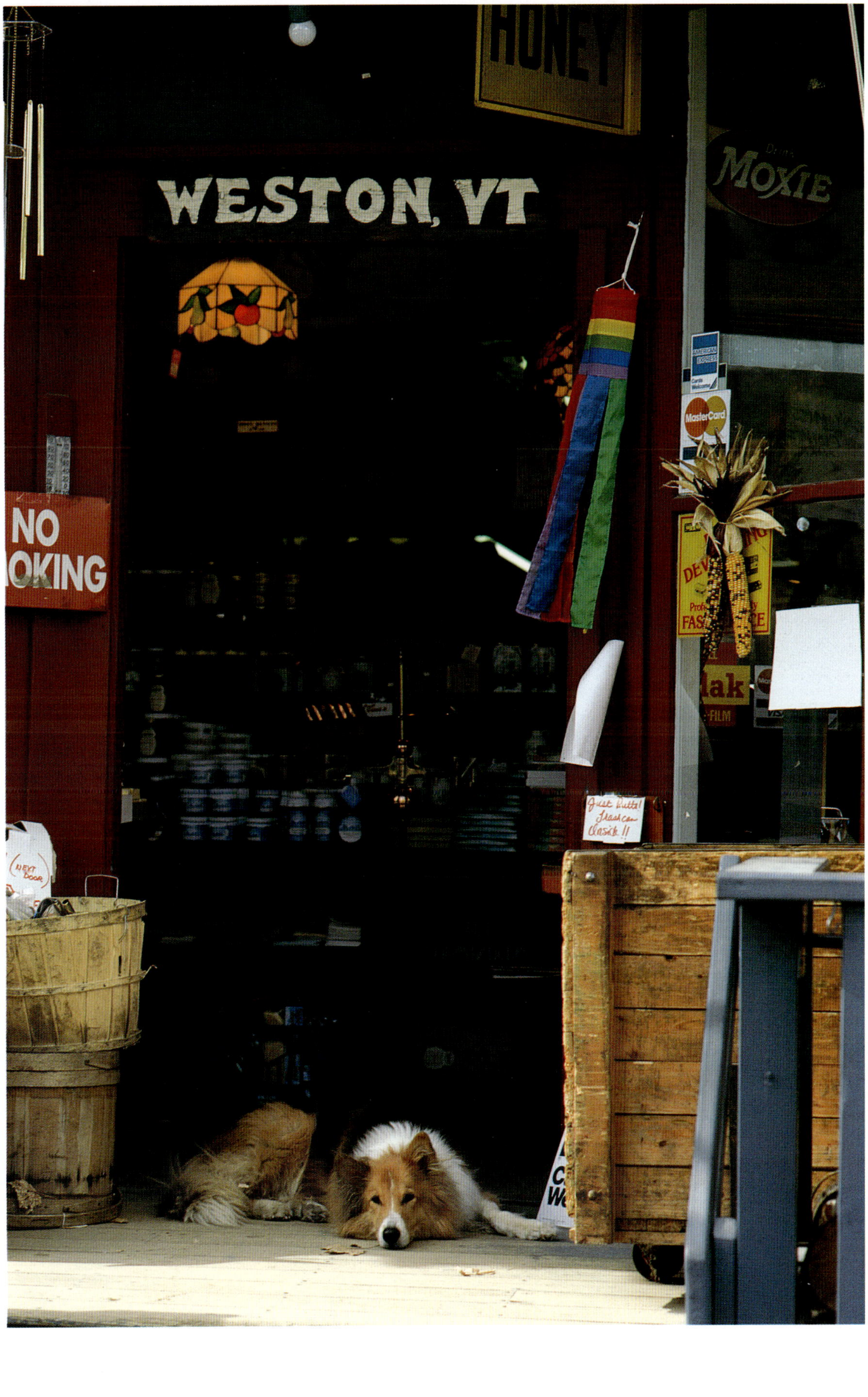

Weston country store

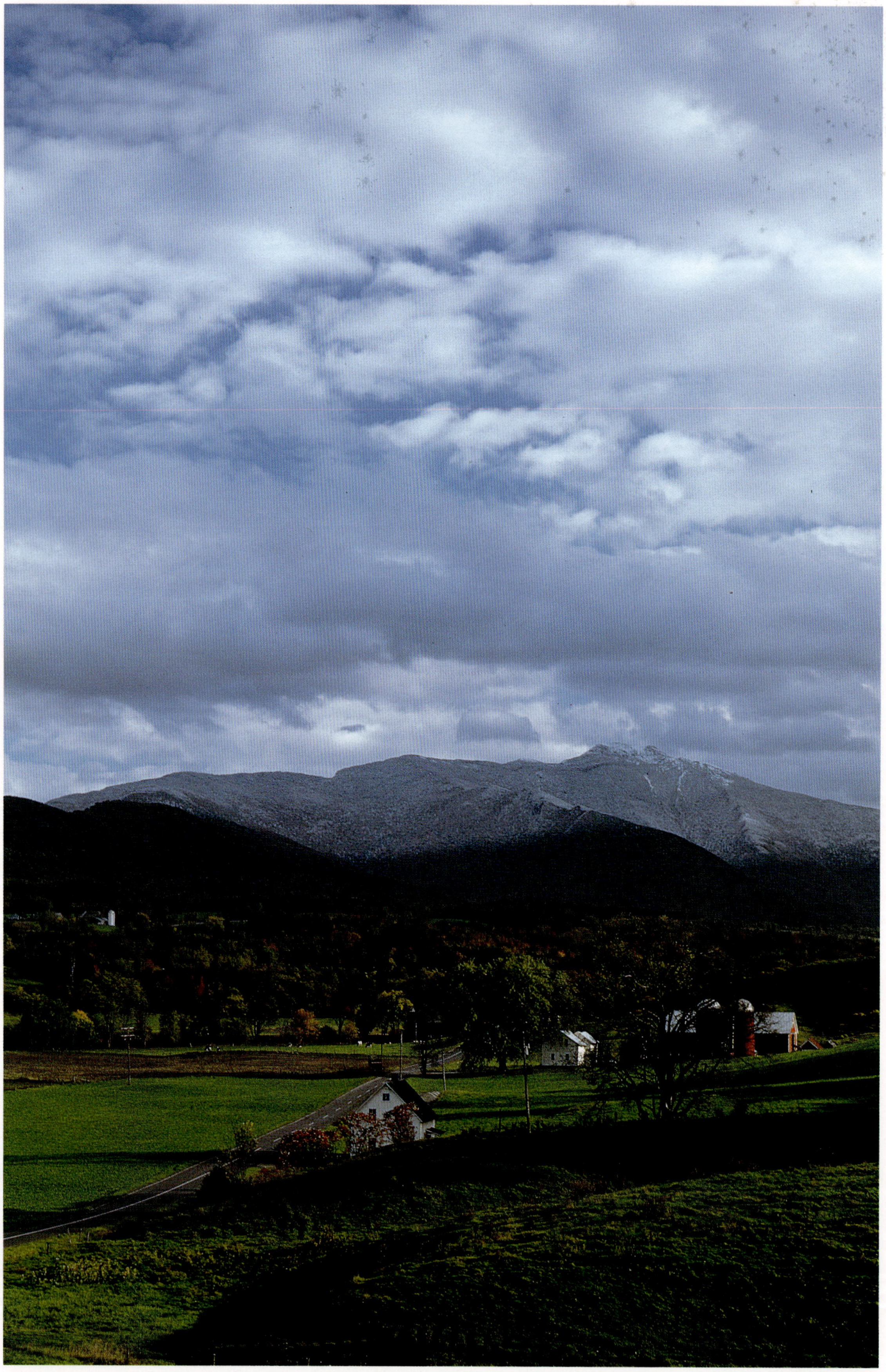

Pleasant Valley